blues
TRAVELING

blues TRAVELING

The Holy Sites of Delta Blues

THIRD EDITION

Steve Cheseborough

University Press of Mississippi
Jackson

www.upress.state.ms.us

First printing 2009

Library of Congress Cataloging-in-Publication Data

Cheseborough, Steve.
    Blues traveling : the holy sites of Delta blues /
Steve Cheseborough.—3rd ed.
        p.   cm.
    Includes bibliographical references and index.
    ISBN 978-1-60473-124-8 (pbk. : alk. paper)
        1. Blues (Music)—History and criticism.   2. Blues musicians—
Homes and haunts—Guidebooks.   3. Musical landmarks—
Mississippi—Guidebooks.   4. Musical landmarks—Tennessee—
Memphis—Guidebooks.   5. Musical landmarks—Tennessee—
Memphis—Guidebooks.   6. Musical landmarks—Arkansas—
Helena—Guidebooks.   7. Mississippi—Guidebooks.
8. Memphis (Tenn.)—Guidebooks.   9. Helena (Ark.)—
Guidebooks.   I. Title.
ML3521 .C53   2009
781.64309762—dc22

                                                        2008023225

British Library Cataloging-in-Publication Data available

To my mom

CONTENTS

ACKNOWLEDGMENTS

Supreme thanks go to two wonderful friends who helped me on all three editions of this book: Milly Moorhead West and Melissa McGuire Bridgman.

Big-time-special thanks go to the other guardian angels who took me in with hospitality and friendship as I blues-traveled for this edition: Terry Buckalew, Bob "The Mississippi Spoonman" Rowell, Gary Bridgman, Eden Brent, and Lucille Ridges.

Super-duper thanks go to people who generously gave their time and information to help me with this edition: "Sunshine" Sonny Payne, James "Gone For Good" Morgan, Roger Stolle, Melvin Burnside, Preston Lauterbach, Marcia Weaver, Richard Ramsey, Stephanie Movre, Scott Barretta, and Art Browning.

And regular heartfelt thanks go to others who helped: Luther Brown, Don Bailey, John Ruskey, Eddie Cusic, Billy Johnson, Andy Hackleman, Steven Johnson, C. W. Gatlin, Dorothy Moore, Ben Payton, George Vasquez, Mary Shepard, Connie Gibbons, Robert Hirsberg, Bubba Sullivan, T-Model Ford, Lightnin' Malcolm, Aikei Pro, Ray Autry, Mary Hurt Wright, Euphus "Butch" Ruth Jr., the staff of Little Rock Airport Enterprise Car Rental, the staff of Blue Moon Camera, Greg Johnson, Helaine Garren, Jimmy

"Duck" Holmes, Kenny Brown, Jules Corriere, Bill Talbot, and Taizz Medalia.

A tear and a smile for my friends David Lee Durham and "Philadelphia" Jerry Ricks, bluesmen who died while I was working on this edition.

And I thank all the bluesmen and blueswomen of Mississippi, living and dead, for inspiring and comforting me every day with their beautiful music.

blues
TRAVELING

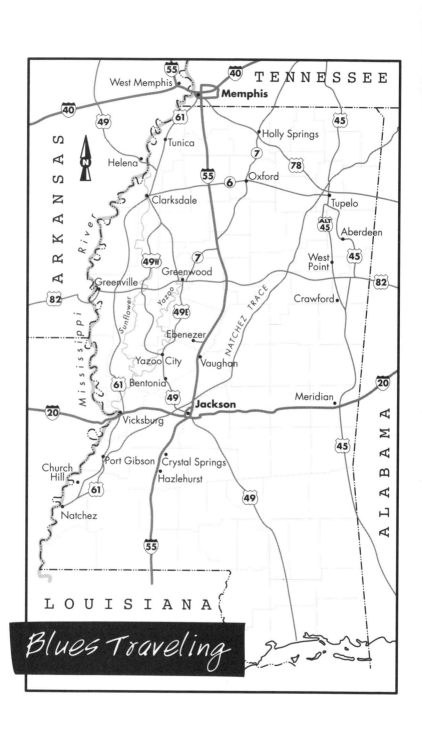

chapter 1

LOOKING FOR THE BLUES

Is the blues still a vibrant tradition as we listen and explore in the twenty-first century? Or is it fading away?

Let's ask George Messenger, the trim sixty-eight-year-old who owns Messenger's Pool Room, the café his grandfather opened more than a hundred years ago on Fourth Street (now Martin Luther King Avenue), the heart of Clarksdale's black community.

"There were businesses all up and down this street," Messenger says, thinking back to his childhood. "On Saturday night the whole area was crowded, food was cooking—barbecue, fish, tamales. The sharecroppers would come into town to have a good time. But the cotton harvester and the casinos ruined business."

The mechanized cotton harvester took away the sharecroppers' work, sending most of them up North for factory jobs. And, more recently, the casinos took away what was left of the Saturday night good-time crowd. And meanwhile, the end of rigid segregation gave black people alternatives to hanging out in jook joints.

"I think the blues is dead, myself," Messenger says. "The blues got started because of the way things were. People were held down. A black person was over here, pushed down. They didn't have nothing else to do but moan."

Still, Messenger doesn't mind the new interest in blues. "It brings people here," he says. "If it hadn't been for the rich white people to talk about blues, and the blues museum, there wouldn't be anything even to talk about anymore."

Jimmy "Duck" Holmes, blues musician and owner of the Blue Front Café in Bentonia, also has seen the local customer base dry up.

"There were eight jook joints in this town and they all used to be full," Holmes says. "Then the interstate came through and people moved to the city. And on the farms, the two-row machinery got upgraded to eight-row. That put people out of work. The jook joint and the general store both are almost gone."

Rather than cry silently about the loss, Holmes does his best to keep both the blues and the jook joint alive. Every day, after working his day job as a school truant officer, he opens up the sixty-year-old jook joint his parents established. His friends and neighbors come in nightly. "This is the nucleus of the community. Always has been," Holmes says. "After a funeral or a church revival, people come here."

These days, travelers who are familiar with Holmes's recent recordings or the town's blues history sometimes augment the local crowd. Holmes doesn't sit around wondering if the blues is still alive. He just gets out his guitar and plays, after making sure everybody has a beer.

Blues Traveling through History

Perhaps the first "blues traveler" in Mississippi was the Harvard archaeologist Charles Peabody, who dug up an Indian mound near Clarksdale in 1901–1902. He looked up from the ground and took careful note of the local black workers' songs.

As Peabody reported in an article he wrote for a folklore journal, the workers sang almost constantly during the day and as they relaxed in the evening. They sang hymns, ragtime pieces, and (what most interested Peabody) "improvisations in rhythm more or less phrased, sung to an intoning more or less approaching melody." The lyrics of those songs were "'hard luck' tales (very often), love themes, suggestions anticipative and reminiscent of favorite occupations and amusements." If that wasn't the blues, it certainly was close. Among the verses he recorded in his notes are some that have become familiar blues lines:

> *They had me arrested for murder*
> *And I never harmed a man*
>
> *The reason I loves my baby so*
> *'Cause when she gets five dollars she give me fo'.*

Some have not entered the blues lexicon:

> *Old Dan Tucker he got drunk,*
> *Fell in de fire and kicked up a chunk*
>
> *Oh we'll live on pork and kisses*
> *If you'll only be my missus.*

According to Peabody's description, the guitar accompaniment also sounded like the blues—"mostly 'ragtime' with the instrument seldom venturing beyond the inversions of the three chords of a few major and minor keys."

In 1903, W. C. Handy, an Alabama-born, African American band musician who had been touring the country for years, settled in Clarksdale to lead an orchestra of black musicians. Handy's first exposure to the blues happened soon after that, while he was waiting for a long-overdue train in the Tutwiler depot:

> A lean, loose-jointed Negro had commenced plunking a guitar beside me while I slept. His clothes were rags; his feet peeped out of his shoes. His face had on it some of the sadness of the ages. As he played, he pressed a knife on the strings in a manner popularized by Hawaiian guitarists who used steel bars. The effect was unforgettable. His song, too, struck me instantly.
>
> *Goin' where the Southern cross' the Dog.*
>
> The singer repeated the line three times, accompanying himself on the guitar with the weirdest music I had ever heard. The tune stayed in my mind.

It certainly did. A few years later, Handy would publish "The Yellow Dog Rag" (which he would rename "The Yellow Dog Blues"), incorporating that line. And he would become known as the Father of the Blues for pieces like that one and "The St. Louis Blues" and "The Memphis Blues"—songs written in standard notation, arranged for bands, and published nationally as sheet music, based on what Handy heard from anonymous guitar-plunking Mississippians like the man in the train station.

Handy's compositions spurred the first blues craze. The word "blues" became nationally known and identified with the twelve-bar, AAB (sing line, repeat line, answer with rhyming line) format—a format that does not apply, by the way, to much of the very real blues of Charley Patton, Skip James, Fred McDowell, R. L. Burnside, and dozens of other genuine down-home blues artists, past and present. But even today, if you ask a rock, pop, or jazz musician to play the blues, that standardized format is what you will get.

The next blues craze began in 1920, when bandleader-composer Perry Bradford persuaded the Okeh record company in New York to make the first recording of a black blues singer. That first recorded singer was not a scraggly, self-taught, guitar-toting southern man of the sort Handy had heard in Tutwiler, though. It was Mamie Smith, a well-dressed woman with a professionally trained voice, singing before a full orchestra. Smith's voice is smooth, lacking what we now consider bluesy effects. Still, blacks who were hearing such a sound on records for the first time were thrilled. It was a huge hit. Smith's recording would be followed by those of other sophisticated blueswomen, or "Classic blues" singers, as they are known, eventually including the great, rougher-voiced Ma Rainey and Bessie Smith.

It wasn't until the mid-twenties that the companies would record the kind of person Handy had seen in Tutwiler and whom we still consider the quintessential blues singer: a self-accompanied male singer. Among the earliest were the banjo-playing (and not scruffy at all) Papa Charlie Jackson of New Orleans, the southeastern guitar virtuoso Blind Blake, and the most popular and influential of them all, the Dallas street singer Blind Lemon Jefferson. Jefferson traveled widely, recorded prolifically, and became the first superstar of the country blues. He showed record companies that there was lots of money to be made in recording male, rural, southern, self-accompanied blues singer-guitarists. So the companies combed the South, auditioning everyone of that description they could find and giving the promising ones tickets to recording studios in the North. Soon they hastened the process by sending the recording equipment south and setting up temporary studios in hotel rooms.

They found the richest mine of bluesmen—and a few blueswomen—in or near the flat, fertile cotton lands of the Mississippi Delta: Charley Patton, Son House, Willie Brown, Louise Johnson, Skip James, Tommy Johnson, George "Bullet" Williams, Rubin Lacy, Memphis Minnie, Kansas Joe McCoy, the Mississippi Sheiks, Kid Bailey, Bukka White, Robert Johnson, Mattie Delaney, Geechie Wiley, Ishmon Bracey, Mississippi John Hurt, William Harris, Eugene "Sonny Boy Nelson" Powell, and many others. These musicians went to Memphis or all the way up to Chicago or Grafton, Wisconsin, to sing and play for a few bucks and the chance to become immortal. As producer Frank Walker said of those sessions: "You might come out with two selections or you might come out with six or eight, but you did it at that time. You said goodbye. They went back home. They had made a phonograph record, and that was the next thing to being president of the United States in their mind."

Commercial country-blues field recording peaked in the late 1920s. By the thirties the record companies, hurt by the Depression, were releasing records only by proven artists, most of whom were southerners transplanted to Chicago, such as Big Bill Broonzy, Memphis Minnie, and Tampa Red. But down in Mississippi, people continued to play the down-home blues in jook joints and on street corners, even if they weren't making it onto record as often.

The blues just might have been born in Mississippi. On the other hand, it might not have. The first blues may have been played somewhere else in the rural South. There are early reports of blues in east Texas, Alabama, Louisiana, and even Missouri.

What is clear is that the blues, since its beginnings, has always found a home here. Mississippians have always made up a large proportion of all blues singers and an overwhelming proportion of the finest blues singers. That includes the whole Chicago blues scene from the 1930s to the present—nearly all its stars have been Mississippi-born. And that is true of both the prewar acoustic period and the later electric period, when Mississippians like Muddy Waters, Elmore James, B. B. King, and Little Milton set the standard.

Mississippi was more rural and agricultural, with a greater concentration of cotton planting, than other states. And it had a large, poor, strictly segregated black population, which was overwhelmingly rural and working in agriculture. In other words, Mississippi has long been more southern than the rest of the South, and that goes double for the Mississippi Delta, which has been dubbed "the most southern place on earth." So the conditions that fostered the blues throughout the South were intensified in Mississippi, especially in the Delta.

When people speak of the delta of a river, they usually mean the area where it washes into the sea or a lake. But the Mississippi Delta is hundreds of miles upstream, in northwest Mississippi (it has a mirror image in northeast Arkansas, but "the Delta" usually refers just to the Mississippi side, and that's how we'll use it here). It's a flat, leaf-shaped expanse of seven thousand square miles, with the Mississippi and Yazoo rivers on its curved sides and Memphis and Vicksburg at its tips.

Thousands of years of Mississippi River floods left the Delta with a thick, dark layer of fertile topsoil. In its natural state, the Delta was a jungly place full of swamps, large trees, vines, and animals. Nineteenth-century settlers quickly perceived its economic value, however. The area was cleared, and it became first a huge lumber camp and then a huge cotton plantation. Both the lumber and the cotton operations were labor intensive, as was the building of levees to protect the settlers and their farms from the regular, gargantuan floods. So tens of thousands of blacks were brought in to work the Delta—first as slaves and later as levee gangs, sharecroppers, tenant farmers, or transient day laborers from the hill country.

Today, the Delta is a sparsely populated, generally quiet place. But back in the twenties and thirties, before the mechanization of agriculture, its fields and now-sleepy towns were alive with people. The crowds and the money attracted musicians (many Delta blues artists were actually born in the hills) who interacted, competed, and innovated. As ethnomusicologist David Evans has explained, the Delta, despite its rural nature, functioned like an urban area, pulling in people from widespread places with diverse musical traditions. In this environment, the famed Delta blues developed.

Outside the Delta, Mississippians also played the blues. The

North Mississippi hill country is home to a droning, hypnotic variety of blues exemplified by Mississippi Fred McDowell, Junior Kimbrough, and R. L. Burnside, among others, as well as to related traditions including African American fife-and-drum bands. The state capital, Jackson, has long been an important recording center, with plenty of live music as well. There and in nearby towns, Bo Carter, the Mississippi Sheiks, and others practiced their smoother blues styles. Bentonia is the birthplace of Skip James and Jack Owens, two artists with styles so similar to each other's yet distinctive from anyone else's that some scholars consider the town a unique blues "school." Jimmie Rodgers, the white singing brakeman whose yodeling versions of black blues songs were the start of country music, came from Meridian, in east-central Mississippi. And Memphis, Tennessee, has always attracted Mississippians, among them musicians who played on Beale Street and heavily influenced that city's sounds.

Mississippi blues reemerged as a national phenomenon in the 1940s, after the young Mississippian Muddy Waters caught the train north, bringing his slide-guitar-driven music style with him. His collaborators and competitors who also made the trip included fellow Mississippians Howlin' Wolf, John Lee Hooker, Jimmy Rogers, Big Walter Horton, Elmore James, Jimmy Reed, and Otis Spann.

The image of Muddy Waters leaving Mississippi and taking the blues with him is a powerful one, but it is not quite true. For one thing, when he arrived in Chicago, the blues was already there—although he did usher in a harder, electric version of it. And, for another thing, Mississippians didn't stop singing the blues after Muddy left.

Popular attention focused again on Mississippi blues—not just on its Chicago outpost—in the folk and blues revival of the 1960s. Young white northerners went south to scout out the old blues records of the twenties and thirties and, in some cases, the old people who had made them. Son House, Skip James, and Mississippi John Hurt were among those found alive and well enough to enjoy new performing and recording careers late in life.

That blues boom faded out soon enough. But there would be yet another in the '90s, kicked off by the re-release of Robert Johnson's complete output as a double-CD box set that turned out to be a smash hit. That set was the first, and still the only, million-seller by an original country-blues artist. A few years later, the Robert Mugge film *Deep Blues* showed that there still were down-home Mississippi blues artists in real life, not just on old records. Other developments include *Living Blues* magazine moving its offices from Chicago to Oxford; new blues record companies setting up shop in Mississippi; a bunch of new and revitalized Mississippi blues festivals and blues museums; the publication of this book, making it easier for blues fans to come visit; the worldwide popularity of North Mississippi Hill Country Blues and rock-based spin-offs; and the state itself putting up blues markers all over the place. Finally, Mississippi blues was enjoying a renaissance—even in Mississippi. And it still is.

But that doesn't mean the Mississippi blues is the *same* as it was in 1929—or 1969. For one thing, you just don't hear much of the complex, solo, acoustic-guitar style that characterized Mississippi blues of the prewar period, except maybe in the hands of a young revivalist in Memphis or Oxford. But then you might hear such a revivalist in Seattle or New York, too. Don't expect to hear a Charley Patton, Robert Johnson, or Memphis Minnie playing on a corner or in a jook joint in Mississippi.

Yes, blues in Mississippi, as elsewhere, generally means electric blues. But even electric blues, sadly, is not easy to find. The best way to get your fill of live music is to schedule your visit around a blues festival. Besides the music at the festival, many local clubs, which otherwise use jukeboxes or deejays, will schedule live performances. When it's not festival time, look for live blues at clubs in the bigger towns and at concerts. Many of the old country jooks have closed or converted to recorded music only.

The physical remains of the old-time blues, such as ever existed at all, also are precarious things. Blues singers were mostly rambling sorts who didn't leave behind much in the way of estates, memoirs, letters, or other personal papers or belongings. They left their music, fortunately, and some sketchy details of the particulars of their lives. So you might not find the house where your favorite blues artist grew up or the joint where he first played your favorite song.

On the other hand, looking at things in a different way, there is much to see. The blues world hasn't changed as rapidly as the rest of the country—in fact, in many ways it hasn't changed a whole lot in the hundred years since the blues began. There are still cottonfields, shacks, and barbecue spots. There are courthouses and jails where defendants—many of them poor and black—receive some kind of justice. There are the roads, narrow, twisting, dark, and poorly marked, leading through fields, woods, and more fields, past cotton gins and over creeks. There are trains. And there is always the river—the Big River, the continent's Main Drain, with its boats, birds, fish, fishermen, levees, and bridges, its precious silt, its threat of flood.

There are old storefronts and depots, in front of which the crowds gathered on Saturday afternoons to listen to Charley Patton, Robert Johnson, or another of the hundreds of blues singers, most of them unrecorded and now unknown, who sang their hearts out as they passed through. And there are places where people still laugh, dance, drink, and listen to the blues.

This book will help you find what *is* left in the Mississippi blues world. And it will help you remember and visualize what is gone and to pick up clues from the songs, the landscape, and literature. Let's go.

State Blues Markers

After a hundred years of ignoring its blues heritage, the state of Mississippi has embarked on an ambitious, million-dollar project to place signs all over the state, marking sites with connections to the blues.

The signs are dark blue, distinguishing them from the green state historic markers. (There are a few green historic markers at blues sites, predating this project, including W. C. Handy's home in Clarksdale and the turnoff to John Hurt's hometown, Avalon.) And they include a lot of detail: the front side has a few sentences of text, similar to a historic marker. But the flip side, vinyl-covered, has photos and much more text in small print, like a magazine page. Later signs might include high-tech features such as music and GPS data.

The state plans to place 130 blues markers, following them up with a series of Civil Rights, Civil War, and literary markers. Expert researchers, working with local sources, make recommendations on the placing and content of the markers.

The markers are well worth reading closely whenever you encounter one—something you will do often as you follow the tour in this book. A list of the markers is available at www .msbluestrail.org.

Planning Your Blues Tour

Unfortunately, the days of local train service to little Mississippi towns are long past. You will need an automobile to get to most of the places in this book.

Chapters 2 through 10 form a rough circle beginning and ending in Memphis. So if you want to see it all, just follow the chapters in numerical order (or reverse numerical order).

If you are flying in from out of state to see Mississippi blues sites, you probably will arrive in Memphis, where you can rent a car and begin the tour. Note that Memphis—*not* New Orleans—is the most convenient major city from which to begin a Mississippi blues tour. The Mississippi Delta and most other areas of interest to blues lovers are in the *northern* half of Mississippi.

But if you happen to be in New Orleans and want to tour Mississippi blues sites, that's okay, too. Just be sure to figure in the extra driving time of about three hours from New Orleans to Jackson, where you would begin this tour (or you could take the train to Jackson and rent a car there). Start with chapter 8 and then follow the circle in either direction, looping from 10 back to 2 or vice versa. Other starting points work just as well. Jackson has an international airport, and there are regional airports in Tupelo, Greenville, and Meridian.

Of course, you don't have to do the whole tour. The places described in this book are close enough to one another that you can get from any spot to any other in four hours or less (in many cases, much less). So you might want to read through the book before starting your trip, and draw your own route. Whatever you choose—take your time, keep your patience and sense of humor handy, and have fun!

TRAINS

There is still one passenger line that might be of interest to blues travelers: Amtrak's City of New Orleans. It runs daily from New Orleans, with stops in Hammond, Louisiana, McComb, Brookhaven, Hazlehurst, Jackson, Yazoo City, and Greenwood in Mississippi, and then Memphis. It continues north to Chicago. Call Amtrak (800-USA-RAIL) for schedules, reservations, and more information.

Sonny Boy Williamson II and Willie Love rode the line from Jackson to New Orleans in April 1953, on their way to Houston for a recording session. On the train, the bluesmen danced, sang, and told jokes to the other passengers. When they got to Houston, one of the songs they recorded was Sonny Boy's "City of New Orleans" (different from the 1970s pop tune by Steve Goodman):

> *I heard the City of New Orleans gonna run today*
> *I got to find my baby before she get too far away.*

Bukka White's 1940 "Special Streamline" also celebrates this train line, re-creating the sounds and feelings of riding it out of Memphis, headed for New Orleans.

Amtrak gives passengers a good dose of New Orleans culture on the trip, with a jazz band playing in the lounge car and Cajun-inspired cooking in the dining car. The company has not yet offered live blues (or barbecue and moonshine) while the train passes through Mississippi, however.

Guidelines for Good Times

Traveling the back roads of Mississippi, you might sometimes feel you've wandered into a foreign country or a different era. Here are some guidelines to help you get along and stay out of trouble.

FEELING THE RHYTHM

If Mr. Turner doesn't feel like playing right now, or if the goat is sold out, or the deejay won't play the kind of music you were expecting—relax or come back tomorrow or next year. And if you want to shoot pictures or video, ask permission and don't block others' views or dance-floor space.

This may be your dream vacation—perhaps you have planned and saved for years, and traveled many miles. But to the local people next to you, it may be a hard-earned night of fun before they head back to work in the morning. So don't expect them to defer to you or entertain you or pose for your picture.

Don't show up with the insulting attitude that this food and drink may be good enough for the locals, but not for you. Even if you eat steamed grains and organic vegetables at home, consider trying the barbecue if that's what's served—or at least don't turn your nose up at it. And even if you drink microbrews back home, have a regular old American mainstream beer. And enjoy it. You can resume your diet and your highfalutin tastes after your visit.

Sitting In

If you are a decent blues musician and currently in practice, feel free to sit in at a jook joint or club performance. But if you haven't touched a guitar in twenty years, have never sung outside the shower, or have had way too much to drink, then resist the urge. And if you do sit in, remember that the idea is not to show off your flashy licks, but to keep the groove going and the people dancing. After one song, leave the bandstand unless the musicians and the crowd ask you to stay for another.

Photography and Recording

Mississippi's stark natural beauty, the endless cottonfields, the colorfully decorated buildings, and the emotion-laden faces of blues musicians all appeal immensely to photographers of any level. But before you whip out your disposable sure-shot or your three-thousand-dollar Nikon, exercise some courtesy. Ask people for permission to photograph them or their businesses, homes, or children. It wouldn't hurt to just hang out for a while first, chatting, before you ask. If they say no, accept that answer. If they ask for money, don't get offended. Just pay up or put away the camera.

Film and video crews have become almost as common as catfish in the Delta. If you are making a documentary, welcome to the pond! And please pay the musicians, actors, tour guides, and other local stars and helpers. Pay them well and pay them up front.

The situation is different at festivals and other public performances. There, you may freely shoot pictures of the performers, as long as you have the management's tacit or explicit permission.

But at such events, make sure to be courteous to your fellow audience members. Just because you have a camera—no matter how big the lens is and even if you are shooting for a publication—it doesn't mean you have the right to push in front of other people, block their view, or disturb them by using a flash.

Overall, unless photography is your life, you'll find you enjoy the trip more when you pay attention to what's going on rather than to whether you're missing a photo opportunity. Plenty of books with fine photographs of blues musicians and Mississippi scenes are available.

ACCOMMODATIONS

A rural, sparsely populated state, Mississippi has fewer hotels and motels than one would expect. A wide range of accommodations can be found in Memphis and in Jackson. You are also sure to find several of the usual motel chains, and perhaps an independent operator or two, represented in large towns (called "cities" here) such as Tupelo, Oxford, Clarksdale, Greenville, Vicksburg, Natchez, and Meridian. But even in those places, a room can be hard to come by if there is a big event going on—a blues festival or a college football game, for example. To be safe, make advance reservations. If you hope to stay in a smaller community, check ahead of time to find out if anything is available. Another option is the large casino hotels along the Mississippi River and on the Gulf Coast.

FOOD AND DRINK

Moonshine—"That's the soul of the blues," one musician says of moonshine. Generally called "corn liquor," "corn whiskey," or simply "corn," homemade spirits are fairly common in rural areas of Mississippi. At a jook joint, private party, or anywhere else, you might see people drinking a clear liquid out of pint bottles that once held factory-made booze—or, in situations where less discretion is necessary, out of a large jar.

Make no mistake, however—even if you're someplace where it seems to be openly tolerated, moonshine is illegal here, as it is everywhere else in the United States. As with other illegal drugs, one doesn't know the strength or quality of homemade corn. It varies by maker and by batch. Some folks say moonshine wreaks a nastier hangover than the legal stuff. Connoisseurs say precisely the opposite, however. They also prefer the taste of corn liquor to that of storebought—besides appreciating the fact that it is generally cheaper. No matter what you're drinking, use your own best judgment, and let someone else drive. As the Mississippi Sheiks sang in "Bootlegger Blues":

> *Bag of whiskey on my back and the sheriffs is on my track*
> *I'm going to make it to the woods if I can*
> *If you can, if you can*
> *You better make it to the woods if you can.*

Barbecue—If corn whiskey is the soul of the blues, barbecue is the heart. Slow-cooked pig meat has been a sacrament at blues performances at least since the days of Charley Patton, who reportedly used to ask for the most fat-laden pieces, which would insulate him against getting drunk. The tradition continues at blues festivals today, where the only problem is deciding among the fragrant smoke-filled booths. Outside of festivals, barbecue is usually better at barbecue joints than at sit-down restaurants. Ask around—or sniff around—for a good one.

If you're lucky, you might find a restaurant or stand serving such downhome delicacies as chitterlings (always pronounced and sometimes spelled "chitlins"), pig ears, or hog maws. All are delicious, especially with a big splash of hot sauce.

Fish—Fried fish is another food with a long connection to blues performances. "When the fish scent fill the air, we'll have snuff juice everywhere. We gon' pitch a wang wang doodle all night long," is how blues songwriter Willie Dixon put it. In recent decades, catfish has become one of Mississippi's prime agricultural products (the fish are raised in ponds) besides remaining a favorite dish. While it turns up in pâtés and other newfangled recipes these days, it's still impossible to beat a plate of plain old fried catfish with hushpuppies, fries, and coleslaw.

When "buffalo" appears on a menu, it does not refer to the meat of the big mammal or to a style of chicken wings but to a locally popular fish. Buffalo is fried like catfish but has a more delicate texture, stronger flavor, and bigger bones. Buffalo was a favorite fish in black communities through the 1950s. "People didn't like catfish then like they do now," says Greenville food writer Kathy Starr. Tony Hollins, who recorded "Fishin' Blues" in 1952, would probably agree:

> *I'm goin' to get my hooks in the mornin', boys, I'm goin'*
>   *down on the bayou*
> *Lord, if I don't catch me a buffalo, I do hope I catch a trout.*

Two festivals celebrating catfish and buffalofish are held on the same day in Belzoni.

Tamales—Hot tamales originated in Mexico but are also standard fare in the Mississippi Delta, and have been at least since the 1930s, when Robert Johnson sang "They're Red Hot" in celebration of this morsel, which were sold at "two for a nickel, four for a dime." The price has gone up since then, but they are still an inexpensive and tasty snack. Delta tamales are about the size of a cigar, much skinnier than the ones you may be familiar with in California or the Southwest. And the vegetarian varieties that have caught on in those places are unknown here.

Plate Lunches—Downhome eateries in Mississippi, as elsewhere in the South, usually offer a "plate lunch" or "meat plus two" in which you get the meat of the day and two choices from a list of vegetables; among these can be such southern specialties as collard greens, fried okra, and several types of peas and beans. A beverage, rolls or cornbread, and sometimes dessert are included. A vegetable plate, with three or four vegetables and without the meat entrée, is an option even if it's not listed on the menu. But strict vegetarians be warned: the vegetables often are cooked with hunks of meat for flavoring. If you order iced tea you'll be asked, "Sweet or unsweet?" Sweet tea, in which the sugar is added while the tea is still hot, so that it dissolves better, is a regional delicacy.

If you don't see a restaurant around—or even if you do—you can often find some excellent eating at the gas station/general stores along the state's two-lane highways. Where you live, food at such places might mean premade sandwiches or microwaveable fare. But in the South, good homecooked food is frequently available at these roadside stops (although not always, by any means). Fried chicken, fried catfish, barbecue, and smoked turkey legs may await you when you stop for gas. Vegetable side dishes might be offered as well. And there probably is a table where you can sit if you don't want to take it to go.

Legal Booze—Liquor laws are left up to individual counties. Some counties are dry, but, fortunately for thirsty blues fans, the Delta and the north Mississippi counties of most interest to them are wet. Some wet counties do not allow the sale of alcohol on Sundays, and a few do not allow the sale of cold beer in stores anytime. In wet counties, beer is available in supermarkets and convenience stores and wine and liquor in "package stores," which are usually small and inconspicuous. The microbrew craze that has swept the country in the past decade has pretty much bypassed Mississippi so far. It can be difficult to find anything but the mainstream brands in stores and bars.

CHURCH MUSIC

Most blues singers received early vocal training in church, and many return to church music toward the end of their lives. Some flip-flop back and forth between blues and gospel throughout their lives, believing that one must choose between the two styles, while others reconcile the two and even throw a church song into their blues performances.

The days of the bluesy, solo singing evangelists are over, however. You won't walk into a little church in Mississippi and hear singing accompanied by slide guitar à la Fred McDowell or Blind Willie Johnson (or, if you do, please notify this author immediately).

On the other hand, you still can hear a lot of powerful, soulful church singing with roots in old-time gospel and connections to the blues. Recommendations of individual churches are outside the scope of this book, but your best bets for such music are Missionary Baptist (look for "M. B." in the name) or Church of God In Christ (COGIC) churches. Services usually start at 10 A.M. Sunday, and often last two or three hours. If you go, dress nicely (no shorts or T-shirts, please) and donate generously when the plate is passed.

Another way to hear gospel music is at a gospel concert. These feature a succession of acts, mostly local but usually with one headliner from out of town, and have less preaching than church services. Still, the idea is to glorify the Lord, not just to dig on the music, so, again, dress and act respectfully. Look for posters advertising these concerts, ask at churches or record stores, or listen to gospel radio programs on Sundays.

Also, some blues festivals include gospel stages.

CASINOS

The state legislature legalized casino gambling in 1990, and old-fashioned, Bible Belt Mississippi quickly became the nation's third-biggest gambling mecca, after Las Vegas and Atlantic City. So as not to pollute the land with their evil enterprise, the casinos must be floating on water, or right next to it. There is a concentration of casinos on the Mississippi River near Tunica, capitalizing on the Memphis market. Another flotilla is around Biloxi on the Gulf of Mexico, attracting gamblers from New Orleans and those who fly in from other parts of the country. The cities of Greenville, Vicksburg, and Natchez also have river casinos, presumably to service their own citizens.

The casinos have had an immediate negative effect on the blues world: they took business away from jook joints, forcing nearby jooks to close or eliminate live music. People who used to pay a cover and then buy drinks in a jook now spend their entertainment dollars gambling at the casino, while drinking on the house and maybe listening to some music in the lounge.

The downhome acts that used to play the jooks are generally not the sort deemed suitable for the slick world of the casino lounges. On the other hand, some casinos present big-name soul-blues acts in concert in their theaters. Call the casinos for schedules or check the listings in the Memphis (for the Tunica area), Greenville, Vicksburg, Gulfport, or Biloxi newspapers.

One casino—the Horseshoe, near Robinsonville—named its theater "Bluesville" and installed a blues museum. Curiously, Bluesville's music programming tends to be less blues-oriented than that of the other casinos. And that museum has closed.

JOOK JOINTS

These places (sometimes spelled "juke joints") are not named after the jukeboxes found in them—rather, it's the other way around. Decades ago, Paul Oliver described jooks as "unappealing, decrepit, crumbling shacks, which never seem to have been built yesterday, but always thirty or forty years ago, and unpainted since."

Many of those shacks have crumbled since, and not been replaced. Others might still be crumbling, and still not been painted. The trouble for today's blues travelers is that most of the remaining jook joints actually have become jukebox-joints, without live music. The jukeboxes are likely to have blues on them, though, and you might get a feel for the kind of places Elmore James or Robert Johnson used to play in. In many Delta towns, the black section—usually across the railroad tracks from downtown—is likely to have a place called a "café" or perhaps without a name at all but with a beer sign and with people hanging out in front. Inside, people sit and drink and talk to their friends. This book includes jooks that regularly feature live music—or have atmosphere, an older clientele, and play recorded blues. But ask around. Places open and close abruptly. You might find one we missed, or one that just happens to have live music the weekend you're in town (and the one that usually has live music just might not have it while you're there).

Danger?

Walking into any bar where you are a stranger can be unnerving. And the apprehension can be magnified when you're far from home and don't dress or talk like the other people there, who all seem to know each other.

Don't, however, mistake your own discomfort for real danger. Chances are, the regulars at any Mississippi jook joint or nightclub will welcome you warmly, and you'll have many new friends by the end of the night. In any poor neighborhood, don't flaunt your cash, jewelry, camera, or other valuables—especially while you're outside the club. Inside, just be nice to everyone, especially the owner, and you'll have a great time.

Some visitors to the South have a fear of the police, worrying that they will be harassed, beaten, or jailed on a trumped-up charge. In reality, the worst problem you are likely to have with law enforcement is getting a speeding ticket—some towns and counties seem to love handing those out. Highway checkpoints for drunk drivers are also common, especially after college football games. So be careful, and mind the laws. If you really are speeding or driving drunk, and an officer cites you, that isn't harassment.

CONCLUSION

Your briefing on history and local customs is finished. With a car and this guidebook, you're ready to hit the highway!

Memphis & Beale Street

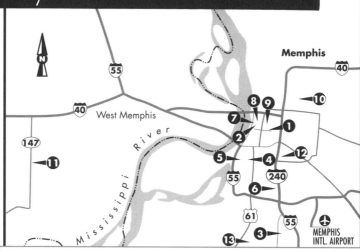

1. Beale Street & Walk of Fame
2. Center for Southern Folklore, Pembroke Square at Peabody Place, 119 S. Main Street
3. Graceland, 3734 Elvis Presley Boulevard
4. Stax Museum of American Soul Music, 926 E. McLemore Avenue
5. Memphis Minnie's final residence, 1355 Adelaide Street
6. Furry Lewis's grave – Hollywood Cemetery, 2012 Hernando Road
7. Memphis Rock 'n' Soul Museum, 145 Lt. George W. Lee Avenue, in the Gibson Guitar Building
8. WDIA Radio Station, 112 Union Street
9. Sun Studio, 706 Union Avenue
10. Wild Bill's Lounge, 1580 Vollintine Avenue (at Avalon Street)
11. Albert King's grave – Paradise Gardens Cemetery
12. Callie & Burnside's, 1243 Walker Avenue
13. New Park Cemetery, 4536 Horn Lake Road

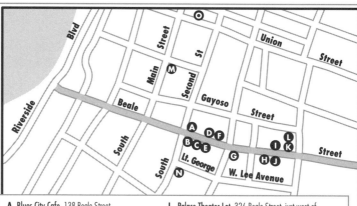

A. Blues City Cafe, 138 Beale Street
B. B. B. King's, 143 Beale Street
C. Black Diamond, 153 Beale Street
D. King's Palace Cafe, 162 Beale Street
E. A. Schwab, 163 Beale Street
F. Rum Boogie Cafe, 182 Beale Street
G. Former site of Mitchell's, Club Handy, and the Center for Southern Folklore, 209 Beale Street
H. Hard Rock Cafe (includes Pee Wee's site), 317 Beale Street
I. Palace Theater Lot, 326 Beale Street, just west of Legends Rhythm and Blues Club
J. Old Daisy Theater, 329 Beale Street
K. Monarch Club, 340 Beale Street
L. W. C. Handy Home, 352 Beale Street
M. Center for Southern Folklore – Pembroke Square at Peabody Place, 119 S. Main Street
N. Memphis Rock 'n' Soul Museum, 145 Lt. George W. Lee Avenue, in the Gibson Guitar Building
O. WDIA, 112 Union Street
   Sun Studio, 706 Union Avenue (see Memphis area map)

chapter 2

MEMPHIS

The railroads, the highways, and the river all lead to Memphis—and bring the people and the music. Although it is in Tennessee, Memphis functions as the cultural and economic capital of North Mississippi.

Memphis has long been one of America's great music cities, where the blues, rock 'n' roll and soul all were nurtured, although it has never managed to polish up its music heritage and turn it into a major industry, the way Nashville has done with country-western.

Beale Street

To get there: From Memphis International Airport, follow the signs onto I-240 west, toward downtown. After 2 miles, switch to I-55 north and take that for 6 miles to Riverside Drive. Continue north on Riverside for about 1 1/4 miles, until you see the Beale Street sign. Turn right onto Beale and park wherever you can on or near the street.

For almost a century, Memphis's Beale Street was the focal point not only of the Mississippi Delta but of black America, eclipsing even Harlem in its crowds, excitement, and music. It left quite an impression on visitors:

You could used to walk down the street in days of 1900 and like that and you could find a man wit' throat cut from y'ear to ear. Also you could find people lyin' dead wit' not their throat cut, money took and everything in their pockets, took out of their pockets and thrown outside the house. Sometimes you find them with no clothes on and such as that. Sometimes you find them throwed out of winders and so forth, here on Beale Street. Sportin' class o' women runnin' up and down the street all night long.
—Will Shade, leader of the Memphis Jug Band

To me Beale Street was the most famous place in the South . . . and it was so much more than I had even envisioned. I don't know if I can explain it to this day—my eyes had to be very big, because I saw everything, from winos to people dressed up fit to kill, young, old, city slickers and people straight out of the cotton fields, somehow or other you could tell: *every damn one of them was glad to be there.*
—Sun Records producer Sam Phillips, who arrived from Alabama in 1945

Beale Street was the black man's haven. When you went to Beale Street and if you had problems or troubles or something away from there, once you got to Beale Street—no problem, no trouble. I told a white fellow once, "If you were black for one Saturday night and on Beale Street, never would you want to be white again."
—Deejay/performer Rufus Thomas

I didn't think of *Memphis* as Memphis. I thought of Beale Street as Memphis.
—B. B. King

A river port surrounded by vast agricultural lands, and the only real city between St. Louis and New Orleans, Memphis was the place to go for a good time. And Beale Street, just off the docks, was the specific destination.

It became the hub of black life for the entire region. And the crowds and the wide-open atmosphere attracted musicians of every stripe. In the late 1920s and early 1930s, Beale Street became home for blues singer-guitarists, mostly from North Mississippi and often in duos: Frank Stokes and Dan Sain, Memphis Minnie and Kansas Joe (who despite their nicknames were both Mississippians), Garfield Akers and Joe Callicott, along with solo acts Jim Jackson, Robert Wilkins, and Furry Lewis. All played on the street, in the park, at parties for whites who would venture onto Beale, on the touring medicine shows that would recruit there, and perhaps in the clubs occasionally, although the club gigs mostly went to pianists and jazz combos.

Jim Jackson's "Kansas City Blues," one of the biggest blues hits of the 1920s, is, despite its title, about Beale Street:

> *I's first on Main Street, started down Beale*
> *I's looking for that woman they call Lucille*

Jug bands also flourished on Beale. These groups, including the Memphis Jug Band, Cannon's Jug Stompers, and Jack Kelly and his South Memphis Jug Band, played the blues as well as waltzes, popular tunes, political jingles, or whatever was required.

The Depression and Boss Crump's reform movement chilled Beale's spirits in the 1930s. In the forties and fifties it sprung back, however, with the new styles of blues and jazz. WDIA had begun its history-making broadcasts of black music with black announcers, and the street swayed to the sounds of Rufus Thomas, Gatemouth Moore, B. B. King, and others.

In the 1960s, Beale hit another lull. Most of its businesses closed, except for a few pool halls and pawnshops. "Urban renewal" came in, demolishing many buildings on Beale and hundreds in the neighborhoods around it. Although Beale Street became a National Historic Area in 1966, it had ceased to exist as a community.

"There isn't much left to Beale Street now," blues writer Samuel Charters sadly observes in the opening line of his 1977 book *Sweet as the Showers of Rain*. Charters had appreciated the street's "looseness—its lack of fuss and pretense. It was a wide-open neighborhood with a lot of music in the clubs or on the street itself, a lot of casual drinking, and a lot of sex that didn't cost much money." He had no idea that it would again become home to blues-filled bars, nightclubs, and outdoor festivals.

Clubs began reopening on the street in 1982, although some of the original buildings are gone and others have been refurbished beyond recognition. The opening of B. B. King's club in 1991 helped make Beale a tourist destination.

The sad thing about Beale these days is that the neighborhoods around it have been torn down. It sits there, all lit up, surrounded by parking lots, office buildings, and newfangled developments. Still, there is some good music on Beale, especially during special events when stages are set up in the park and on the street, and usually in the clubs on any weekend.

Beale Street

- ## B. B. King's
  143 Beale St.
  (901) 524-5464

The name "B. B. King"—the name most identified with the blues—boosts the reputation and popularity of this club and, by extension, all of Beale Street. Strategically located, neon-bedecked, with outdoor speakers blaring the blues and its own gift shop next door, the club, which opened May 3, 1991, lets you know, loud and clear, that you're on Beale Street, land of the blues.

Don't walk in expecting to see B. B., though—he plays there only a few times a year, and those high-ticket shows generally sell out early. There is live music nightly, however, from Preston Shannon or another high-energy local blues act.

- ## Other Clubs

Other places that regularly present blues include the **Black Diamond**, 153 Beale St. (901-521-0800), the **Blues City Cafe**, 138 Beale St. (901-526-3637), and the **Rum Boogie Cafe**, 182 Beale St. (901-528-0150), which has part of the original Stax neon sign inside, as well as guitars signed by Son Seals, Ike Turner, Stevie Ray Vaughan, and many others.

- **King's Palace Cafe**
162 Beale St.
(901) 521-1851

The upstairs of this building once housed Hooks Brothers, a black-owned photography studio where Robert Johnson is believed to have posed for the 1935 pinstripe-suit photo that was on the cover of his 1990 *The Complete Recordings* boxed set—one of only two known photos of Johnson. The one common photograph of Tommy Johnson was also made here in 1928.

- **A. Schwab**
163 Beale St.
(901) 523-9782

Schwab's is open from 9 A.M. to 5 P.M. Mondays through Saturdays. An old-fashioned general store, this is the only remaining original business on Beale, a holdover from the street's glory days and before. Alsatian immigrant Abraham Schwab founded the store in 1876 at 142 Beale. It moved to 149 Beale in the 1890s and to its present location in 1911. The founder's grandson, Abe Schwab, runs the store today.

In the 1990 documentary *Deep Blues,* narrator Robert Palmer begins his exploration of the Mississippi Delta at Schwab's. Abe Schwab tells him that the store used to sell blues 78s (at three for a dollar) and people poured in, lured by the music playing on the speakers. When the store became overcrowded, the Schwabs would put on church music for a while to thin out the crowd.

The family learned that the people who bought blues records were also interested in voodoo. Schwab's began carrying bottled potions, candles, soaps, and other voodoo supplies, and still does. It also still carries music, on CDs and tapes instead of 78s. And it seems to have everything else—hardware, cleaning supplies, souvenirs, clothing. "If you can't find it at Schwab's, you're better off without it" is the slogan. The second-floor landing has an exhibit recreating the music and goods of the old days.

- **Former site of Mitchell's, Club Handy, and the Center for Southern Folklore**
209 Beale St.

The building dates from 1896, and was originally a drugstore—one of the first twenty-four-hour drugstores in the country, providing around-the-clock emergency service on rough Beale Street. In the 1940s, the building housed Sunbeam Mitchell's third-floor hotel and second-floor lounge, famous for hospitality to poor or stranded musicians and for its chili. It later became the Club Handy, where jazz and blues musicians performed and jammed after hours.

Mitchell's and the Club Handy are fondly remembered in the Center for Southern Folklore's documentary *All Day and All Night: Memories From Beale Street Musicians,* which may be viewed at the center's new location. The Center for Southern Folklore occupied this building from 1996 to 1999, when it lost its lease and was kicked out to make way for Wet Willie's, a branch of the frozen-daiquiri bar chain.

• Third and Beale

This intersection is mentioned in many blues lyrics and was the heart of the community. Memphis Minnie and Little Son Joe lived in an apartment at this corner after moving from Chicago back to Memphis in the late 1950s.

• Handy Park
Between Third and Beale streets, Peabody Place, and Rufus Thomas Blvd.

The park once was the site of the Beale Street Markethouse and Cold Storage Plant, an indoor/outdoor market that was torn down in 1930. It became a park that year, and was dedicated to Handy on March 29, 1931. The statue of Handy went up in 1960, two years after his death. Mahalia Jackson sang at the statue dedication ceremony.

Cast in bronze and standing on a marble pedestal, Handy holds a trumpet and looks sternly across the park onto Beale Street. His wordy plaque reads:

FATHER OF THE BLUES
William Christopher Handy
Born November 16, 1873 Florence, Ala.
Died New York City, March 28, 1958

Enshrined forever in the hearts of the nation are his immortal songs, "Memphis Blues," "St. Louis Blues," "Beale Street Blues" and those who sow in tears shall reap in joy with his golden trumpet he gave everlasting voice to these and folk songs of his people in the south land. His music is known and beloved throughout the world as an inspiration to youth and as an enduring gift to America's treasury of songs. For more than thirty years he was a distinguished member of the American Society of Composers, Authors and Publishers (ASCAP) which proudly joins the citizens of Memphis in erecting this everlasting tribute to his memory.

You still can hear musicians playing for tips on the hallowed ground of Handy Park. It's generally an electric band these days; amplification is required if those playing are to be heard above the din of traffic and recorded music emanating from the street-facing speakers of nearby businesses. During festivals, there often are free performances by scheduled acts.

• Rufus Thomas Monument
Rufus Thomas Blvd. just north of Beale St.

Rufus Thomas, who died December 15, 2001 at age eighty-four, is perhaps the epitome of Memphis entertainers. A minstrel-show veteran, deejay, singer, dancer, comedian, bandleader, and wild-dressing World's Oldest Teenager, Thomas was best known nationally for his dance hits "Do the Funky Chicken" and "Walking the Dog." He is recognized with a state historic marker in front of the Palace Theater site, a marker in Handy Park near the Handy statue, and in this tall concrete monument, which describes him as follows:

Rufus Thomas
Ambassador of Soul
The King of Rhythm and Blues
The funkiest chicken of the South
A star and veteran of service to this community
A man whose talents have endured
And whose performances have spanned generations
Out spoken and outta sight

• Pee Wee's
317 Beale St.

Pee Wee's—or "P. Wee's," as the sign read—was the hangout and unofficial office of many musicians, because the staff would take messages for them. Pee Wee's is where Will Shade met Charlie Burse and asked him to join the Memphis Jug Band.

Legend has it that this is also where W. C. Handy wrote "Mr. Crump," which later became "Memphis Blues." Handy explains in his autobiography, however, that he "often used to use his cigar

stand to write out copies of the following lyric for visiting bands."
Note that he says "write out copies"—of a song that he had already written.

Of course, people did more than hang out and write music at Pee Wee's. It also was a rough gambling den, with the house joke "We can't close yet—no one has been killed." Handy used that as a slogan for the whole street in his "Beale Street Blues":

> *You'll meet honest men and pickpockets skilled,*
> *You'll find that business never closes till somebody*
> *gets killed.*

The building has been demolished, and its lot is underneath part of the Hard Rock Cafe, 315 Beale St. (901-529-0007). There is a historical marker about Pee Wee's on the sidewalk.

• Palace Theater Lot
326 Beale St., just west of Legends Rhythm and Blues Club

Once the largest black-entertainment venue in the South, the Palace was affiliated with the Theater Owners' Booking Association. The TOBA circuit provided national tours for black performers including Bessie Smith, Alberta Hunter (from Memphis), Butterbeans and Susie, and Ma Rainey. The Palace outlasted TOBA, and continued to bring in top touring jazz acts such as Duke Ellington, Count Basie, and Ella Fitzgerald.

Beginning in 1935, the Palace featured a weekly amateur night, at which Rufus Thomas worked first as the comic, then as emcee. Performers competed for small cash prizes, hoping not to be booed offstage. Later, the policy was changed so that every performer received one dollar.

Some of those contestants would later become famous. Others were already established performers, but they would come by anyway when times were hard. Frank Stokes, Bukka White, Robert Nighthawk, and Earl Hooker were among the contestants. To this day, B. B. King thanks Thomas for allowing him to compete every week, so that he could collect that dollar. On another night of the week was the "Midnight Ramble," when all-white audiences came to see black acts.

The Palace has been demolished. The covered patio of Legends Rhythm and Blues Club is on its lot. There is a state historic marker on the sidewalk.

- **Old Daisy Theater**
  329 Beale St.

Another grand old theater where movies and touring acts played, this one is pretty much closed but still standing. You can look at the mosaic entranceway and old ticket booth under the painted ceiling of the outdoor foyer. It houses some offices, and shows are held there occasionally, but the building is generally closed to the public.

The 1929 short film *St. Louis Blues,* starring Bessie Smith, had its world premiere at the Daisy, and Bessie attended.

- **Monarch Club**
  340 Beale St.

Currently occupied by a bar called the Double Deuce, this is perhaps the street's loveliest building. In its heyday, from 1902 to about 1920, the Monarch Club was the fanciest joint on Beale—and the most notorious. It was dubbed the "castle of missing men" because so many murders were committed there. Owned by politician and alleged gangster Jim Kinnane, it is probably the club where Robert Wilkins wishes he were in his 1935 "Old Jim Canans":

> *I wisht I was back at Old Jim Canans*
> *I'd stand on the corner and wave my hand*
> *And if you don't b'lieve that I'm a drinkin' man*
> *Said, baby, stop by here with your beer can.*

Born in Hernando, Mississippi, and resident of Memphis for many years, Wilkins later became the *Reverend* Robert Wilkins and changed the words of his old blues numbers to make them religious (such as "That's No Way to Get Along," about women mistreating him, which became the biblical "Prodigal Son"). But he certainly bragged about partying down at Jim Kinnane's. The song refers not only to beer drinking but also to whiskey, playing the dozens, and sniffing cocaine. Perhaps that was just to please the audience, though—Ishmon Bracey, another bluesman-turned-minister, said of Wilkins, "Didn't drink nothing but a little wine. I never saw a man drink so little."

Delta blues-singing pianist Louise Johnson also liked the Monarch, or knew that her audiences did. She opens her 1930 "On the Wall" (with Charley Patton in the studio making spoken comments) by announcing:

Well, I'm going to Memphis, gon' stop at Jim Kinnane's,
I'm going to show these womens how to treat a man

Another verse has her stopping at "Church's hall" to show the women "how to cock it on the wall." "Church's hall" was the auditorium in **Church's Park**, east of Fourth Street on Beale. Established in 1899 by Robert Church, a real-estate magnate said to be the South's first black millionaire, the park was an early center of black social life. The auditorium is no longer standing.

• W. C. Handy Home
352 Beale St.
(901) 522-1556

The building is open from 10 A.M. to 4 P.M. Tuesdays through Saturdays. An admission charge includes a tour.

The delightful, thorough tour of W. C. Handy's home given by Mattie Sengstacke is probably the best deal in town. Mrs. Sengstacke is familiar not only with Handy's life but also with Memphis history, the Civil Rights Movement, and the African American press, among other subjects.

The house is tucked into the corner of the Beale Street Historic District, back a way from the street. It was moved to Beale from its original location at 659 Jennette Street, ten blocks to the south, which is where Handy actually lived while he was in Memphis—from about 1905, when he came here from Clarksdale, Mississippi, until 1918, when he moved to New York.

A simple brick shotgun house, it is painted plain gray on the outside and white on the inside. Visitors can see musical instruments and clothing of the type associated with Handy, but not his actual belongings (some of those are in another Handy museum, at his birthplace in Florence, Alabama).

A trained, professional musician, Handy championed and commercialized the blues, which had been a folk music passed on strictly through the oral tradition. He wrote and published compositions with elements of the blues in their melodies and lyrics and with the word "blues" in their titles, thus bringing that form into the mainstream of popular music and creating the first blues craze. Although he accepted the title "Father of the Blues," even using that as the name of his autobiography, Handy did not create the blues and never claimed to.

The Handy house in Memphis contains the published sheet music of many of his songs, photographs of him and his family throughout their lives, and some of his letters. Handy tapes, books, and T-shirts are available for purchase.

• The Midway
357 Beale St.

Many musicians claimed to have played at the Midway. Memphis Slim insisted, however, that he and Roosevelt Sykes were the only two blues singers who played there, "because guitar players couldn't play nowhere in those days but in the park or in the street somewhere." The Midway remained open as a pool hall into the late 1960s, when most of the other joints had become pawnshops, barber shops, laundries or were closed.

The building has been demolished. The site lies outside the Beale Street Historic District, which ends at Fourth Street.

• Solvent Savings Bank
386 Beale St.

Walk across Fourth Street—the limit of the usual tourist section of Beale Street—to find this handsome red-brick two-story building that once housed Pace and Handy Music Publishing. Solvent Savings itself was the city's first black-owned bank, established in 1906. Pace and Handy Music opened shop as a tenant upstairs, 392 Beale, the following year.

• Center for Southern Folklore
Pembroke Square at Peabody Place, 119 S. Main St.
(901) 525-3655

The Center for Southern Folklore (not to be confused with the Center for the Study of Southern Culture at the University of Mississippi) is a nightclub, coffee bar, art gallery, and bookstore with live music and other cultural events at noon and in the evening. It also is a nonprofit corporation that aims "to preserve, defend and protect the music, culture, arts and rhythms of the South." It produces the annual Memphis Music and Heritage Festival, held on Labor Day weekend.

The center often features live blues at lunchtime. The late Mose Vinson was a regular until his death in 2002. Vinson, a native of Holly Springs, Mississippi, was a longtime participant in the Memphis music scene—he played on such 1950s Sun recordings as James Cotton's "Cotton Crop Blues" and Jimmy DeBerry's "Take a Little Chance." The Fieldstones, longtime house band at the beloved Memphis jook Greens Lounge (destroyed by fire in 1998) also play at the center.

• The Peabody
149 Union Ave.
(901) 529-4000

The Peabody's giant neon sign glows above Beale Street. An elegant and expensive old hotel, the Peabody might seem a world apart from the raucous street life of Beale. But it has an important place in blues history as a site of field-recording trips by northern record companies in the 1920s and 1930s. The companies would rent a room at a hotel in a southern city, then call for blues singers for auditions and on-the-spot recording sessions.

Among the artists who recorded at the Peabody in 1929 were Furry Lewis, Charlie McCoy, Walter Vincent (aka Vincson), Speckled Red, Robert Wilkins, Jenny Pope, Big Joe Williams, Jed Davenport, Garfield Akers, Jim Jackson, Joe Callicott, and Kid Bailey.

Mississippi bluesman Eugene Powell, who recorded as Sonny Boy Nelson at the St. Charles Hotel in New Orleans in 1936, provides some insight into a process that was probably about the same at the Peabody, the King Edward in Jackson, or any of the other hotels that served as temporary recording studios:

> I remember we worked all night. The machine was sitting in the middle of the room, but we was way upstairs in the air, in another part of the house. The place was about seven or eight stories high, and we was way up there, playing music, to be out of the noise and other stuff, cars, or they would get caught on tape—they put those big sheets up over the windows to muffle all that music and stuff. The guys that recorded us they were nice fellas, they just recorded whatever we wanted to play. They didn't tell us how to do nothing. So we was making some good records.

The Peabody also sometimes provided work for Memphis jug bands at stag parties for white businessmen. Those were good gigs, because the businessmen would get drunk and tip well, especially when the bands played requested pop hits.

The beloved live ducks in the Peabody lobby fountain are a tradition that began in 1932, originally as a prank by the manager.

Best times to watch are when they leave the elevator at 11 A.M., or when they get back on it to return to their rooftop roost at 5 P.M.

Now inside the Peabody lobby, **Lansky's** still features the flashy men's clothing it has specialized in since the 1950s, when it was the place where Beale Street's hippest bought their threads. At least one dreamy-eyed young white boy—Elvis Presley—would gaze into the store's windows and say hello to its proprietors. As soon as he got a few bucks, Presley began buying clothes at Lansky's. Even before he started performing, Presley stood out from the white working-class crowd for his unconventional dress, which, like his music, derived almost directly from blacks. Bernard Lansky, who still owns and operates the store, proudly proclaims himself "Clothier to the King" on his signs and business cards. B. B. King, Bobby "Blue" Bland, and Rufus Thomas have also shopped at Lansky's.

When Elvis was hanging out there, Lansky's was at 126 Beale Street. That building, appropriately, became Elvis Presley's nightclub, recently renamed EP Delta Kitchen. Love Me Tender gifts and clothing, in the same building, offers Elvis-style duds at lower prices than Lansky's. Nearby and across the street stands a giant Elvis statue that was unveiled during Elvis week 1997.

- ## Beale Street Walk of Fame

Brass notes on the sidewalk honor people who have been important in Memphis music history. Many blues musicians as well as those from other genres are so recognized, as are business people, public officials, and other nonmusicians who have had significant roles on Beale.

- ## Gayoso Street

North of Beale and parallel to it, this street was full of high-class whorehouses around the turn of the twentieth century. It was the Memphis equivalent of New Orleans's famed Storyville district. Like Storyville, it featured light-skinned black prostitutes who catered to wealthy white customers. And, as in Storyville, each club had a pianist playing standards, ragtime, and early forms of blues and jazz.

- ## Memphis Rock 'n' Soul Museum
  145 Lt. George W. Lee Ave., in the Gibson Guitar Building
  (901) 543-0800

The Smithsonian Institution designed this as a traveling exhibition, but Gibson provided a permanent home at its plant in Memphis, which opened in 2000.

The admission price includes an audio tour, featuring speech and music, through the museum's photos, artifacts, and re-creations. The portable CD players also allow visitors to listen to a choice of dozens of classic Memphis tunes, including such obscure gems as Elder Curry's "Memphis Flu" and Phineas Newborn, Jr., and Trio's "No Moon at All," as well as the standard classics. The opening video is a good introduction to Memphis music—make sure to stay for Carl Perkins's "Matchbox" at the end. Among the museum's treasures are a piece of the Grand Ole Opry transmitter, a 1934 Seeburg jukebox, the drums Al Jackson played on "Dock of the Bay" and "Green Onions," and the sax on which Ben Branch played "Precious Lord, Take My Hand" for Martin Luther King, Jr., just before King was killed. Hours are 10 A.M. to 6 P.M. Sundays through Thursdays and to 8 P.M. Fridays and Saturdays. Tours of the plant also are available.

FESTIVALS

The Memphis Music and Heritage Festival (Labor Day weekend), International Blues Challenge (in late January), the Handy Awards (in April), and Memphis in May's Beale Street Music Festival (early in May) are blues-filled festivals held on and around Beale.

The **Music and Heritage Festival**, presented by the Center for Southern Folklore, is Memphis's answer to the New Orleans Jazz and Heritage Festival. Both are celebrations of the music and folk traditions of their area. But while the event in New Orleans draws hundreds of thousands, the Memphis fest attracts small, mostly local audiences. It is delightful and free, held on outdoor stages and inside the center.

International Blues Challenge, presented by the Blues Foundation, combines a conference for blues societies and fans with a competition for unsigned blues acts. It all happens along Beale Street. The Blues Foundation also presents the Handy Awards, the blues world's equivalent of the Grammys. The awards event features plenty of live music. Tickets and information on both events are available through the Blues Foundation's web site, www.blues.org.

Memphis in May is the city's biggest celebration, and includes many other events besides the two-day music festival, which is held in the riverside Tom Lee Park and on Beale. There are several pop headliners, but also a blues stage with national and regional acts.

Away from Beale Street

• Crump Boulevard

This street is named after Edward Hull Crump, who was born in Holly Springs, Mississippi, in 1874, moved to Memphis as a young man and became mayor in 1909. He was reelected twice, then resigned in 1916 amid legal pressure over his refusal to enforce state prohibition law. However, like other local political bosses in U.S. cities, Crump firmly controlled Memphis politics until his death in 1954.

W. C. Handy composed "Mr. Crump Don't Like It" as an *instrumental* campaign ditty for Crump in his first campaign. Listeners, however, would sing along, expressing their feelings about Crump's reform plans. Those comments became the lyrics to the song:

> *Mr. Crump won't 'low no easy riders here*
> *We don't care what Mr. Crump don't 'low*
> *We gon' to bar'lhouse anyhow—*
> *Mr. Crump can go and catch hisself some air!*

Handy transformed the song into his "Memphis Blues." But "Mr. Crump" lived on as a Memphis staple, notably in a 1927 recording titled "Mr. Crump Don't Like It" by the Beale Street Sheiks (Frank Stokes and Dan Sain).

• Bridges

Bluesman-turned-rock pioneer Chuck Berry wrote the classic "Memphis, Tennessee" about trying to reach by phone a little girl who lived "on the south side, high upon a ridge, just a half a mile from the Mississippi bridge." The location of the fictional girl's home is probably not specific. The bridge, however, would be the Memphis-Arkansas Bridge that crosses the Mississippi River at Crump Boulevard—*not* the flashy new M-shaped Hernando de Soto Bridge farther north. The Memphis-Arkansas Bridge, originally named the E. H. Crump Bridge, was completed in 1949. To cross Berry's bridge, take Interstate 55 north. Half a mile south of there would put you at about McLemore Avenue.

The Hernando de Soto Bridge was completed in 1972, too late for Chuck Berry's song. But it does have a music-oriented **welcome sign**. Driving over the bridge into Memphis from West Memphis, notice the sign that greets you from atop a storage silo to the right: "Memphis, Home of the Blues, Birthplace of Rock 'n' Roll." The "I" in Memphis is in the form of a guitar. The sign, installed in September 1999 by Shelby County government with private donations, lights up at night.

- **WDIA**
  112 Union St.

A state historic marker here identifies WDIA as "the Goodwill Station" and notes that its all-black format made it the top-rated Memphis station in the early 1950s. The sign names Nat D. Williams as the station's first black deejay and identifies some of its other well-known deejays from over the years, including blues singers B. B. King, Rufus Thomas, and Dwight "Gatemouth" Moore (although his name is spelled incorrectly and his nickname is left off). This is WDIA's second location, where it was based from 1981 to 2004. It started at 2267 Central Ave. In 2004 it moved to its current location, 2650 Thousand Oaks Blvd. #4100.

The best way to appreciate WDIA is to turn your radio to 1070 AM and listen to it—especially on Saturdays, when it plays all blues.

In 1949, WDIA became the first black-format (although white-owned) radio station. It billed itself "The Mother Station of the Negroes." Joe Hill Louis, "the Be-bop Boy," a one-man band who played the blues in parks and at ball games (and recorded at Sun Records) was the station's first Pep-ti-kon Boy, singing live commercial jingles for the patent medicine. The next Pep-ti-kon Boy was B. B. King.

King, a new arrival from Mississippi, had played one night at the Sixteenth Street Grill in West Memphis, filling in for regular performer Sonny Boy Williamson. The club's owner, a Miss Annie, told King he could work there six nights a week if he, like Williamson, had a radio show on which to publicize the cafe gigs.

Sun Studio, 706 Union Avenue, Memphis

King scrambled to WDIA, where he won the radio spot by instantly writing a Pep-ti-kon jingle. King biographer Sebastian Danchin cites that moment as "the point where his career really took off." King worked at the station until 1953, when he turned his show over to Rufus Thomas.

- **Sun Studio**
  706 Union Ave.
  (800) 441-6249 or (901) 521-0664

Bob Dylan reportedly kissed the studio floor when he visited. Best known as the place where Elvis Presley made his first recordings, Sun Studio would be a major musical shrine even if Elvis had never stopped by.

At Memphis Recording Service (as it was called in its first few years, before the Sun label was founded), Sam Phillips oversaw raw, wild blues sessions, including the wonderful early recordings of Howlin' Wolf, "Dr." Isaiah Ross, B. B. King, Big Walter Horton, James Cotton, Rufus Thomas, Little Junior Parker, and Little Milton. Jackie Brenston's 1951 "Rocket 88" (featuring Ike Turner as pianist and bandleader), often considered the first rock 'n' roll record, was another in the series of important, influential, and just plain great tracks recorded here.

On the eighteen-year-old Presley's first session at the studio in 1953, he chose to record the decidedly non-blues, non-rock 'n' roll "My Happiness" and "That's When Your Heartaches Begin." Presley returned to Sun on July 5, 1954, however, with Scotty Moore and Bill Black, and cut a cover of Mississippi bluesman Arthur Crudup's "That's All Right" that would launch Presley's career and the national rock 'n' roll craze.

Phillips soon sold Elvis's contract to RCA. But Phillips's attention had shifted from blues to white rock 'n' roll. He recorded hits for Carl Perkins, Johnny Cash, Jerry Lee Lewis, Roy Orbison, and Charlie Rich. Despite all his success with rockabilly, however, Phillips always called Howlin' Wolf his greatest discovery.

"My feeling was that there was more talent, innately natural, in the people that I wanted to work with—Southern black, Southern country white—than there was in the people who wrote down arrangements," Sam Phillips told an interviewer in 1994, concisely stating the philosophy that guided him and his studio.

Phillips moved his operations to 639 Madison Avenue in 1960 and kept Sun going there until 1968, but the company was no longer a vital force in popular music. Phillips retired in 1969 and died in 2003. His son Knox still operates the Madison Avenue studio as Phillips Recording Service.

Except for occupation by a few short-lived businesses, the original Sun Studio was empty and unused from 1960 to 1985. Looking much the way it always did, it has reopened as an active recording studio as well as a tourist attraction. B. B. King returned to Sun in 1987 to record "When Love Comes to Town" with Irish rock superstars U2, who also recorded three other songs here for their album *Rattle and Hum*. Bonnie Raitt, Ringo Starr, and the Stray Cats also have recorded here in recent years.

If you get inspired, studio time is available at competitive prices. You can also book a special souvenir session, in which you sing to a prerecorded background and take home a CD or tape of yourself.

In the half-hour studio tour, for which there is a fee, you can pose for pictures at the microphone Elvis used. The guide tells the amazing history of Sun, and plays samples of many of the songs recorded here, including some blues numbers. Tours are given from 10 A.M. to 6 P.M. daily.

Entrance to the gift shop, upstairs, is free, and it has exhibits of photographs and equipment. Tapes and CDs of all the Sun artists are available. In the 1950s, the gift shop space was Taylor Boarding Home, where many of the white artists stayed while they were recording. Blues pianist Mose Vinson worked there as a custodian. Vinson did get to play on some of the sessions.

The Sun Studio Cafe, downstairs, is a working restaurant that also has a small gift shop. It looks about the way it did in the old days, when it was the Taylor Cafe, where the studio staff and artists would hang out and work out deals.

- **Graceland, Elvis Presley's home and grave**
  3734 Elvis Presley Blvd.
  (800) 238-2000 or (901) 332-3322

The most visited place in Memphis and probably the most popular music-related site in the world, Graceland is the house Elvis bought in 1957, when he was a twenty-two-year-old star. He lived here until he died twenty years later.

You can get a free peek at the outside of the house by walking across the street from the parking area and looking over the stone wall. The wall and sidewalk in front of the house are covered with graffiti from fans. A state historic marker there sums up Presley's career:

Elvis Aaron Presley

Elvis Presley was born in Tupelo, Mississippi on January 8, 1935, the son of Vernon and Gladys Presley. He moved to Memphis in 1948. Soon after signing a contract with Sun Records in 1954 he achieved tremendous popularity. His musical and acting career in records, movies, television, and concerts made him one of the most successful and outstanding entertainers in the world. He died on August 16, 1977 and is buried here at his Memphis home, Graceland.

The Meditation Garden, which contains the graves of Presley and his mother, father, paternal grandmother, and a monument to his stillborn twin brother, is open free of charge from 7 to 8:30 A.M. daily.

To see any other part of the property, you must take a tour. The tours are offered from 9 A.M. to 5 P.M. Mondays through Saturdays and 10 A.M. to 4 P.M. Sundays. Graceland is closed on Thanksgiving, Christmas, and New Year's Day. The mansion tour is not given on Tuesdays from November through February. There are various tour packages at different prices, allowing visitors to choose parts or all of the mansion tour (the house, grounds, and grave), the Elvis Presley Auto Museum, the Lisa Marie and Hound Dog II airplanes, and the Sincerely Elvis exhibit of artifacts. Photography is permitted at Graceland, but only without flash. Video and audio recording are prohibited.

Built in 1939, Graceland already had its name when Elvis purchased it for a hundred thousand dollars and moved his family into it. It became the hangout for his large entourage of male friends, along with a changing cast of women. Fans would wait outside, hoping to catch glimpses of Elvis, and he often obliged them by coming out to chat and sign autographs.

The house is a palace of period kitsch. It has stained-glass peacocks, a Hawaiian-themed Jungle Room with an indoor waterfall and green shag carpeting on the floor and ceiling, a basement poolroom with fabric-covered walls, a firing range, and televisions everywhere (including three side by side in one room, so Elvis could watch all three channels simultaneously, an idea he got from President Lyndon Johnson). Much of it is left as it was when it was a family home. Other areas display gold records, portraits made by fans, clothing from Elvis's movies and concerts, guns given him by police officers, and other goods.

The mansion tour includes an audio guide with comments from Elvis's ex-wife, Priscilla, about life at Graceland: "One time it was meatloaf. Meatloaf every night for six months."

Many visitors become teary-eyed at the end of the tour when they arrive at the Meditation Garden, the final resting place for Presley and his family members. (Minnie Mae Presley, who died May 8, 1980, about a month before her ninetieth birthday, outlived her son, daughter-in-law, and famous grandson to become the most recent occupant of the garden.)

August 10–16 of each year is Elvis Week; it draws thousands of hardcore fans for special events, including an overnight candlelight vigil at the grave beginning on August 15.

- **Stax Museum of American Soul Music**
  926 E. McLemore Ave.
  (888) 942-SOUL or (901) 946-2535

Memphis is known for the blues and rock 'n' roll. But in the 1960s and '70s, it also was home of the great soul record company Stax. Jim Stewart (the "St") and Estelle Axton ("ax"), brother and sister, turned an old movie theater into "Soulsville USA," as its marquee proclaimed. With house band Booker T and the MGs, Stax created a Memphis soul style that challenged Detroit's Motown artistically and financially.

Stax also made some records of specific interest to blues lovers: a 1963 comeback album by the banjo-playing jug-band star Gus Cannon. And the company's biggest hit ever was the 1968 "Who's Making Love" by urbane bluesman Johnnie Taylor, who later made many successful records for Jackson-based Malaco. And the great Albert King was a Stax artist.

The company started in 1957 and folded in 1974. Although white-owned, Stax drew on the talents of the surrounding black community. As a map in the museum shows, many of its musicians grew up in the immediate area. Booker T Jones was a highschooler who came in to try out the instruments and never left. The neighborhood even was home to some prominent musicians without Stax connections: Aretha Franklin (although she and her family moved out when she was two) and Memphis Slim (his house is across from the museum parking lot at 1130 College Street, and supposedly due for restoration).

After Stax went out of business, its historic building was repossessed by a bank that sold it, for $10, to Southside Church of God in 1980. The church never followed through on its plan to turn it into a community center. The church also refused to sell it to anyone who wanted to make it a monument to Stax, allegedly because the company's product was the devil's music.

The building was torn down in 1988. **Shangri-La Records** (1916 Madison St., 901-274-1916) sold Stax bricks as mementos, and part of the original neon sign wound up inside **Rum Boogie Café** on Beale Street. All that remained at the hallowed site were the remains of the lobby's checkerboard slate-tile floor and parts of a concrete foundation. In front went a state historic marker that reads:

On this site stood Stax Records, Inc. which boasted such stars as Otis Redding, Rufus and Carla Thomas, Isaac Hayes, the Staple Singers, Albert King, the Bar-Kays and many others. It relied upon its deep soul roots to carry it through struggling from a back-street garage in 1957 to become a multi-million-dollar organization.

The lot sat empty and forlorn until 2000, when a group came along to develop it as a museum. Financed by the city and private donors, the multimillion-dollar museum opened in 2003. The idea was that it would rejuvenate the neighborhood. But the neighborhood stubbornly and happily retains its funky charm, with beauty shops, barbecue joints, and other urban splendor all around the sparkling new museum.

The self-guided museum tour starts with a movie including footage of B. B. King and Ray Charles, along with Rufus Thomas's terrific explanation of the difference between Motown and Stax.

Highlights of the collection include a whole country church, which was moved there from Duncan, Miss.; some Ike and Tina Turner performing outfits; the organ Booker T played on "Green Onions"; Albert King's first guitar, a Sears Werco electric (and for denser visitors, a museum note pointing out that King's "Crosscut Saw" is one of many blues songs that "hide sexual innuendo behind everyday imagery"); and Isaac Hayes's fur-lined, gold-plated Cadillac. There also is a dance floor where you can dance with a projection of *Soul Train*.

The tour finishes in the gift shop, which, appropriately, occupies the space where Satellite Records used to be.

• Callie & Burnside's

1243 Walker Ave. (off Bellevue Avenue—look for big milk bottle on a pole at an old dairy, and turn across from that onto Walker)
901-281-3202

This urban jook joint is owned by blues royalty: the late R. L. Burnside's oldest son, Melvin. The "Callie" in the joint's name is Melvin Burnside's fiancée, who works the kitchen, cranking out pig-ear sandwiches (fried or regular), burgers, and catfish and pork-chop sandwiches. The kitchen is open until 11 P.M., and the music usually goes much later—except on Sundays, when things start about 5 or 6 P.M. and end by midnight.

And this classic jook does full justice to the Burnside name.

Jim Townsend, owner of building that houses Callie & Burnside's jook joint, Memphis, outside his building

There is sometimes live music (often including members of the Burnside family) but even when it's deejay only, it's real blues. A mellow, friendly, and well-dressed older crowd dances to Bobby Blue Bland and Howlin' Wolf. It's a small place with only about ten tables, and not much of a dance floor, but people manage to dance wherever they can. There are red lights for atmosphere, and some fine photos on the wall, including one of actor (and blues musician and Memphis resident) Steven Seagal with Melvin, at a Seagal party where R. L. played.

Beer is sold by the quart, glasses provided. You can bring your own liquor and order mixers.

- **Memphis Minnie's Final Residence**
  1355 Adelaide St.

This is where Memphis Minnie and Ernest "Little Son Joe" Lawlers, her final husband and musical partner, lived from about 1960 to the end of their lives, staying with Minnie's sister Daisy. Having had a stroke and suffering from asthma, Minnie was in a wheelchair by then. Photos of her from that period, sitting on the house's porch, have been published in books and magazines. Lawlers died in 1961. Minnie lived until August 6, 1973. The old, white, wood house is near the corner of Olive Street. It has red-and-white awnings and well-maintained shrubs and lawn; the porch still looks inviting. Resist the temptation, though, because this is a private residence.

- **Wild Bill's Lounge**
  1580 Vollintine Ave. (at Avalon St.)
  (901) 726-5473

This north-of-Midtown jook joint is in a long, old commercial building that also houses a dry cleaner, a deli, and three beauty shops. Founder "Wild" Bill Storey died in 2007 at age eighty-eight, but his family has kept the business going.

Inside, it's a box about thirty feet wide by seventy feet long, with a kitchen in the back that cooks up chitterlings, beef stew, fried chicken, and all the trimmings. The room is bright orange, with Christmas lights strung all about and dozens of photos on the walls. It's full of long rows of tables—if you come alone, you'll be seated with other people.

And, now that the place has been discovered by the outside world, some of those people at your table might be well-to-do Memphians or visitors from another country. It's still a fun place, but the customer base has expanded well outside the neighborhood.

The live music happens most Friday and Saturday nights, with good local blues acts. You walk in right onto the dance floor. Either start dancing immediately or take your seat and order a drink. The beer prices still can't be beat. You order it by the quart or the forty-ouncer. Liquor, wine, and champagne also are available.

- **Blues Night Club (formerly known as the Blue Worm)**
  1405 Airways Blvd.
  (901)-454-4858

This club features live blues on Friday and Saturday nights, with the music usually starting after midnight. It is a very big room with little atmosphere and very late hours. It's open other nights except Mondays for deejay or jukebox music, which are blues-ish. Cover charge on weekends.

- **Live Blues Elsewhere in Memphis, Off Beale Street**

There are occasional visiting blues acts at Midtown clubs including Otherlands, Murphy's, Huey's, the Hi-Tone, and the Young Avenue Deli. The Boss Lounge, 912 Jackson Ave., sometimes features jazz-blues sessions on Thursdays. Check the weekly

Memphis Flyer or the Friday edition of the *Commercial Appeal* to find out who is playing where.

- **Place where Casey Jones began his fateful ride**
  Front Street just north of Poplar Avenue

Memphis's Poplar Station is where engineer John Luther "Casey" Jones began his final ride on April 29, 1900. He was riding Engine 383, the Illinois Central Cannonball.

Jones was not scheduled to work that day. He replaced the scheduled engineer who had called in sick. Outside Vaughan, Miss., the train crashed and Jones was killed. It remains unclear why Jones couldn't stop the train.

The crash became famous after Wallace "Wash" Sanders wrote a song about it, which has been loosely interpreted by many blues artists. (For more on the crash and the songs, see Water Valley Casey Jones Museum entry in Chapter 10.)

There is a state historic marker about Jones's ride on the west sidewalk of Front Street, just north of Poplar. If driving, you probably will have to park a few blocks away and walk to the sign, which is in the midst of the convention-center complex. Look past the sign to see a section of the old station's brick wall.

- **Graves of Bukka White, Rufus Thomas, several of the Bar-Kays, Al Jackson Jr., and others**
  New Park Cemetery
  4536 Horn Lake Road
  (901)785-7150

The cemetery is always open, but it is staffed 8:30 A.M. to 4 P.M. Mondays through Fridays.

It might seem odd to talk about a great cemetery. But this one, for blues travelers, is excellent. It contains the graves of two major blues musicians, and a handful of other prominent musicians. And the cemetery has done great work in making the graves accessible to the public. It prints a brochure of the "legends, heroes and influential talents that are buried at our facility." The staff will direct you or accompany you to the graves you are looking for (and in a huge cemetery like this, you need the help).

And best of all, the cemetery took the responsibility and the cost of buying and erecting a grave marker for Bukka White, who had lain here in an unmarked grave for many years. The stone's inscription reads:

Booker W. White
1909-1977
Loved by all

Yes, White's first name actually is "Booker," but the record company misunderstood his pronunciation and listed him as "Bukka." His date of birth might actually be 1906.

Blessed with a powerful voice and powerful arms that got a lot of sound out of a metal guitar, White first recorded in the 1930s, doing both blues and gospel. During that era he recorded the original version of the much-copied "Shake 'Em On Down." The song became a hit, but White had gotten into a scrape and been imprisoned at Parchman in the meantime. Upon his release in 1940, he recorded again, with the record company bringing in Washboard Sam to modernize the sound.

Those recordings are highly regarded by blues fans, but White temporarily left the music world after making them. He took a job at Newberry Tanks & Equipment Inc. (The company is now at 205 N. Walker Ave., West Memphis, Ark., but at that time it was at Lauderdale and Vance in Memphis.) For a while, White took in his young cousin B. B. King, who had gotten into trouble with his boss in Mississippi, and helped King get a job at Newberry. King admired White's slide-guitar style but was unable to copy it. Instead, King developed his trademark finger vibrato as a way to simulate the sliding. In the 1960s and '70s, White was a hit on the folk circuit nationally and overseas. He lived in California for a few years, but moved back to Memphis late in life and died here.

The Bar-Kays were a hot funk band that recorded instrumentals and backed vocalists at Stax. Four of them died, along with singer Otis Redding and several other people, in a plane crash on December 10, 1967. Three of those—drummer Carl Lee Cunningham, saxophonist Phalon Jones, and guitarist Jimmie King Jr.—are buried at New Park. Trumpeter Ben Cauley, who survived the crash, and bassist James Alexander, who missed the plane because he was returning a rental car, re-formed the group.

The graves of Cunningham and King are near each other, as is that of King's valet, Matthew Kelly, who also died in the crash. Jones's is separate from the rest.

Another Stax artist, drummer Al Jackson Jr. of Booker T and the MGs, also is buried at New Park. He died October 1, 1975, murdered at age thirty-nine.

Johnny Ace, a singing sensation of the early 1950s, who died playing Russian roulette on Christmas 1954, also is buried at New Park. His gravestone gives his real name, John M. Alexander Jr. It is a double marker with his mother, Maggie Newsom.

Gospel composer the Rev. William H. Brewster Sr. and gospel singer Mattie Wigley also are buried at New Park.

- **The Cotton Museum at the Memphis Cotton Exchange**
  65 Union Ave.
  (901)531-7826
  Admission charge

This fine small museum is on the floor of the actual cotton exchange, where brokers sampled, bought, and sold cotton, and worldwide prices were chalked onto a blackboard. The cotton business still goes on in Memphis, but the sampling is done by machine and the blackboard has been replaced by a computer.

The museum lets you look up at the board, feel samples, and talk with retired brokers who serve as volunteer guides.

There is an introductory film connecting blues, jazz, and rock 'n' roll to the cotton industry. And there are blues posters, some signed guitars, sheet music, a phonograph, and some African musical instruments.

But more interesting, even for the blues traveler, are the nonmusic items: boll weevils (a real one and a giant model), a scale model of a plantation, a slave bill of sale, manacles, and "manillas"—the money traded for slaves in Africa.

There also are phone booths where you can watch excellent video oral histories of people in all aspects of the cotton industry. And there is a gift shop with clothes, books, and bales.

- **Furry Lewis's Grave**
  Hollywood Cemetery, 2012 Hernando Road

Park at the entrance and walk around the office and straight up the path that leads into the cemetery. Turn left at the third intersection and then look to the left. Furry's gravestones (one upright and one flat) are there, facing away from the entrance.

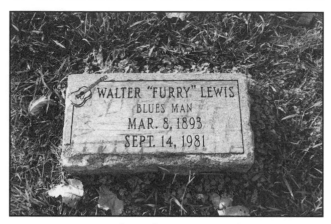

Furry Lewis's grave, Hollywood Cemetery, Memphis

The flat one reads:

> Walter "Furry" Lewis
> Blues Man
> Mar. 8, 1893
> Sept. 14, 1981

The upright stone disagrees on the birthdate, listing it as March 6 (the more commonly accepted date). It also says, "When I Lay My Burden Down," with an etching of a guitar.

Walter "Furry" Lewis, street sweeper on Beale Street for forty years, also was a bluesman who recorded in the 1920s, playing delicate guitar arrangements on such pieces as "Kassie Jones" and "Turn Your Money Green."

Furry emerged from a long musical retirement to become the star of the blues revival of the 1960s and 1970s. He not only made new recordings and played concerts and festivals but also appeared on *The Tonight Show* with Johnny Carson (where he quipped, "Why should I marry when the man next door has a wife?") and in *W. W. and the Dixie Dance Kings* with Burt Reynolds. He was also an opening act for the Rolling Stones.

• Xanadu Books and Music
2200 Central Ave.
(901)274-9885

John "Johnny Lowebow" Lowe, proprietor of this store, also is a maker of electrified, multiple-neck cigar-box guitars, and a one-man band who performs on those instruments.

The cigar-box guitar is a myth, in the true sense, of American music. The idea of an impoverished-but-handy musician turning a cigar box into an instrument is charming. Some elderly musicians actually claim to have made them in their youth, but actual photos, recordings, or other evidence is hard to come by. One gets the idea that the concept didn't work out so well in practice, and that the early cigar-box guitars were plunked a few times and set aside.

Instrument maker and musician John "Johnny Lowebow" Lowe, at his shop, Memphis

But a concept that did work well is the one-string guitar or "diddley bow." Made by nailing a wire to a wall and tautening it with a can or other object stuck underneath, the diddley bow is played with a slide. It has a long history as a children's instrument in parts of the U.S. South, the rest of the Americas, and Africa. Many professional blues guitarists cite it as their first instrument, and some continued to play it into adulthood—notably, Napoleon Strickland and Lonnie Pitchford.

In recent years, Lowe and a handful of other makers and players—including Richard Johnston, who won the International Blues Competition playing one of Lowe's instruments—have combined the cigar-box guitar and the diddley bow, usually adding modern tuning pegs, electric pickups and other far-from-the-backwoods features. For a neck, Lowe and other makers often use a pool cue.

At his store, Lowe sells his "Lowe Bows" and also will play for you. While singing and playing the Lowe Bow, he also manages to play the drums with his feet and one hand. He gets a postmodern, rocked-up sound, although he feels connected to the early bluesmen and the rockabilly artists. "I think the blues guys who were famous then were the innovators," Lowe says. "They took what came before and changed it up." Lowe constantly experiments with his designs, lately adding moveable bridges so more chords are playable.

Xanadu also sells old normal guitars, records, amps, strings, and other accessories and includes a small general bookstore. Lowe also repairs guitars. And he hosts a Lyon-Pitchford Award for cigar-box or diddley-bow music during the annual International Blues Competition.

• West Memphis, Arkansas

West Memphis, Arkansas, sits right across the Mississippi River from Memphis, Tennessee. In the 1940s through the 1950s, West Memphis was a hotbed of blues. Sonny Boy Williamson II, Howlin' Wolf, and B. B. King all played in its clubs. Most of the action was on Eighth and 16th streets south of Broadway. KWEM, the radio station where B. B. King was a guest on Sonny Boy's show in 1948, was at Broadway and 12th Street. It is gone, replaced by a large bank building.

• Albert King's Grave

To get there: From Memphis, take Interstate 55 north across the river into West Memphis, switch to Interstate 40 west and continue to exit 271, which is Arkansas Highway 147. Drive south on 147, through the Arkansas Delta, which is even more desolate and less populated than its Mississippi equivalent across the river. After 3 miles you will come to Paradise Gardens Cemetery, a huge burial ground in the midst of this isolated area. Turn into the cemetery.

Albert King is buried in the right front corner, near the Dr. Martin Luther King Jr. Park and a large, white, raised monument, surrounded by benches, honoring Martin Luther King. There are wooden street signs inside the cemetery marking the paths Martin Luther Kingsway and Albert Kingsway. (Martin Luther King is not buried here.) Although he is in a huge cemetery, Albert King lies alone; no other graves are in his part of the grounds, which he shares only with the Martin Luther King monument.

Albert King's gravestone is flat, and the whole grave is covered with gravel and bordered by two rows of raised bricks. A bronze plaque on the marble stone depicts King's trademark Flying V guitar, properly oriented for a left-handed player. It reads:

Sign near Albert King's grave, Paradise Grove Cemetery, Edmondson, Arkansas

'I'LL PLAY THE BLUES FOR YOU'
Albert Nelson King
April 25, 1923–December 21, 1992
Born under a bad sign in the Mississippi Delta, Albert King rose to greatness as a true giant of blues music. With his commanding presence, powerful voice, and stinging single-note guitar style, Albert King played the blues for the world, and forever changed the way the world would play the blues.
Dedicated to the memory of Albert King from his many fans and friends.

Early in his career, Albert King tried to pass himself off as fellow Indianola native B. B. King's brother, even changing his last name from Nelson to King. There was no need for the charade. Albert was a fine singer and a killer guitarist with a style all his own, based on bending the strings *way* across the fingerboard. He found his greatest success in the late 1960s, on Memphis's Stax label, where he recorded such songs as "Born Under a Bad Sign" and "I'll Play the Blues for You" backed by Booker T and the MGs. King has greatly influenced many blues and rock guitarists, including Eric Clapton, Robert Cray, and Stevie Ray Vaughan.

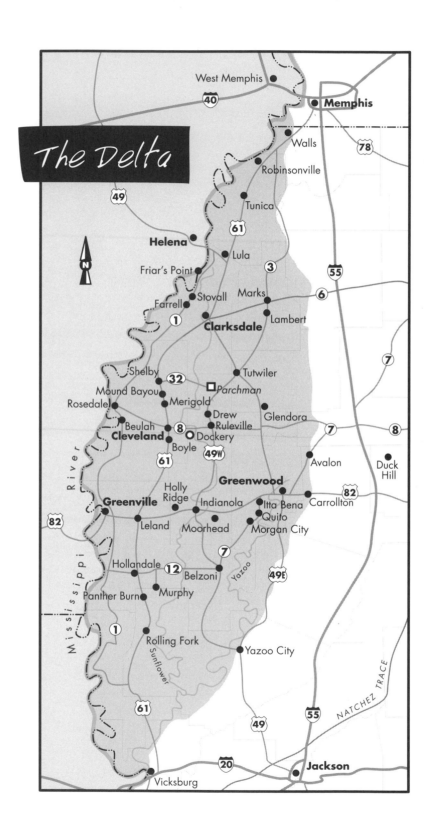

The Delta

chapter 3

DOWN HIGHWAY 61

Highway 61

To get there: Memphis's Third Street becomes Highway 61. From downtown Memphis, head south on Third Street. From Memphis International Airport, take I-240 west toward downtown; after 2 miles switch to I-55 north, and then, after another 1 1/2 miles, take the Highway 61 south exit.

> *61 Highway is the longest road I know*
> *She run from New York City down to the Gulf of Mexico*

Thus sang Mississippi Fred McDowell. Other versions put the starting point in Detroit and have it end at the border of New Mexico. Actually, it extends past Duluth, Minnesota, up to Thunder Bay, Ontario, Canada, and down to New Orleans. Highway 61 runs the full length of the Mississippi Delta, Memphis to Vicksburg, passing through or near most major towns.

Big Joe Williams and Howlin' Wolf sang of the other main Delta highway: "I'm going to get up in the morning, hit Highway 49." Since most bluesmen were rambling types, their songs often mention 49, 61, or 51, which skirts the Delta's east border and connects Jackson to Memphis.

Old Highway 61

Highway 61—"Highway 61, here I am. Get my picture taken by the highway sign. Walk in the footsteps of the great blues players. Maybe sneak into a field and pick some cotton." Except then you get on it and it's a regular four-lane highway. Sure would be dangerous to try to stop, much less walk.

Here's a tip: get off Highway 61 and onto Old Highway 61. It's right nearby, just to the west.

Old 61 is really the road they're singing about in all those songs (or an even older version of it, since it has been realigned several times over the years). And it is still there. Traffic is slower. It has stop signs and dogs crossing the road. And there are shotgun shacks, abandoned cotton gins and working ones, and old churches with little cemeteries beside them. There are homes and cotton fields and horses and all manner of life that you will not see on the quicker, safer new Highway 61. So, if you are really in a hurry—or if it's late at night, foggy, or your driving is impaired for any reason—stay on the modern four-lane Highway 61. But otherwise, try Old 61 for at least part of the trip.

Walls

- ### Memphis Minnie's Grave

  To get there: Take the Walls exit from highway 61 and go through the town and continue past it on Old Highway 61. Proceed 2 miles to an intersection with a sign reading "Church." The sign refers to a church different from the one you are seeking, but turn right at that intersection anyway, onto Norfolk Road. Follow Norfolk for less than a mile, until you see New Hope M. B. Church on the right, with a cemetery before it. There is a state blues marker at the site.

Minnie's grave has the tallest stone in the small cemetery. After parking in the church lot, walk parallel to the road you came up, in the direction you came from, until you get to that tall stone.

Two pink roses, with green leaves, are painted into the angled top of the stone, which stands about four feet tall. Commissioned by the Mount Zion Foundation, it also features a photo of Minnie and reads:

Church cemetery where Memphis Minnie is buried, Walls

Lizzie "Kid" Douglas Lawlers
AKA
Memphis Minnie
June 3, 1897
Aug. 6, 1973

The back of the stone features this lengthy, philosophical inscription:

The hundreds of sides Minnie recorded are the perfect material to teach us about the blues. For the blues are at once general and particular, speaking for millions but in a highly singular, individual voice. Listening to Minnie's songs, we hear her fantasies, her dreams, her desires, but we hear them as if they were our own.

One of the few female singer-guitarists in blues, and one of the very best blues guitarists of either gender, Lizzie "Memphis Minnie" Douglas was born in Algiers, Louisiana, in 1897, and moved to a farm near Walls with her family around 1904. By the time she was in her teens, she was slipping off to Memphis to play on the street around Handy Park.

When she started recording in 1929, at age thirty-two, Kid Douglas became Memphis Minnie, a Chicago-based blues star who would record about two hundred sides. "Memphis Minnie can make a guitar speak words, she can make a guitar cry, moan, talk and whistle the blues," wrote Big Bill Broonzy, himself no slouch. Minnie bested Broonzy in a blues contest in 1933 in Chicago, although he stole her prize, ran off, and drank it.

Lovely, petite, hard-drinking, hard-cursing, tobacco-chewing, and ready to fight if necessary, Minnie was a musical genius, a celebrity and a real character. Although she had a long career with many hits, Minnie fell into poverty in her old age. She moved back to Memphis in the 1950s and died there in 1973. Her family brought her body back to Walls for burial.

The **town of Walls** itself is small and unremarkable, with an auto-body shop, a dense trailer park, a bank, a church, a gas station, and a tavern making up its business area. Across the tracks, on West Railroad Avenue in the town's old black section, is a closed-up cafe that might be the sort where Minnie played on her visits. She toured the South regularly after becoming a successful, Chicago-based musician. Minnie would also come home to Walls to visit, sometimes for weeks or months, when she wasn't touring.

Robinsonville

To get there: If you ask at one of the casinos how to get to Robinsonville, you will probably get a puzzled look and be told, "You're in Robinsonville." But the casinos actually are a few miles from the town itself. From the intersection of highways 61 and 304, go west 1 mile on 304 to the first light, which is Old Highway 61. Turn left and you are in Robinsonville.

This tiny town, now ringed with casinos, is where young Robert Johnson bombed out when he took the stage at a jook joint where Son House and Willie Brown were playing. Howlin' Wolf also farmed and played in the area. "A lot of corn whiskey was cooked around Robinsonville" is how one longtime resident explained the town's great number of musicians.

The Hollywood Cafe, on the left, is a real restaurant, not a jook joint. Turn left at the Hollywood Cafe and then immediately right onto Front Street to see Foster's Cafe, an abandoned and very dilapidated old jook joint with a still-readable sign. That is the only reminder of the days when some of the Delta's greatest bluesmen lived near this town and played in the jooks and on the streets.

- ### Kirby-Wills Plantation

To get there: A modern Kirby-Wills Plantation sign, lettered vertically on a pole on the east side of Highway 61, can be seen across from the Tunica Visitors Center, 2.4 miles north of the intersection of highways 61 and 304. There is a smaller, older sign in front of a group of buildings 1.1 mile farther north.

Foster's Cafe, an abandoned jook joint on Front Street, Robinsonville

Charley Patton's 1929 "Joe Kirby Blues" refers to the owner of this plantation, who apparently gave Patton the blues, although the song doesn't provide specifics. It does mention a girlfriend in the area:

> *I'm goin' where the Green River never do run down*
> *'Cause the woman I love, Lordy, she's living in Robinsonville*
> *town.*

(Green River, which also gets a Patton song of its own, "Green River Blues," was a stream near Lake Cormorant, with a mill owned by the Memphis-based Green River Lumber Company.) The woman Patton sings about is likely singer-pianist Louise Johnson, who lived at Kirby-Wills and entertained at a jook there. Besides being a fine musician, Johnson is significant as one of the few women who played self-accompanied Delta blues. This concept was so unfamiliar to scholars and fans that for years they tried to determine which male pianist had backed Johnson on her records. Son House cleared up the mystery by explaining that she backed herself.

Johnson was also part of the most famous love triangle in the blues world. In 1930, Charley Patton recruited her and Willie Brown, who were both living at Kirby-Wills, to join him and Son

Plantation where blues singer-pianist Louise Johnson lived, Robinsonville

House on a trip to record at the Paramount studio in Grafton, Wisconsin.

Johnson, who was about twenty-five, had been romantically involved with blues-star Patton, about fifteen years her senior. The two of them began the trip sitting together in the front seat of the chauffeur-driven, moonshine-stocked car. But they began arguing after a while, and Johnson switched seats with Brown. House, who was closer to Johnson's age, began sweet-talking her in the back seat. Even House was surprised, however, when they got to their hotel in Grafton and Johnson told him the two of them would share a room.

The romantic intrigue didn't stop anyone from recording top-quality music the next day. You can plainly hear the men shouting in the background on Johnson's songs. It's hard to tell if they are being encouraging or rude.

- ### Abbay and Leatherman Plantation

  To get there: From highways 61 and 304, head west on 304 (Casino Strip Boulevard) for 4.0 miles. The two buildings are on your right, on the north side of the road.

This is where Robert Johnson spent most of his childhood. His mother, Julia Dodds, and stepfather, Dusty Willis, brought Robert here from Memphis (where he had been living with his mother's

Plantation where Robert Johnson grew up, Robinsonville

previous husband) in about 1918, when he was seven. Robert grew up here, picking up the jew's harp, then the harmonica, and then the guitar, and pestering Brown and House to teach him more about music.

Johnson left the area to return to Hazlehurst, his hometown, sometime after 1930. He came back to Robinsonville a few years later and astounded everyone with his guitar virtuosity, provoking the idea that he might have struck a bargain with the devil.

Abbay and Leatherman once employed 450 families, but the number is down to 11. The original plantation office building, a white-painted brick building with a sign reading "Abbay and Leatherman," is standing and still in use as the office. The plantation is still owned and operated by the Leatherman family, which bought the land from the Indians around the 1830s. The office, which dates from that era, also used to serve as the commissary where the workers shopped with scrip. Next to it is a small county jail of the same vintage.

- ● **Commerce**

  To get there: The land that once was Commerce is on the north side of Casino Strip Boulevard (Highway 304) just east of the levee, or kitty-corner from the Exxon/Full House store two lights west of the Abbay and Leatherman plantation building. The only reminders of the town are the Commerce Landing

Center, a Commerce Development sign, and Commerce Baptist Church, all along Casino Strip Boulevard.

This settlement was where many of the workers at Abbay and Leatherman Plantation lived. Robert Johnson lived here as a boy and attended school here. Writer Samuel Charters visited Commerce in the early 1970s and wrote that it "isn't much more than two rows of shacks," with a dirt road that led from Commerce past the plantation buildings to Robinsonville. The settlement has since been demolished.

• Bluesville

To get there: From Casino Strip Boulevard (Highway 304), follow the signs to the Horseshoe Casino.

The *name* of this thousand-seat nightclub inside the Horseshoe Casino may be a tribute to the area's blues traditions. And its décor follows a blues theme, with faux peeling-plaster walls and tin roofs over guitar-, harmonica- and piano-shaped bars. But its entertainment lineup generally is anything but the blues. LeAnn Rimes, Martina McBride, the Doobie Brothers, and Ronnie Milsap were the coming attractions advertised recently.

The Horseshoe did put together an excellent Blues and Legends Hall of Fame Museum, with such treasures as W. C. Handy's 1929 bill of sale for "St. Louis Blues" to RCA for $200; a Lightnin' Hopkins song list that includes "Please Release Me" and "Jolie Blonde"; Memphis Minnie's hand-lettered wood grave marker (which has been replaced by a stone at her grave); Big Mama Thornton's bitten-up harps; and what appear to be two of Furry Lewis' guitar cases.

But unfortunately the museum has been closed for the past few years, even though it persists for some reason in the casino's brochures. The collection is supposed to move to another Tunica location, perhaps the visitor's center on the highway.

• Clack's Grocery site

To get there: ½ mile north of Casino Center Blvd. on Old Highway 61. Or take Grand Casino Parkway from Grand Casino, go west to Old 61, and go slightly south. There is a state blues marker there. It is on the west side of the road in a field opposite the Grand Casino water tower and the Willows sign.

Clack's Grocery was a general store and train station at this site. Like most such places, it probably had blues players dropping by frequently to play on the porch or the platform—and this one probably had some very fine blues because several great artists were from the immediate area: Memphis Minnie, Willie Brown, and Son House.

But Clack's looms large in blues history not because of the music that might have happened there, but because of some that definitely did. It was here, on September 3, 1941, that folklorist Alan Lomax, working for the Library of Congress, recorded House, with Brown adding second guitar on some numbers along with Fiddlin' Joe Martin on mandolin and Leroy Williams on harmonica. The Clack's recordings, along with some other House recordings that Lomax would make the next year in Robinsonville, are available on *The Complete Library of Congress Sessions, 1941–1942*. House had recorded commercially in 1930, and this was his first "rediscovery." Another would happen in the 1960s.

Lomax would later reminisce about the Clack's session: "Of all my times with the blues, this was the best one." House also liked to talk about the session, noting that Lomax paid him with only a Coke, and joking that at least the Coke was ice cold.

The Clack's building is gone, but the sign from it is at the Delta Blues Museum in Clarksdale. There is a state blues marker here at the site and a faint handmade sign for Simuel MB Church.

Tunica

Now known mainly as the center of the casino region, Tunica once was a lively blues town, with a number of clubs and gambling dens run by a man named Hardface. The north end of Main Street has some old storefronts reminiscent of these days.

The Tunica area has come a long way, economically, since 1985, when it was reportedly the poorest county in the United States, and *60 Minutes* covered Jesse Jackson's visit in which he declared it "America's Ethiopia." The coming of the casinos, whether good or bad for the culture and for many individuals, has certainly boosted the local governments' coffers, enabling them to build roads, schools and museums.

- ## Tunica Museum
  1 Museum Blvd. (next to Paul Battle Arena on Highway 61 about 4 miles north of Tunica's commercial strip)
  (662) 363-6631

Even though this town now boasts another, larger museum (Tunica RiverPark Museum, see below), the Tunica Museum is still worth a visit. Its well-made exhibits cover the natural and cultural history of the area, starting with prehistory.

It includes several items of special interest to blues fans: a mule cart, a reproduction of a plantation commissary, and a jook-joint reproduction that includes old whiskey bottles and an old slot machine, with recorded commentary by blues drummer Sam Carr, a local resident.

There are exhibits for locally connected bluesmen James Cotton (a Tunica native who still comes to visit regularly), Skip James (who was living in this area when he was "rediscovered" in the 1960s), "Dr." Isaiah Ross, Willie Brown, and Robert Johnson.

There also is an exhibit about Harold "Hardface" Clanton, a gambler and jook-joint owner who died in 1982 after forty successful years in the business. B. B. King, Howlin' Wolf, and Roosevelt Sykes are among the many musicians who played at Hardface's establishments in Tunica.

Hardface's exit from the scene was timely, as the casinos that sprung up a few years later probably would have curtailed his business. The museum includes machines and tables from Splash, the area's first legal casino, which drew long lines of people when it opened in 1991.

- ## Tunica RiverPark Museum
  1 RiverPark Drive
  (888)517-4837 or (662)357-0050
  Admission fee

This museum building has a beautiful modern design that perfectly fits its dramatic riverfront setting. There are nature trails outside and observation decks where you can sit in a rocking chair and watch the Mississippi flow. It also has its own small paddlewheel riverboat, the *Tunica Queen*, which offers sightseeing, dining, and dancing day cruises. (These are priced separately from museum admission; call 866-805-3535 or 662-363-7622 for cruise tickets and information.)

The exhibits touch only a little bit on the blues—there are a couple of strange electric guitars and a nice video of old blues photos and narration, backed by blues licks from a Japanese guitarist.

But the rest of the museum is certainly worthwhile if your interest extends out to the area's history and wildlife. There are well-made exhibits on the Indians, early settlers, steamboats (with a fun diving-bell simulation to enter), bridges, levees, floods (with a replica of a flood-demolished house), cotton, and the Civil War.

And there is a fine aquarium showing what lurks beneath the Mississippi's dark surface: softshell turtles, alligator snapping turtles, bowfin, and big catfish in various shades from white to black.

Lula

To get there: From Highway 61, take Highway 49 west and follow the sign into town.

Son House and Charley Patton were both living in Lula in about 1930, and both composed songs about the town's severe dry spell and recorded them that year. House's "Dry Spell Blues" declared that it was

> *So dry old boll weevil turn up his toes and die*
> *No, ain't nothing to do—bootleg moonshine and rye.*

While Patton's "Dry Well Blues" observed:

> *Way down in Lula, hard living has hit.*
> *Lord, your drought came and caught us and parched up all*
> *the trees.*

The Lula well that "was gone dry" in Patton's song was probably the main one for the town, which feeds the water tower that stands today. You can wash your clothes in that well's water and then give them a "dry spell" at the town's laundromat.

Friar's Point

Before the construction of the Highway 49 Bridge between Lula and Helena, Friar's Point was where people caught the ferry over to Helena. It also was a major river port for shipping cotton and wood. Therefore there were crowds working there and waiting for the ferry, and the crowds attracted blues players.

Stormy sky over the Delta, at railroad crossing on Highway 1 near Friar's Point

This town is mentioned in several blues, including Robert Johnson's "Traveling Riverside Blues," in which he brags about his Friar's Point woman who "hops all over me." Muddy Waters recalled seeing Johnson play in Friar's Point and being intimidated by Johnson's fierceness and musicality. Drummer Sam Carr was born in this town on April 17, 1926. Carr's dad, Robert Nighthawk, a Helena native, used to hang out here too and recorded a "Friar's Point Blues." Country star Conway Twitty also is from Friar's Point.

Municipal workers outside Friars Point Museum, Friar's Point

Drummer Sam Carr at dedication of state blues marker honoring his father, Robert Nighthawk, Friar's Point

- ## Hirsberg's Drug Store
  649 Second Street
  (662)383-2420

It was on a bench in front of Hirsberg's that Waters heard Johnson. T-shirts commemorating that event are for sale inside the store, which remains open and in the hands of the Hirsberg family who took it over in 1935. The current owner, Robert Hirsberg, born 1934, is the son of original owner Sol Hirsberg. There are some benches outside the store. Although they are not the same ones that Johnson would have sat on, they still make a fine place to sit and play the blues. "Philadelphia" Jerry Ricks used to do exactly that, carrying on the tradition, while he was living in the Delta in the late 1990s.

Outside the store, there is a state blues marker for Robert Nighthawk, who lived in the area and wrote "Friar's Point Blues."

- ## North Delta Museum
  700 Second Street
  (662)645-9251

The museuam is open 10 A.M. to 4 P.M. Thursdays through Saturdays, 9 A.M. to noon Mondays through Wednesdays, and by appointment.

An article in the Memphis *Commercial Appeal* said of this museum, "It's like crawling through someone's attic." It is a true com-

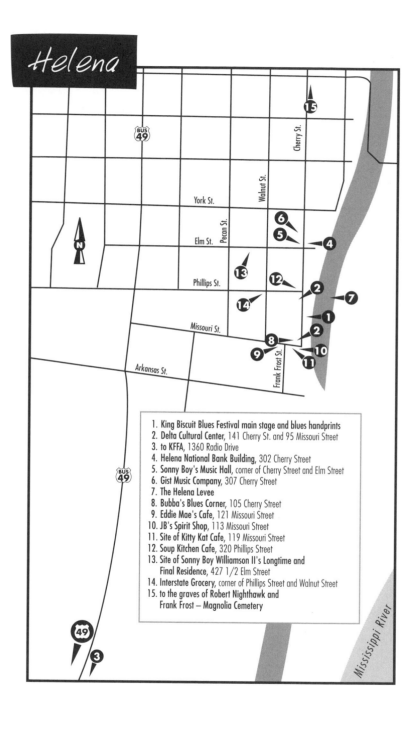

Helena

1. King Biscuit Blues Festival main stage and blues handprints
2. Delta Cultural Center, 141 Cherry St. and 95 Missouri Street
3. to KFFA, 1360 Radio Drive
4. Helena National Bank Building, 302 Cherry Street
5. Sonny Boy's Music Hall, corner of Cherry Street and Elm Street
6. Gist Music Company, 307 Cherry Street
7. The Helena Levee
8. Bubba's Blues Corner, 105 Cherry Street
9. Eddie Mae's Cafe, 121 Missouri Street
10. JB's Spirit Shop, 113 Missouri Street
11. Site of Kitty Kat Cafe, 119 Missouri Street
12. Soup Kitchen Cafe, 320 Phillips Street
13. Site of Sonny Boy Williamson II's Longtime and
    Final Residence, 427 1/2 Elm Street
14. Interstate Grocery, corner of Phillips Street and Walnut Street
15. to the graves of Robert Nighthawk and
    Frank Frost — Magnolia Cemetery

munity museum, volunteer-run, with an attic-y feel but much more interesting items than you find in most attics: fossils, Indian pottery, waffle irons, washing machines, radios, phonographs, butter molds, dough bowls, telephones, and a hand-cranked cotton gin. There is a small exhibit dedicated to Waters hearing Johnson in Friar's Point and an exhibit about the blues-related book *Beale, Black and Blue* by Margaret McKee and Fred Chishenhall, who are Friar's Point residents.

Helena, Arkansas

To get there: From Highway 61, take Highway 49 west, crossing the bridge into Arkansas. At the T in the road, turn right and drive about two miles, into Helena.

In the 1930s through the 1950s, this Mississippi River port town was notoriously "wide open"—an easy place to get your fill of liquor, gambling, prostitution, and music.

Bluesman Cedell Davis, who was born in Helena in 1926, remembered the old days in a 1976 interview: "They could go to town and stay there 'til maybe 9 or 12 o'clock [in Mississippi towns], they'd get out, you see. But now, Helena, you didn't have to worry about no time, see, wasn't no time—all night, see, because the joints stayed open all night, all day, you know what I mean like that. Well, anything that you wanted to spend money on or buy, it was there. All you had to do was look around, it was there."

Robert Johnson lived here for much of the last five years of his life, which ended in 1938. He stayed with girlfriend Estella Coleman, who was fifteen years his senior, and gave music lessons to her son, Robert Lockwood, Jr., who was only four years younger than Johnson. Howlin' Wolf is another blues star who was a resident of Helena for a while. Slide guitar master Robert Nighthawk was a native. Pianist Roosevelt Sykes was born here and started his career by playing in Helena joints for "a dollar and a red pop." Countless others stopped by to play in its many clubs.

Memphis Minnie not only played in Helena but apparently was stopped there by a tall, tough cop nicknamed "Reachin' Pete." In her 1935 song of that name she describes him as the "baddest copper" on Cherry Street, and tells what happened when she and a female friend ran into Pete and his partner:

> *He met me one Sunday morning, just about the break of day*
> *I was drinking my moonshine, he made me throw my knife*
> *away*

Minnie got off easier than her friend, who was taken to jail.

But the town's proudest blues son, the king of Helena's blues scene and the man who broadcast it over the air, was Sonny Boy Williamson II, aka Rice Miller. Star of *King Biscuit Time*, the first blues radio show, Williamson was the center of a group of musicians that included Lockwood, Pinetop Perkins, Houston Stackhouse, Johnny Shines, Dudlow Taylor, and Peck Curtis. Although he was born in Glendora, Mississippi, it was in Helena that the great blues harpist became widely known. Through his radio fame, he attracted the attention of Jackson record producer Lillian McMurry, who would record him.

Downtown Helena retains its blues-soaked quality, probably more than anywhere else. The buildings, the river, the levee, the people, the museum, the festival, and the radio programs all cast a spell that make it easy to dream you're back in 1929. Unfortunately it is also desperately poor and seems to be crumbling almost as you watch. Restoring the old buildings seems an insurmountable task, although the Delta Cultural Center and Main Street Helena do what they can. But who knows? KFFA announcer "Sunshine" Sonny Payne, who has lived in Helena for all of his eighty-plus years, says he has seen the town's economy decline and spring back several times, and expects it to spring back again. In the meantime, take your time in Helena and enjoy it while you can.

- ### Arkansas Blues and Heritage Festival (formerly the King Biscuit Blues Festival)

In a move that caused consternation to local residents and blues fans everywhere, this long-running festival was forced to give up the "King Biscuit" name a few years ago. The festival is held on the second weekend of October.

The *King Biscuit Time* radio show started on Helena's KFFA in 1941 and still happens daily on that same station. The show is named for King Biscuit Flour, a locally produced brand that originally sponsored the show, on which Sonny Boy Williamson and his King Biscuit Boys were the house band. The festival, which started in 1986, was named after the radio show. But it turned out that no one at the station ever thought to copyright the name. Meanwhile, someone else in another part of the country did copyright it and asked the festival to change its name, although the radio show has been able to keep its name.

But while the name has changed to the prosaic "Arkansas Blues and Heritage Festival" (officially, anyway, although blues fans still call it King Biscuit), the festival is still going strong. It is arguably the world's major blues festival, in terms of the quality and authenticity of the performers, the number of attendees over its three days, and its historic, downhome setting. And it's free!

The festival runs for three days on three stages in downtown Helena. The setting contributes as much as the music to the good feeling of this festival. At the main stage, the audience sits on the levee. Vendors set up in the streets, including local folks selling home-cooked foods. Musicians, too, are allowed to set up and play in the street, and some topnotch ones do. (Note: If you plan to play music on the street during the festival, you probably will need a sound system and an agreement with a local business to plug in to its electric outlet. Unfortunately, an unplugged acoustic performer cannot be heard over the sounds of the festival stages and the plugged-in street performers.) Local stores, bars, and restaurants stay open, many of them enjoying their busiest days of the year.

Besides the main stage, there is an acoustic/heritage stage and an emerging-artist stage. (The gospel stage was discontinued a few years ago, but the town now has a separate gospel festival in May.) The spirit of Sonny Boy Williamson seems to hover over the proceedings, inspiring the performers and relaxing the audience.

One problem you might have at King Biscuit is finding a place to stay. Try to make your reservations early, and look for rooms in communities within an hour's drive (in Arkansas or Mississippi), since there aren't many right in Helena. There's also the option of low-cost camping at the volunteer fire department's campground across the levee. The campground becomes a musical scene of its own, with plenty of jamming until all hours. Make sure to gather up your belongings and leave the campground on the morning after the festival ends, however, as there is no security provided after that.

- ● **Delta Cultural Center**
  141 Cherry St. and 95 Missouri St.
  (870) 338-4350
  (800) 358-0972

This superb, state-funded multi-facility museum is dedicated to the history of the Arkansas Delta. And, wisely recognizing that music is a key part of that history, the center devotes one whole building—the Visitor's Center on Cherry Street—to the area's musical heritage. The center's other major facility—the Depot, a block away on Missouri Street—covers other aspects of Delta life and history, including prehistory, Indians, farming, logging, the river, the Civil War, and home life, in a restored 1912 train depot. Both buildings are open 10 A.M. to 5 P.M. Mondays through Saturdays, 1 to 5 P.M. Sundays. Admission is free.

The Visitor's Center features a permanent "Sounds of the Delta" exhibit and changing art exhibits. Blues is not the only thing on the menu. There are photos of East Arkansas–connected musicians in various genres, including Louis Jordan, Levon Helm, Al Green, and Rosetta Tharpe, along with bluesmen Johnnie Taylor, Howlin' Wolf, Albert King, Robert Lockwood Jr., Robert Nighthawk, Cedell Davis, Harmonica Frank Floyd, Roosevelt Sykes, and Junior Wells.

And it tells the story of *King Biscuit Time.* The radio program started in November 1941 and became such a hit that Interstate Grocer soon was selling Sonny Boy Meal besides its King Biscuit Flour (both are still available in local groceries).

The announcer would start the program by saying, "Pass the biscuits, 'cause it's King Biscuit Time," and then Sonny Boy Williamson and Robert Lockwood Jr. would sing:

> *Good evenin' everybody, tell me how you do*
> *We're the King Biscuit boys and we've come out to play*
> *   for you.*
> *Every mornin' for my breakfast, put King Biscuit on my table*
> *I'm invitin' all my friends and all my next-door neighbors.*

The museum has the drums that Peck Curtis played on the show. And, best of all, it still has the show itself. Yes, *King Biscuit Time* came back on the air in 1986, after six years off. And "Sunshine" Sonny Payne, who took over from original announcer Herb Langston in 1953, is still the host. He broadcasts live from the Delta Cultural Center on Cherry Street 12:15 to 12:45 P.M. weekdays— unless there is a St. Louis ballgame—on KFFA, 1360 AM. Visitors are welcome, and Sonny will likely ask you to say a few words on the air.

Payne also co-hosts, with DCC Assistant Director Terry Buckalew, the Delta Sounds program, which is broadcast live from the DCC Visitors Center 1 to 1:30 P.M. Fridays.

The DCC hosts concerts, classes, lectures, contests, and other events throughout the year, many of them blues-related, and is especially active around the Arkansas Blues and Heritage Festival.

The DCC also sponsors two other annual music festivals, so if you don't make it down for the big festival in October you might tie your visit to one of these: the Arkansas Delta Family Gospel Fest in May and the Mother's Best Music Fest (named after another local brand of flour) in June.

The Visitor's Center includes a nice gift shop with books, videos, and T-shirts, relating to music and Delta history, as well as official KFFA merchandise. The DCC also is a good place to find out about events and music going on throughout the area.

- **KFFA**
  1360 Radio Dr.
  (870) 338-8361

  To get there: From downtown Helena, head south on Highway 49B, past the turnoff for the Mississippi Bridge and on toward West Helena on Highway 49. Turn right at a light 3.0 miles past the bridge turnoff, and then bear to the right at the fork, onto Highway 185. Go 0.7 miles and look for the Sonny Boy trailer in a field on the right. The station's offices and transmitter are just past that, on Radio Drive.

"Oh, yes! I used to listen to Sonny Boy and them all the time . . . When *King Biscuit Time* was on, everybody stopped working in the fields to listen to them," said B. B. King.

The original KFFA building, on Walnut Street, has been torn down. Its next home, starting in the 1960s, was on the fifth floor of the tallest building in town, the **Helena National Bank Building** (then called the Solomon Building), 302 Cherry St. KFFA's

"Sunshine" Sonny Payne, longtime host of King Biscuit Time, at his booth, Delta Cultural Center, Helena

studio and offices are now based in a trailer outside of town, next to its transmitter.

When he's not downtown doing *King Biscuit Time*, Sonny Payne works at the office, selling ads for the station. The original Sonny Boy logo-painted King Biscuit trailer, from which Sonny Boy and his comrades would play at gas stations and grocery stores throughout the countryside, is parked in a field near KFFA. It comes into town for the blues festival.

- **Sonny Boy's Music Hall**
  Corner of Cherry St. and Elm St.
  (no phone)

An old mosaic in the walkway gives away this building's early existence as a J.C. Penney's. The blues murals give away its later existence as Sonny Boy's Music Hall, where the Sonny Boy Blues Society held shows, meetings, and jam sessions. The building has fallen into disrepair and is closed.

- **Gist Music Company**
  307 Cherry St.
  (870) 338-8441

Sonny Boy Williamson II, Robert Lockwood, Jr., and the other *King Biscuit Time* entertainers used to stop by this store after doing their show at the building across the street.

"They didn't buy much," says owner Morris Gist. "They didn't have much money." They would even repair a broken guitar string if possible, by tying a knot in it.

Gist started in the music business by selling records on Helena streets, with a windup Victrola to play them on, as a child during the Depression. From there he got a jukebox route, and eventually opened this store in 1953. "We didn't change a thing," Jean Gist says of the furnishings. "We like it like this." It still has the original high ceilings, old wood cabinets, and friendly owners.

• Blues Handprints

Ten major performers, one dog, and one announcer all made handprints in cement at one of the early King Biscuit festivals, apparently at the request of the then-director. The prints were stowed away for years and then discarded into an alley, only to be rediscovered by a sharp-eyed Delta Cultural Center employee. The prints were recently installed near the festival main stage, across from 141 Cherry St. The hands (or paws) belong to: Big Jack Johnson, Rufus Thomas, Jessie Mae Hemphill and her dog, Sam Myers, Sam Carr, Robert Lockwood Jr., Frank Frost, Pinetop Perkins, Sonny Payne, Lonnie Shields, and Levon Helm.

• The Helena Levee

A brick walkway along the levee affords fine views of the harbor, the river, and some of Mississippi on the other side. Also notice the mural of blues artists on the levee wall near the Delta Cultural Center.

• Bubba's Blues Corner
105 Cherry St.
(870) 338-3501

Bubba Sullivan sells CDs and vinyl, vintage and current, as well as videos, posters, books, and other blues-related items from his corner of his wife's antique store. Sullivan has been part of Helena's blues scene for many decades, and he is happy to discuss local history, the King Biscuit Festival, 1930s blues legends or the latest hits with visitors.

- **Frank Frost Street**
  Off Missouri Street, just west of Walnut Street

"Home of Bluesman Frank Frost," proclaims the window painting at Eddie Mae's Café, 121 Missouri St. (corner of Frank Frost Street), above an airbrushed portrait of the late singer-harpist-keyboardist. Frost lived and died in the apartment above this restaurant/jook, run by his longtime girlfriend Eddie Mae Walton. The cross street was named after Frost after he died in 1999. Walton died in 2002. The club continued for a while under new management but has closed again. Like many Helena businesses, it might reopen around festival time.

Bullock's Café, another eatery across from Eddie Mae's, is renowned not only for its good downhome food, but for cook-owner Cora Bullock's way of explaining the menu—she'd take each customer back into the kitchen, open up the pots and have you select what you wanted ladled onto your plate. The place has mostly been closed since Bullock's death in 2007, but her son, also a fine cook, sometimes reopens it, especially around festival time.

- **JB's Spirit Shop**
  113 Missouri St.

In Chris Hunt's 1992 documentary film *The Search for Robert Johnson,* John Hammond, Jr., interviews Johnny Shines inside this liquor store. In the film, Hammond and Shines also go outside onto two corners of Missouri and Frank Frost streets to play the blues, separately, simulating an old-fashioned "cutting contest." They wind up playing together in front of Eddie Mae's Café.

- **Site of Kitty Kat Cafe**
  119 Missouri St.

This abandoned storefront, with no sign, was a jook joint where Robert Johnson used to play, according to Bubba Sullivan.

- **Site of Sonny Boy Williamson II's Longtime and Final Residence**
  427½ Elm St.

Helena was where Sonny Boy first made his fame, on the *King Biscuit Time* broadcasts. And the town was his home, on and off,

Former site of Interstate Grocer, the company that sponsored the radio show *King Biscuit Time,* featuring Sonny Boy Williamson II, Helena

throughout his life. From 1941 on, whenever he was staying in town, he rented a room in the boardinghouse on this site. In 1964 he came back for what he somehow knew was the final time. He told people he had come home to die. On May 25, 1965, he died in his sleep in his room in the boardinghouse.

The Sonny Boy Blues Society tried to raise funds to buy the building and restore it as a museum and concert hall. The effort failed, and the owner demolished it. The tile floor is about all that remains.

- **Soup Kitchen Cafe & Pool Room**
  320 Phillips St.

James "Gone For Good" Morgan, a local deejay and singer who had a 1986 semi-hit song called "Gone For Good," runs this jook joint with owner Barbara Marshall. Despite the name, you usually can't order soup or any other food here. Marshall named her place the Soup Kitchen because she periodically opens it up to the needy, serving free meals.

The rest of the time it's a safe, comfortable, lively club for dancing and having a beer. It draws a middle-aged crowd that comes to dance and dig the blues and soul that Morgan spins on the turntable. The club is opens 5:30 P.M. to midnight daily. The inside walls have murals by J. C. "Ratt" Smith, airbrush artist

Singer-deejay James "Gone for Good" Morgan outside his
club, Helena

extraordinaire, whose work graces many Helena business windows and signs. (Smith also has canvases on display at the Delta
Cultural Center.)

Morgan, a Helena native, knows a lot about local history from
about the 1960s on, especially as it relates to music, nightclubs,
and race relations and is happy to talk about it with visitors. He
also hosts Sunday Night Blues Party, 5-8 P.M. on KFFA and fills in
for Sonny Payne on *King Biscuit Time* as needed.

• Other nightclubs in Helena

Fonzie's Blues & Jazz Club, 400 Cherry St., has been presenting
occasional shows from touring soul-blues acts. It also is open, with
a deejay, most weekends and especially during the blues festival. En-
terprising Helena residents turn several other storefronts on Cherry
Street into nightclubs and restaurants to cater to blues-festival
crowds. If you visit at another time of year things are much quieter.
The clubs on Walnut Street tend to attract younger crowds, and
their deejays play funk and rap rather than soul and blues.

• Site of Interstate Grocer Co.
Corner of Phillips St. and Walnut St.

This is the site of the company that made King Biscuit Flour
and Sonny Boy Meal and sponsored the *King Biscuit Time* radio
program starting in 1941. In fact, Sonny Boy Williamson and

Robert Lockwood Jr. auditioned for owner Max Moore in the Interstate Grocer building to persuade him to sponsor a radio show. Some of the show's musicians worked at the plant in addition to playing on the radio show. The huge brick building stood vacant for many years, until the owner donated it to the Delta Cultural Center a few years ago. The DCC was unable to maintain or restore the building, and it was a safety hazard to leave it as it was, so the museum demolished it.

- **Graves of Robert Nighthawk and Frank Frost**
  Magnolia Cemetery

  To get there: From the north end of Cherry Street, circle around onto Perry Street. Three blocks past the traffic light, turn right onto College Street. Continue 0.8 mile, through residential neighborhoods, until you see the sign for Magnolia Cemetery. Turn at the sign and go another 0.2 mile to the cemetery.

From the cemetery entrance, proceed up the first hill and look to the left of the road for these large two grave markers next to each other. Nighthawk is buried in this cemetery, but the exact location of his grave is unknown. His marker was placed next to fellow bluesman Frost's by the Sonny Boy Blues Society, which paid for both markers.

Robert Nighthawk, a Helena native who lived from November 30, 1909, to November 5, 1967, was a distinctive and influential musician on both the harmonica (on which he recorded as Robert Lee McCoy) and the guitar. He first recorded on May 5, 1937, with Sonny Boy Williamson I and Big Joe Williams, and continued to record into the 1960s. He is most famous for his slide-guitar work, which influenced Muddy Waters, Elmore James, and Earl Hooker. He took the name "Nighthawk" while he was playing regularly on KFFA, after his signature tune, "Prowling Nighthawk." He is the father of the great Delta blues drummer Sam Carr, who worked with Frank Frost until Frost's death in 1999.

Frost, who was sixty-three when he died, was an Arkansas native who learned harmonica from Sonny Boy Williamson II. He also sang and played keyboards. Frost, Carr, and guitarist Big Jack Johnson made up the Jelly Roll Kings, who recorded several albums together and were a longtime favorite in Delta jook joints. Frost also recorded several albums under his own name, and was in the 1986 film *Crossroads*.

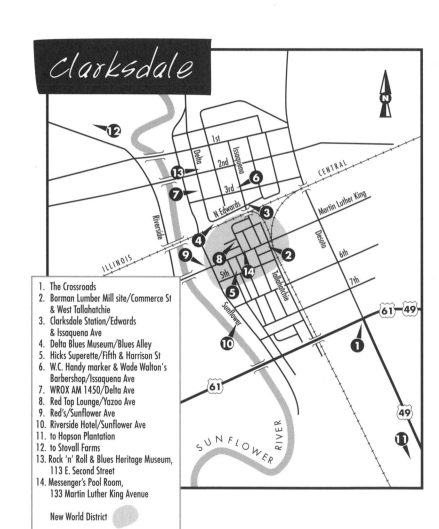

Clarksdale

1st
2nd
3rd
Delta
Issaquena
N Edwards
Riverside
ILLINOIS
CENTRAL
Martin Luther King
Desoto
6th
7th
Tallahatchie
Sunflower
5th
SUNFLOWER RIVER
61
49
61
49
N

1. The Crossroads
2. Borman Lumber Mill site/Commerce St & West Tallahatchie
3. Clarksdale Station/Edwards & Issaquena Ave
4. Delta Blues Museum/Blues Alley
5. Hicks Superette/Fifth & Harrison St
6. W.C. Handy marker & Wade Walton's Barbershop/Issaquena Ave
7. WROX AM 1450/Delta Ave
8. Red Top Lounge/Yazoo Ave
9. Red's/Sunflower Ave
10. Riverside Hotel/Sunflower Ave
11. to Hopson Plantation
12. to Stovall Farms
13. Rock 'n' Roll & Blues Heritage Museum, 113 E. Second Street
14. Messenger's Pool Room, 133 Martin Luther King Avenue

New World District

chapter 4

THE CLARKSDALE AREA

Clarksdale

When the railroads supplanted the river as the area's main artery, inland Clarksdale's importance surpassed that of older riverside towns like Vicksburg and Natchez. Clarksdale's location became even more strategic when the highways came in. The Illinois Central Railroad and highways 61 and 49 all intersected here, helping make it the richest town in the Delta, the cotton capital.

Naturally, the music followed. "I made more money in Clarksdale than I had ever earned," W. C. Handy boasted. "This was not strange. Everybody prospered in that Green Eden." A cultural hot spot even in Handy's day, Clarksdale was already an important blues town in the mid-1920s, when Son House learned to play guitar there from a man named Lemon (who had earned that nickname by mastering Blind Lemon Jefferson's recordings). The torch would pass when Muddy Waters learned from House in a nearby plantation jook a decade later.

The town's blues heritage continued through the postwar electric period, when Clarksdalians Junior Parker and Ike

Old Greyhound bus station, Third Street and Issaquena Avenue, Clarksdale (The station has since been restored and is now part of the Delta Blues Museum.)

Turner, among others, would make their names. In recent years such artists as Big Jack Johnson and James "Super Chikan" Johnson have come from Clarksdale. One native Clarksdalian who left town in 1931, at age fourteen—John Lee Hooker—became a superstar in his old age.

With twenty thousand residents, Clarksdale is one of the Delta's larger cities but still a small town. (The motto that appears on signs— "Welcome to Clarksdale, Home of the Big Frog"— does *not* refer to a blues artist named the Big Frog. It's an invitation to companies to move to a town where they can be big frogs in a small pond.)

• The Crossroads

When local residents speak of the Crossroads, they mean the intersection of the Delta's two main highways, 49 and 61. That intersection is clearly *not* the place Robert Johnson sang about in his "Cross Road Blues":

> *I went to the cross road, fell down on my knees*
> *Asked the Lord above, "Have mercy, save poor Bob if*
> *you please."*

Johnson was almost certainly referring to a lonely country crossroads, not a busy intersection next to a big town. If Johnson or any other bluesmen sold their souls to the devil at a crossroads, they would probably have picked a more remote location. And even though the devil appears in some other Johnson songs (especially "Me and the Devil Blues"), "Cross Road Blues" makes no such reference. "The Lord above" is the only supernatural being Johnson deals with in this song.

Still, this Crossroads is important for what it is: the intersection of the two main blues highways, the roads on which countless blues singers and other Delta folks walked or rode as they sought work, migrated north, or just rambled. The highway alignments have changed over the years, however, so the Crossroads hasn't always been in this spot. With the new bypass outside town, the Crossroads may be relocating again.

The intersection itself isn't so romantic to look at these days. Delta Donuts and Abe's Bar-B-Q ("get your souvenir T-shirts here") are somewhat more interesting than the chain gas stations and convenience stores. The highway sign itself, with both numbers on it, might be worth stopping at for a moment of silence or a photo. Just be careful if you stop—it's a very busy intersection. A garish "crossroads" sign, twenty feet high with lights and blue guitars, also marks the spot.

And before you get down on your knees, one more point: this juncture is not technically a crossroads of 49 and 61. It's actually only a T-intersection of the highways, because what looks like the extension of 49 is Desoto Avenue west of 61. The two highways join into one as you head north from this spot. They break apart again twenty-two miles north, near Moon Lake, where 61 continues north and 49 heads west to the Helena bridge. So if a three-way intersection is enough for you, that spot is another Crossroads.

The 1986 movie *Crossroads*, starring Karate Kid Ralph Macchio as a Juilliard student who hooks up with Willie Brown to seek a lost Robert Johnson song, revived the pop-mythology concept of a bluesman going to a crossroads to make a deal with the devil. (The crossroads in the movie was in Beulah, Mississippi.)

Throughout rural Mississippi, people refer to the intersection of the two most important roads in their area as "the crossroads." Since Robert Johnson was a rambling guy, it is impossible to tell which crossroads he is talking about, if any in particular, in his song.

Arkansas bluesman Robert Lowery, who sings a version of Johnson's "Cross Road Blues," introduces the song by explaining that one is sometimes torn between two women who live down different roads, so you stand at the crossroads wondering which to visit.

Years before Johnson's recording, Charley Patton had referred to the crossroads in his 1929 "Joe Kirby Blues":

> *I was standing at the crossroad bidding my rider goodbye*
> *Train blowed for the crossroad, Lord, she started to fly.*

Patton's verse contains no suggestion of anything supernatural. Yet he does cast the crossroads as a significant and dramatic place, a place where you might bid a lover goodbye and start a new phase of life.

In the West African Yoruba religion—elements of which persist in African American folk belief—crossroads belong to the god Eshu, also called Elegba, Elegbara, or Legba. The crossroads is where one recognizes truth and makes life-changing decisions. Eshu is the messenger god, a childless wanderer, a mischievous and creative spirit. Missionaries and others familiar with both Yoruba and Christian beliefs sometimes equated Eshu with the devil. So, by the 1930s in Mississippi, the Yoruba concept of going to the crossroads to pray to Eshu for inspiration had changed into meeting the devil there to exchange one's soul for musical gifts.

There is no evidence that Robert Johnson ever claimed he had made a crossroads deal with the devil or anyone else. Some other people attributed such a deal to him, however, to account for his seemingly overnight transformation from inept to masterful musician. Son House and Willie Brown had known Johnson as a pesky kid who would pick up their guitars and make unmusical noise while they were on break. But one day, after they hadn't seen him for a year or so, he picked up a guitar. "And man! He was so good!" House related many years later. "When he finished, all our mouths were standing open. I said, 'Well, ain't that fast! He's gone now!'" But what had actually made the difference, of course, was another age-old tradition: sitting down and practicing for hours on end, or "woodshedding," as jazz musicians call it.

Another Delta bluesman *did* claim to have made a supernatural deal. That was Tommy Johnson (no relation to Robert). Tommy Johnson's brother, LeDell, told researcher David Evans the exact procedure:

> He said the reason he knowed so much, said he sold hisself to the devil. I asked him how. He said, "If you want to learn how to play

anything you want to play and learn how to make songs yourself, you take your guitar and you go to where a road crosses that way, where a crossroad is. Get there, be sure to get there just a little 'fore 12 o'clock that night so you'll know you'll be there. You have your guitar and be playing a piece there by yourself. You have to go by yourself and be sitting there playing a piece. A big black man will walk up there and take your guitar, and he'll tune it. And then he'll play a piece and hand it back to you. That's the way I learned to play anything I want."

Note that LeDell did not specify a particular crossroads. So if you're interested in trying it, any lonely Delta crossroads ought to work. And by the way—it wouldn't hurt if you also spent several years practicing every day.

• Abe's BBQ
616 State St. at the Crossroads
(662)624-9947

Abe's has been open since 1924 and at this location since 1937, the year before Robert Johnson went to his final crossroads. In a blurb on the menu, the owners carefully avoid embracing the Crossroads myth, while still taking pride in their location's supposed significance in that story: "This is where legend has it that Delta Blues King Robert Johnson sold his soul to the devil, and Abraham Davis surrendered his soul to God, and his family business still prospers after 75 years."

This is a classic barbecue restaurant, very popular with locals. Tamales, chili, and burgers are on the menu as well.

• The Clarksdale Mill

In "Moon Going Down," Charley Patton sings:

Oh where, where were you now, baby, Clarksdale mill
    burned down?
Oh where, where were you now, baby, Clarksdale mill
    burned down?
(Spoken: Boy, you know where I was) I was way down Sun-
    flower with my face all full of frown.

He apparently was referring to a fire at the Borman Lumber mill, which once occupied the now-vacant lot at Commerce Street and West Tallahatchie. The mill burned down shortly before Patton recorded the song, in 1930. It is unclear what business Patton had on nearby Sunflower Avenue. But a clue might come later in the song, when he sings about the green house over yonder full of the "finest young women, Lord, a man 'most ever seen." The Bottoms, the area along the Sunflower River now occupied by the Martin Luther King Community Park, was once a red-light district.

• Clarksdale Station

At Edwards and Issaquena avenues sits Clarksdale Station, built in 1926. This is the passenger depot where Muddy Waters bought his ticket, sat in the colored waiting room, and boarded the train to Chicago in 1943. Thousands of other black Clarksdalians, probably including other blues singers, made that trip from the same spot. And tens of thousands of others began the same kind of trip from similar train stations in other towns. But somehow Muddy is the classic example of that whole mass migration—the rural southerner saving up to buy the ticket, quitting his job at the plantation, packing up his guitar and a few other belongings, telling his woman he'll send for her. Of course, Muddy *did* find fame and fortune in Chicago. Many did not, and some soon made the return trip back south.

Coahoma County and the county chamber of commerce have purchased and renovated the depot as part of the Blues Alley project that also includes the Delta Blues Museum. Clarksdale Station has spaces for a nightclub, restaurants, and shops, which are for lease to private tenants.

There hasn't been passenger service to Clarksdale for several decades. But if the county's plan is carried out, the trains may roll again—to take tourists from Clarksdale to Lula, where they will be shuttled to the casinos along the Mississippi River.

• Delta Blues Museum

Old Freight Depot, 1 Blues Alley. The museum also has public archives on the second floor of the Carnegie Public Library, 114 Delta Ave. (662-627-6820; the Web site is www.deltablues museum.org). The renovated Greyhound Station at Third St. and Issaquena Ave. is also part of the Delta Blues Museum and hosts free traveling exhibitions and special events.

Hours are 10 A.M. to 5 P.M. weekdays, to 2 P.M. Saturdays, with extended hours during festivals.

Illinois Central Railroad Freight Depot, built in 1918, home of the Delta Blues Museum since 1999, Clarksdale

In October 1999, the Delta Blues Museum finally made its long-planned move to the Freight Depot, from its original home in the library. A 1918 brick building, the new digs are grander and more suitable to the museum's subject matter. However, the twelve-thousand-square-foot space is *too* big for the museum's modest collection. The staff is filling the extra space with changing photo exhibits while it tries to raise the $1.2 million needed for new permanent exhibits.

The small but interesting collection includes an oil drum from the company Big Jack Johnson, "the Oil Man," used to drive a truck for. The old gravestone for Mississippi Fred McDowell (misspelled "McDewell") is here. There are a metal guitar slide Lonnie Pitchford made from a leg of his kitchen table and a beat-up barber chair once used by singing barber Wade Walton. A rather creepy wax likeness of Muddy Waters sits in a chair. And there are signs from buildings that no longer exist, such as Clack's Grocery, where Alan Lomax recorded Son House.

A series of panels uses words and photos to showcase the astounding number of Mississippi musicians—in blues and other genres—who have achieved national renown. Another exhibit shows the development of stringed instruments, beginning with the African gourd banjo. And a display case is devoted to the underappreciated singer-drummer-harpist Big Mama Thornton. The changing blues-related photo exhibits generally are by nationally prominent photographers.

The museum gift shop is a great place to buy books, magazines, calendars, CDs, tapes, postcards, T-shirts, or hat pins. Many of the books and recordings are local or otherwise hard to find.

The museum also functions as a crossroads for blues travelers from all over. Blues-influenced rock stars Jimmy Page and Robert Plant shopped enthusiastically when they stopped by in 1998, fulfilling the title of their album of that year, *Walking into Clarksdale*. Many blues musicians drop in occasionally. And foreign visitors come in a steady stream to this little museum in a small Mississippi town.

From 3 to 5 P.M. Mondays through Thursdays, Clarksdale bluesman "Dr." Mike James uses the museum as a classroom where he teaches schoolchildren to play the blues on various instruments. Those who learn their lessons well may be asked to join James's band, the Interns. Some of the students also have formed their own bands, including Pure Blues Express, an all-girl group. Others have joined established groups in the area. The class sessions are open to the public.

- ### Sunflower River Blues and Gospel Festival
  (800) 626-3764

Probably because it happens in the dead of the Delta summer, early August, Clarksdale's annual blues festival has always drawn far fewer people than the festivals in Greenville (September) and Helena (October).

Don't let the heat scare you off, though. The smaller attendance at Sunflower gives it an intimate charm that the other two major Delta blues festivals lack. At Sunflower, it is easy to get close to the stage, to run into a performer in the crowd, or to get to a portable toilet.

The music also sets Sunflower apart. Its performers all are Mississippi natives or have strong connections to the state. The emphasis is on deep, traditional blues, not the blues-rock or soul-blues that dominate other festivals throughout the country. And admission is free!

•Juke Joint Festival

Held in mid-April, this festival puts music in all the jook joints in town—and in all the sort-of jook joints. That is, anyplace that usually or occasionally hosts live music, or seems like the kind of place that should have live music, gets live music for this weekend. That makes for about a dozen joints. You buy a wristband and ride a shuttle around among them all night. Plus there are outdoor stages with daytime music, as well as storytelling, films, pig races, and other activities.

• New World District

The railroad tracks separate Clarksdale's downtown (which was traditionally for whites only, except for blacks who had jobs there) from the longtime center of black life, commerce, and music, the New World. Fourth Street (now Martin Luther King Avenue) is its main drag.

Although bandleader W. C. Handy mainly made his living at plantation dances, store openings, and political rallies when he lived in Clarksdale in the first decade of the century, he also jammed in New World joints—apparently playing something other than blues, however. In his autobiography, Handy praised the neighborhood's brothels full of "lush octoroons and quadroons from Louisiana, soft cream-colored fancy gals from Mississippi towns," and noted that "just beyond this section lived some of the oldest and most respectable Negro families."

The New World was still hopping in 1942, when folklorist Alan Lomax visited on a song-collecting trip and caught a young Honeyboy Edwards singing an Uncle Sam blues on a street corner. Lomax observed, "Peanut vendors and Mexican hot-tamale salesmen peddled their wares. Fried catfish was proclaimed available in every restaurant window. Wagons bulging with huge green watermelons stood at every corner. Inside the bars—the Dipsie Doodle, the Red Wagon, the Chicken Roost, and Catfish Bill's—jukeboxes moaned and blasted."

These days, the cathouses are gone and the food and drink choices are more limited, although a tamale man still sets up his

Window of business in the New World district, Clarksdale

cart at MLK and Issaquena. The New World is still the liveliest part of town. People walk in and out of bars or nearby churches, chat on the sidewalks, or drive slowly through. In the bars, gamblers will offer to play you a game of checkers, dominos, or Ping-Pong, as well as dice or cards. The blues is still heard, but usually only on jukeboxes or deejay turntables. Another part of Lomax's description could almost apply today: "Slick young sheiks in Harlem drape-shape coats, watch chains hanging below the knees of their peg-top trousers, watched the chicks go by, some in poor cotton dresses, some in the latest fashions."

On July 6, 1999, President Bill Clinton strolled down Issaquena Avenue in one stop on his tour of the nation's poorest places. Clinton posed for photographers in front of the New Roxy theater. Later he and his party ate ribs and tamales in a back room of **Hicks Superette**, Fifth and Harrison streets. A board near the counter commemorates that occasion with photos and a copy of a handwritten letter of thanks from Clinton. After Clinton's meal, at owner Eugene Hicks's suggestion, the president went outside and shook hands with townspeople who had been waiting in the heat to see him. (Clinton apparently had left his saxophone at home—there is no record of him playing the blues in Clarksdale.) Something about this downhome eatery attracts big names—John F. Kennedy, Jr., and his date dined there, sitting at a counter in the main room, during their 1991 visit to the town. There are no photos of Kennedy because, Hicks says, "I didn't know who he was, until later."

- **Messenger's Pool Room**
  133 Martin Luther King Ave.
  (662)624-2305

"If you are looking for a nice quiet place to go and enjoy yourself then you are at the right place. We appreciate your business. However, on the other hand, if you are looking for a place (followed by a faded, long list of bad things to do in a bar) then you are at the wrong place. Your business is not welcome. Take it elsewhere."

So reads the sign on the front door of Messenger's (open nightly at 5 P.M.), considered the oldest continuously-run business in Clarksdale. An article on the wall shows a liquor license for Messenger's from 1907, so the place has been around for quite a while. It moved to the current location in 1948, having outgrown the original location, right next door (the original building has since burned down). George Messenger, grandson of the original owner, owns it now with his wife, Myrta.

Messenger's is a holdover from the glory days of Fourth Street (now Martin Luther King Ave.), when country people came to town on weekends to shop, eat out, and have fun. The vintage cash register helps re-create the mood, as do George Messenger's frank reminiscences about good and bad times.

Messenger's serves barbecue and beer (no hard liquor). One room, the café, has tables and chairs. The other room has pool tables. There is no live music, except during the Juke Joint Festival, when Messenger's is one of the festival venues, and occasional special events. But it is not a jook joint and never was one. Messenger explains that his grandfather didn't allow dancing because he couldn't spare the space. As the sign states, Messenger's is a quiet place to sit and drink a beer and listen to the jukebox (which does have a lot of blues) and maybe shoot a game of pool. Nothing wrong with that.

- **W. C. Handy Home Marker**
  Issaquena Ave. near Third St.

Handy, the "Father of the Blues," was a native of Florence, Alabama, and is most associated with Memphis. But he also lived in Clarksdale for a few years, beginning in 1903, when he was thirty, and took a job leading a black Knights of Pythias band—a non-blues, society band that he built up into a nine-piece orchestra. It was while Handy was living in Clarksdale—but waiting for a train at the Tutwiler depot—that he had the dramatic, career-changing introduction to the blues he describes in his autobiography.

A historical marker stands in front of the empty lot where Handy's house was.

• Wade Walton's Barber Shop
317 Issaquena Ave.

The late Clarksdale barber Wade Walton was "discovered" as a musician by British blues scholar Paul Oliver in 1960. He made a fine album on Bluesville, *Shake 'Em on Down*, shortly after that, and sang and played guitar and harmonica at local nightspots and festivals. But, as he humbly admitted, barbering was his occupation and music just a pastime.

Even if he hadn't been a musician, Walton would merit a place in blues history as the barber to such luminaries as Sonny Boy Williamson II, Ike Turner, and Howlin' Wolf. When Allen Ginsberg visited Mississippi in 1983 or 1984, Wade Walton's Barber Shop was the first place he wanted to go. The blues-singing barber cut the beatnik poet's hair.

Walton appears in the documentary film *Deep Blues*, wearing an impossibly loud suit—plaid, with huge lapels—as he works and plays in his shop. He managed to combine both his interests when he played percussion by sharpening his razor against a leather strop, scraping, clanging, and swishing out a beat, as he did with guitarist Big Jack Johnson on "Close Shave Boogie" on the 1990 compilation album *Clarksdale, Mississippi: Coahoma the Blues* (available at the Delta Blues Museum gift shop) and with guitarist R. C. Smith on "Barbershop Rhythm" on the 1960 compilation *I Have to Paint My Face*. The 1990 album also includes Walton accompanying himself on guitar as he sings "Leaving Fourth Street," his lament about being forced to relocate from his longtime location at 304 Fourth St. in 1989. It concludes with the lines:

> *I knew all the time that I wasn't treated fair*
> *But if you come to 317 Issaquena, I can still cut your hair.*

All of Walton's musical instruments are depicted in the mural on the building: a harmonica, a guitar, and a razor strop, with razor. "Attention: No cameras or any recording devices beyond this point," warns a sign at the front door.

Walton died January 10, 2000, at age seventy-six, at a hospital in St. Louis, after a brief illness. He is buried at McLaurin Gardens in Lyon, just north of Clarksdale on Highway 61. The barbershop has closed. It has reopened as a nightclub but with spotty hours.

• WROX

621 Desoto Ave.
(662) 627-1450

WROX began broadcasting on June 2, 1944. Three years later, Early "The Soul Man" Wright began working there and stayed for fifty-one years, finally retiring at age eighty-three. Wright was one of the first black deejays in the country on one of the first stations to play blues records (KFFA in Helena already had a blues program, which was rebroadcast on other stations including WROX. But KFFA's announcers were white.) Wright's charming style and format remained virtually the same throughout his five-decade career.

WROX was originally based at 321 Delta Ave., in the building now occupied by Bluestown Music and Studio 61 recording. It then moved down the street to 257 Delta for a time in the 1950s, a time when Ike Turner worked there first as a janitor, then as a deejay. Elvis Presley gave a live performance on the station during that time. Then it relocated to the second floor of the McWilliams Building (Third Street and Delta Avenue) and stayed there for most of Wright's reign. In the early nineties it moved back to 317 Delta. In 1998, an out-of-town chain purchased WROX and converted it to talk format with off-site programs. In 2003 WROX returned to local ownership but moved to this new location.

Its programming is mostly oldies these days. But Saturday is blues night, kicking off with the *Cat Head Delta Blues Show*, hosted by Cat Head Delta Blues & Folk Art owner Roger Stolle, 6-8 P.M. That program focuses on local artists and ones who are coming to town. Two syndicated blues programs follow it. Stolle also goes on air at 8:10 A.M. Thursdays to talk about live blues in Clarksdale that weekend. And there are local church-service broadcasts, often including excellent music and stirring preaching, on Sunday mornings.

The station broadcasts at 1450 AM and 92.1 FM and online at wrox.com

Wright's daily blues and gospel shows were a favorite of residents and visitors alike. Teenagers in the fifties and sixties would honk their horns from the street outside the studio (which was not soundproof) in the McWilliams Building, hearing the horns on the air and shouting their requests to Wright when he came to the window. Howlin' Wolf, B. B. King, Little Milton, Bobby Rush, and Clarksdale native Ike Turner were among the blues artists who would stop and visit with Wright, live on the air, whenever they were in town. The not-so-famous—friends, strangers, locals, and tourists—also were welcome as guests on Wright's show.

Wright's on-air manner defied radio convention and delighted his listeners, many of whom made tapes of his shows. In a deep, slow voice, he spoke in a downhome vernacular. And he left long breaks of silence when he stopped to look for a record or take a drink of water. Wright and his studio—at the McWilliams location—are in a scene in the film *Deep Blues,* in which Wright interviews Big Jack Johnson on the air. "Ladies and gentlemen, I got a very extinglished guest here in the studio with me tonight," Wright begins.

Wright died December 12, 1999. He is buried at Heavenly Rest Cemetery, on Highway 61 just north of Clarksdale.

- ### Cat Head Delta Blues & Folk Art
  252 Delta Ave.
  (662) 624-5992

In an appropriately weathered building, this store is a treasure house for blues lovers. It stocks blues recordings, folk art, photographs, and related books and magazines. Fill in your Blind Lemon Jefferson collection, pick up a hand-labeled CD by an obscure local act, or maybe even find an out-of-print blues book here. There is a good selection of blues videos, too. Owners Roger and Jennifer Stolle are founts of knowledge on live blues and other events throughout the Delta. They post such information on their web site, www.cathead.biz, and also e-mail regular updates on blues happenings. The store also hosts frequent in-store performances and book signings, especially around festivals and holidays.

The **Cat Head Mini Blues Fest** is a wonderful festival held three times a year in front of the store. Each festival features a handful of topnotch acts. The setting is terrific and so is the price—free. The mini fests are around the Juke Joint Festival (April), Sunflower River Blues Festival (August), and Arkansas Blues & Heritage Festival (October).

- **Rock 'n' Roll & Blues Heritage Museum**
  113 E. Second St.
  (901)605-8662

Theo Dasbach, a Dutch music fanatic, moved to Clarksdale with his American wife and opened this fascinating museum in 2006.

His collection includes records and other recording media from the earliest days on, focusing on the blues and rock 'n' roll eras. Phonographs, posters, and other art and artifacts also are part of the collection. It is organized so as to show the connections among different artists and eras. And, even more interesting to us provincial Americans, it shows the worldwide impact of blues and rock.

Since moving to the U.S., Dasbach continues to add to his collection, especially adding material on Mississippi musicians. And Dasbach himself is the knowledgeable tour guide. Museum hours are 11 A.M. to 5 P.M. Thursdays–Saturdays April–October; shorter hours November–March. Tours also are available by appointment.

- **Ground Zero Blues Club**
  0 Blues Alley
  (662) 621-9009

This large club and restaurant, decorated jook-joint style, opened in 2001. One of its owners is actor Morgan Freeman, who grew up in Greenwood and lives in Charleston, Mississippi. The club was featured in the 2003 Starz! TV documentary *Last of the Mississippi Jukes*, including a scene of Alvin "Youngblood" Hart, Sam Carr, and Clarksdale bassist Anthony Sherrod playing on the Ground Zero stage.

Ground Zero presents live blues Wednesday through Saturday nights, including open jams on Thursdays. And if you want the full Ground Zero experience, you can even rent a room upstairs from the club.

- **Red Top Lounge (aka Smitty's)**
  377 Yazoo Ave.
  (no phone)

This nightclub's facade was the backdrop for the wild cover photo on the Jelly Roll Kings' 1979 album *Rockin' the Juke Joint Down*. The three Kings—Big Jack Johnson, Frank Frost, and Sam Carr—stand in front of the Red Top Lounge with their instruments, Jack looking especially dapper in a pink suit, wicked process, and oversized sunglasses, and playing a Beatle-style bass.

The Jelly Roll Kings were the house band for years at this large club, which also hosted shows by many other local and traveling blues acts. The club closed permanently in 2003.

• Red's
395 Sunflower Ave.
(no phone)

From the outside, Red's looks like it has been closed for years. But make sure to stop in on a Friday or Saturday night for excellent live blues in a super-authentic jook joint. So authentic, in fact, that the place seems about to fall apart. Insulation and ceiling tiles are falling from the ceiling, and there are leaks when it rains. The owner hopes to fix these serious problems and accepts donations for the cause.

In the meantime, enjoy the red glow, the lazy disco ball, the buckets to catch leaks, and the music—T-Model Ford, Big Jack Johnson, Wesley Jefferson, and Robert Belfour are among the regular performers at Red's.

• Riverside Hotel
615 Sunflower Ave.
(662) 624-9163

In the predawn hours of September 26, 1937, Bessie Smith, the Empress of the Blues, and her friend and driver, Richard Morgan, were driving from Memphis to Clarksdale on Highway 61, riding in Bessie's old Packard. They planned to stop in Clarksdale before heading to Darling, Mississippi, for a show there.

But somewhere about sixteen miles north of Clarksdale (the exact spot is unknown and the question is probably meaningless now, because the road has been widened and realigned several times since), the Packard struck a stopped truck that was partly blocking the narrow highway. The car rolled over and its wood roof was sheared off. Morgan was unhurt, but Smith's arm was badly injured, and she was bleeding profusely.

The truck driver drove off toward Clarksdale. Morgan flagged down a car that came by immediately; amazingly, it contained a physician, Dr. Hugh Smith, who was going fishing with his friend Henry Broughton. Smith and Broughton moved Bessie Smith to the shoulder of the road, and then the doctor tended to the injured singer while Broughton walked to a house to call for an ambulance.

But it took Broughton a long time to make the call, and then the ambulance didn't arrive very quickly. Bessie's condition was deteriorating. So the men started moving the fishing tackle out of the back seat and into the trunk, to make room for Bessie in the car.

As they were doing that, a fast-moving car slammed into Hugh Smith's car, which was in the middle of the road. That car's occupants, a white couple who had been out partying, were not seriously injured but were hysterical. As the doctor examined them, the police and an ambulance arrived, followed by a second ambulance (summoned by the truck driver after he drove to Clarksdale). All three patients were driven to Clarksdale hospitals. Bessie Smith was taken to the G. T. Thomas Afro-American Hospital, where she was pronounced dead at 11:30 A.M., of shock, possible internal injuries, and compound bone fractures. She was forty-three.

The story is tragic but straightforward. But it became controversial a month later, when John Hammond, Sr., erroneously wrote in *down beat* magazine that the great singer "was refused treatment because of her color and bled to death while waiting for attention." That indictment of a racist system was so tantalizing that it hung on in popular mythology for years, despite Hammond's admission of error. It even became the essence of a 1959 play, *The Death of Bessie Smith*, by the distinguished playwright Edward Albee. The play reinforced the myth; it includes a scene in which Bessie's companion drives her to a white hospital in Memphis and is repeatedly told by a nurse to sit down and wait, even though he explains that he has a seriously injured woman in his car.

Hugh Smith explained long after the accident that no ambulance driver would have even tried to take a black person to a white hospital—and, at any rate, the black hospital and the white hospital in Clarksdale were less than half a mile from each other. A curious footnote to the story is that Hugh Smith, even though he was a part-time jazz pianist, had never heard of Bessie Smith, and had no idea who the woman was until much later.

The G. T. Thomas Afro-American Hospital opened just before World War I and closed about 1940. A few years later, Z. L. Hill bought the building and turned it into the Riverside Hotel, which she operated until her death in 1997. Among the guests Hill was proudest of were two decidedly non-blues duos: John F. Kennedy, Jr., and a date (in 1991), and a pair of Siamese twins. But years before that she also had housed Ike Turner and his band, Robert

Nighthawk, and Sonny Boy Williamson II, who used to come by the hotel to serenade her.

Although it is well past its prime, the Riverside remains open as a no-frills place where rooms can be rented by the night, week, or month. Within walking distance from the festival grounds, it is a popular place to stay during the Sunflower River Blues Festival. For blues fanatics, the building's history, convenient location, and low price override its shabbiness.

- **Stackhouse Records/Rooster Blues Building**
  232 Sunflower Ave.

From 1988 until it closed ten years later, this steamboat-shaped building was the place to go in Clarksdale if you wanted to run into blues musicians, find out what was going on over the weekend, shop for old 78s, new CDs, photos, posters, mojos, or maps, or just hang out. It also housed Rooster Blues record company's office and recording studio. Stackhouse/Rooster was owned and operated by Jim O'Neal, a major blues buff who also founded *Living Blues* magazine (which he has since sold to the University of Mississippi). Lonnie Pitchford's *All Around Man*, Super Chikan's *Blues Come Home to Roost*, Robert "Bilbo" Walker's *Promised Land*, and other great Mississippi blues albums of the 1990s were recorded for O'Neal's Rooster Blues label. Bluesmen Pitchford and Lonnie Shields helped construct the studio.

The store reopened for a while under new management but has closed again.

- **Sarah's Kitchen**
  276 Sunflower Ave.
  (662) 627-3239

A longtime cook for the county jail, Miss Sarah also cooks here at her restaurant, although the place's hours have been irregular lately. If you find Sarah's open, ask about music. There used to be Thursday night blues jams/open mikes and occasional Saturday night special performances. Sarah's still has a blues-laden jukebox and a bulletin board of photos of musicians playing there.

Robert "Bilbo" Walker, a flamboyant Clarksdale-born bluesman who has relocated to Bakersfield, California, usually holds court at Sarah's around festival time.

A mural of John Lee Hooker, Muddy Waters, and Bessie Smith—three famous blues musicians associated with Clarksdale—is on the side of **Carmen's Pawn Shop**, Sunflower Avenue at East Second Street.

• Second Street

Muddy Waters sang about this street in his 1949 "Canary Bird":

> *Well, canary bird, when you get to Clarksdale, please fly down Second Street*
> *Well, canary bird, when you get to Clarksdale, please fly down Second Street*
> *Well, you know I don't want you to stop flying until you take the letter out to Stovall for me.*

The street leads to a bridge across the Sunflower River and connects to the highway to Stovall Farms.

• Hopson Plantation and the Shack-Up Inn

1 Commissary Circle (on the west side of Highway 49, 2½ mi south of town) (662) 624-8329

It is ironic that this plantation is becoming a center for blues tourism, because its history is connected with the exodus of blues culture from the South.

Hopson is the site of the first mechanically planted and harvested cotton crop in 1941. That original harvesting machine is on display near the Hopson Commissary. The machine broke the age-old relationship between human hands and the cotton plant. "The farmers run the black folks away when they got them mechanicals in the fields, those machines to pick cotton," is how bluesman Honeyboy Edwards explains it in his autobiography. The migration of black people to the North accelerated, and the music went with them.

In the late 1990s a group of business partners, including some with connections to the plantation's original owners, began moving old sharecropper shacks here, renovating them (including features the sharecroppers never had, such as plumbing and air conditioning), and renting them out as the Shack-Up Inn. The shacks were so popular that they kept acquiring more, then turning the plantation's cotton gin into more accommodations. Now they are building old-looking shacks from scratch, incorporating "green" features to make them energy-efficient.

Bluesman Pinetop Perkins, who played piano with Sonny Boy Williamson and Muddy Waters and has continued an active musical life into his nineties, lived and worked at Hopson in the 1940s. Another Clarksdale musician, Ike Turner, credited Perkins for teaching him boogie-woogie piano in the 1940s. And one of the shacks for rent (not where he actually lived) is named for Perkins and includes a piano.

Hopson hosts an annual **Pinetop Perkins Homecoming** on the Sunday after Helena's Arkansas Blues & Heritage Festival (the second weekend of October). It has become a notable festival in its own right, with several stages of music including open mics and jam sessions, barbecue for sale, craft booths, and other attractions. Perkins himself, dressed to the nines, plays the gracious host. Since his religious beliefs discourage playing music on Sundays, it takes some begging before he takes the stage to play a few numbers.

• Quapaw Canoe Company
291 Sunflower Ave
(662)627-4070

Okay, you've driven around, walked the dusty roads, maybe even hopped a train, and you want to try a new way of exploring the Delta. How about paddling around on the Mississippi by canoe or kayak?

John Ruskey has been doing just that almost every day for years, starting with a teenage adventure when he and a friend tried to re-create Huck Finn's journey (they almost made it, until the raft hit something near Memphis and split into pieces). He knows the river, its islands and currents. On a canoe trip with Ruskey, you feel—well, about as safe as you could feel riding in a tiny boat on a giant, barge-trafficked river.

Day trips, and longer ones in which you camp out on islands, are available. A musician himself and director of the Delta Blues Education Program, Ruskey also can talk blues with you, help you find live blues in the area, or sing you a song.

Stovall

• Stovall Farms

To get there: From downtown Clarksdale, head west on First Street, across the bridge over the Sunflower River. Turn right immediately onto Riverside Avenue, then left immediately onto Oakhurst Avenue. It will change names a few times, eventually becoming Stovall Road. Stay on it past a cemetery and out of town. About three miles out, at the corner of Farrell Road, you will see a Stovall Farms sign in an orchard on the left.

The Stovall family took this land over in the 1840s, hung onto it through the Civil War, and still owns it. A member of the family, Howard Stovall (grandson of Muddy Waters's employer), occasionally plays with local blues bands and has served as director of the Blues Foundation, a Memphis-based organization that works to promote and preserve the blues worldwide. (Despite growing up at one of the blues' holy places, however, Stovall says he never heard any blues as a child. He finally met Muddy Waters in 1983, at Yale.) Stovall is one of the owners of Ground Zero nightclub in Clarksdale.

Muddy Waters, born April 4, 1915, in Rolling Fork, moved to the Stovall Plantation with his grandmother in 1918. At a jook joint on the plantation, Waters heard Son House play, and switched from harmonica to guitar. That jook may have been the one at Stovall Road and Highway 1, where a store now stands.

This plantation also is where the Chatmon brothers—Bo (who later would adopt the surname Carter), Lonnie (later one of the Mississippi Sheiks), Sam, and others—sharecropped in 1917–18 before returning to their hometown, Bolton, to go into music more seriously.

Past the sign is an iron fence in front of a big house. That is the spot where folklorist Alan Lomax inquired about a blues singer he had heard of who worked on the plantation—a young man named Muddy Waters. Another local bluesman, David Honeyboy Edwards, had said Waters was the best around. The Stovalls (their descendants still live there) directed Lomax to the sharecropper cabins nearby.

• Muddy Waters Home Site

To get there: From the Stovall Plantation's big house, keep going down the road. Just past the row of brick houses on the left is a dirt road, Burnt Cane

Road. At the right of that road, on the main road, is where the cabin was. Grass has grown back over the site. Look closely and you may see some signs of the foundation, some depressions the building left in the earth. There is a state blues marker here. Look out into the fields and see where Waters worked, driving a tractor for 22½ cents an hour.

Muddy Waters grew up and made his first recordings in a cabin on this site. In about 1918, when Waters was three, his family moved here from Rolling Fork. Waters, his wife, his uncle, and his grandmother all were still living in the cabin in 1941, when Lomax arrived with a portable recording unit. Although Waters thought the folklorist was really an undercover revenuer out to bust him for his moonshining, he couldn't resist the opportunity to record anyway. Using his bottleneck slide on Lomax's Martin guitar, Waters made his recording debut with tunes like "Country Blues" (which he would rename "Walkin' Blues" when he rerecorded it, on electric guitar, in Chicago) and "I Be's Troubled" (which would become his first big hit, rerecorded and renamed "I Can't Be Satisfied"). One of the songs Waters recorded for Lomax, "Burr Clover Blues," pays tribute to his employer and to a crop raised there (Stovall, who had patented the burr-clover harvester in 1935, asked Waters to compose a song about the crop):

> Man, I told a man way up in Dundee
> Well, "You go out on Mr. Howard Stovall's place, he got all
>   the burr clover you need."
> Well, now, the reason I love that old Stovall's Farm so well
> Well, you know we have plenty money and we never be rais-
>   ing hell.

When asked to identify himself during an interview portion of the recording session, Waters confidently announced, "Name, McKinley Morganfield. Nickname, Muddy Waters. Stovall's famous guitar picker." Hearing his own recordings after Lomax sent them back would inspire Waters to head into town to make the trip north: "When Mr. Lomax played me the record I thought, 'Man, this boy can sing the blues!'"

Originally a one-room cabin of ax-hewn cypress planks, the Waters home had three additional rooms when Waters and his family occupied it in the 1940s. It had become a tin-roofed, tar-papered house much like countless others used by sharecroppers throughout the South. When the rock group ZZ Top visited it in 1983, however, a tornado had just knocked down the addition, leaving only the solid, antebellum original part. The band took some of the original wood that was lying about and had it made into "Muddywood" guitars, including one donated to the Delta Blues Museum.

Souvenir-seeking vandals (despite a sign that read "Please do not deface this sight, we will lay a Big Nasty Mojo on you if you take anything") and the elements were eroding the rest of the house. So, in a move controversial to blues lovers, the Stovall family struck a deal with the House of Blues nightclub chain in 1996 to dismantle the Waters cabin, restore it, and take it on tour. Builders using materials from another sharecropper shack at Stovall Farms restored the house to a half-size replica of its four-room, Muddy-era state. It was displayed at the 1996 Olympics in Atlanta and the 1997 Chicago Blues Festival, then packed away in a New Orleans warehouse. The house has returned to Clarksdale and now stands inside the Delta Blues Museum.

Farrell

About four miles south of Stovall on Highway 1, this community is the one Henry Sims sang about in "Farrell Blues." Sims, who played the fiddle on some of Charley Patton's recordings, took a rare turn at the vocals on this track, and Patton accompanied him:

> *I'm goin' to Farrell, where I can have my fun.*
> *Gon' get me a gal and I can have a run.*

Sims had a knack for playing with great bluesmen. A few years later, Alan Lomax would record him, as Son Simms, playing with Muddy Waters at Stovall.

Lambert

- ### J. B.'s Blues School
  721 Darby Ave.
  (662) 436-7802

  To get there from Clarksdale, take Highway 6 east to Marks. From Highway 6, head south on Highway 3, through Marks. Lambert is 4 miles south of Highway 6. When you get into the town, you will go by the large Lambert Auto Parts building on the right. Soon after that is an old gas station on the right. At that intersection (which is Darby Avenue, but lacks a street sign there), turn left. Past the Union Planters Bank is a strip of old storefronts, in-

Club on Darby Avenue, Lambert

cluding B&P Club on the right. The Entertainment Club is in a plain white building, without a sign or visible address, three doorways past the B&P Club. If it is during lesson time, you probably will hear music and see the "J. B. and the Midnighters Delta Blues Education Fund" van parked in front.

After a long career as a blues musician and auto mechanic in Mississippi and Chicago, Johnnie "Mr. Johnnie" Billington settled into a life of teaching children the blues business in the late 1970s. In November 1998, he relocated his blues school here from the Delta Blues Museum in Clarksdale (although one of Billington's former students, Michael "Dr. Mike" James, continues the program there).

Visitors are welcome to observe or participate in Billington's classes. Free of charge, he trains students to play guitar, bass, drums, and keyboards. The instruction goes way beyond musical notes, covering how to dress and act like a musician and, especially, how to make money as a musician. Within a few months, good students are accompanying Billington on paying gigs.

As of this writing, Billington was moving his operation to another building on Darby Avenue. He also planned to develop his space into a club with live music, food, and drink. Call the number above to get the address, class times, and other details before heading to Lambert.

chapter 5

THE MID-DELTA

Tutwiler

To get there: Take Highway 49—*not* 49E or 49W—from where those three roads meet with Highway 3. Bear left toward town and follow the guitar-shaped sign to "town center and blues sites." Drive through the downtown to its end, then turn left around behind the buildings. You will see some large murals and the railroad tracks.

Tutwiler is where W. C. Handy had a blues epiphany. While waiting for a train here in 1903, he heard a "lean, loose-jointed Negro" play knife-slide guitar and sing, over and over, "Goin' where the Southern cross the Dog." Handy considered that "the weirdest music I had ever heard." He soon wrote and published some of the first compositions based on the blues and using the word "blues" in the title. One of those was "Yellow Dog Blues," incorporating the verse of his anonymous depot-mate.

One mural depicts Handy's magic moment. Another is about Sonny Boy Williamson II, and includes a large, good map to his grave. Still another proclaims Tutwiler the "Wood Duck Capital of the World."

Tutwiler no longer has a train station. However, there is a

Sonny Boy Williamson II mural, Tutwiler

concrete slab, next to the tracks near the murals, that used to be the foundation of a train depot. That one was newer than the one where Handy waited, which was somewhere in this same area of track.

- **Tutwiler Community Education Center**
  301 Hancock St. (the large, modern building on Tutwiler's main street)
  (662) 345-8393

The concrete slab has a Tutwiler family quilt painted by the Tutwiler Quilters, a women's cooperative. Their quilts—as well as quilted pot holders, bags, and place mats and blues-themed cards and T-shirts—are available at this center.

- **The Grave of Sonny Boy Williamson II**

  To get there: From the murals, cross the tracks and head straight up Second Street, pausing to look at the intricately decorated house and car of Preston Smith at 405 Second Street. Continue up Second Street for 0.4 mile, to an intersection with a gas meter. Turn right and drive 1.5 miles, bearing to the right onto Prairie Place Road at the fork. Williamson's grave is in a small cemetery on the right, back from the road and in front of the woods.

The great Sonny Boy Williamson II has connections to many places. He was born near Glendora. He lived much of his life, and became famous, in Helena. He was living in Belzoni when Lillian

Grave of Sonny Boy Williamson II, Tutwiler

McMurry encountered him. He recorded in Jackson and Chicago. Toward the end of his life he lived in London, playing with rock musicians and wearing tailored suits and bowler hats. He returned to Helena to die in 1965.

But he is buried near Tutwiler, on a small family plot in a church cemetery whose church has fallen down and disappeared. Visitors often leave harmonicas as offerings. The grave remained unmarked until 1980, when Lillian McMurry of Trumpet Records erected a marker that reads:

Aleck Miller
Better known as
Willie "Sonny Boy" Williamson
Born Mar. 11, 1908
Died June 23, 1965
Son of
Jim Miller and Millie Miller
Internationally famous harmonica and vocal, blues artist discovered and recorded by Trumpet Records, Jackson, Miss., from 1950 to 1955.

The stone has an incorrect date for Williamson's death. He died May 25, 1965. The actual year of his birth is uncertain—1897, 1899, 1901, and 1911 all are possible, as is the date on the stone. Bill Donoghue, a Williamson biographer, picks December 5, 1912, as the most likely birthdate. Williamson's first name is often spelled "Alec" or "Alex," and he went by the name "Rice" Miller.

Yellow Dog Railroad flag stop sign, along Highway 49W, south of Tutwiler

There is a double tombstone in front of Williamson's for Mary Ashford and Julie Barner. They are two of his sisters, who both died October 11, 1995, in a fire in the house they shared.

As you drive south of Tutwiler, you may start noticing catfish ponds in the fields along the highways. Farm-raised catfish from these ponds are a big industry for Mississippi. Note the herons and other large birds hanging around for a snack. As the blues line goes:

> *I wish I was a catfish, swimming in the deep blue sea*
> *I'd have all these good-looking women fishing after me.*

On Highway 49W about four miles south of Tutwiler, there is a Yellow Dog flag stop sign, with a little red building near it where people once waited for the train.

Parchman

Mississippi State Pententiary
(662) 745-6611

To get there: Parchman shows up as a dot on highway maps, as if it were a town, but the dot represents just the main entrance and a few buildings. The prison grounds cover forty-six square miles to the west of the entrance. That entrance, with a dramatic-looking gate labeled "Mississippi State Penitentiary" in very large letters, is on the west side of Highway 49W, at the intersection with Highway 32. There is a sign telling you not to stop for photographs—so if you want to shoot a picture of the gate, do it while your car is moving. And yes, the people you see wearing striped outfits, working in the fields, are prisoners. Group tours of the prison may be arranged by calling Linda McIntyre at (662) 745-6611.

From its beginning in 1904 until reform finally came in the 1970s, the main purpose of Mississippi's state prison was not to rehabilitate or even to punish the convicts, but to make money by growing cotton. And it did so, pouring millions into the state treasury. While other state prisons cost the public money, Parchman *made* money for Mississippi. According to most descriptions, it closely resembled an antebellum plantation, with prisoners replacing slaves. (However, it has always housed white and black inmates.)

Because the prisoners worked in organized gangs, as slaves had, Parchman became a kind of preserve for group work songs, which scholars consider an influence on the blues. Folklorists such as John and Alan Lomax visited the prison to document the songs. "What makes it go so better when you singing, you might nigh forget, and the time just pass away," a prisoner named Bama told the Lomaxes. Swinging their axes to chop wood, they sang verses such as these:

> *Big-Leg Rosie with her big-leg drawers*
> *Got me wearin' these striped overalls.*
> *When she walks she reels and rocks behind*
> *Ain't that enough to worry a po' convict's mind?*

A re-creation of a Parchman work song, sung by elderly ex-cons as they chop, appears in Alan Lomax's 1981 documentary, *The Land Where the Blues Began.* The blues is not the same as work songs. But the possibility of going to Parchman hung over the state's black men, including the bluesmen, and sometimes came out in their music. Charley Patton's "A Spoonful Blues," about the power of love over men, includes the line "It's mens on Parchman—doing lifetime—jus' 'bout a" with his slide guitar pronouncing "spoonful" to complete the sentence.

Son House admitted to spending two years in Parchman, from 1928 to 1930, although the details of his case are unknown.

Another inmate/blues singer was Booker T. Washington "Bukka" White, an older cousin of B. B. King. Born in 1909 in Houston, Mississippi, White had recorded a pair of religious songs in 1930—"I Am in the Heavenly Way" and "Promise True and Grand"—and in September 1937 made his big hit, "Shake 'Em on Down."

But the next month, White was indicted for murder. He was convicted on November 8 in Aberdeen and sentenced to life in Parchman. Somehow, however, he was released in 1940—apparently through a pardon from Governor Paul Johnson, according to researcher Gayle Dean Wardlow. The pardon likely was related to White's status as a recording artist. Immediately upon his release, White went to Chicago to record again. He was ready to cut versions of standard and popular blues songs, but producer Lester Melrose put White up in a hotel and gave him two days to write some original songs. "So help me God, I got down to it," White later recalled. He came up with twelve new compositions, including two related to his stay in Parchman.

In "When Can I Change My Clothes?" White dreamed of the day he could get out of the striped prison garb:

> Never will forget that day when they had me in Parchman jail
> Wouldn't no one even come and go my bail
> I wonder how long, baby, before I can change my clothes?

In later verses, White laments that he has to go out and work in the rain and cold wearing only those same flimsy clothes.

In that same 1940 session, White also recorded "Parchman Farm Blues," which opens:

> Judge give me life this morning down on Parchman Farm
> I wouldn't hate it so much but I left my wife and home

Despite writing these melancholy songs, White told an interviewer in 1963 that he had been treated better inside Parchman than he often was after his release. As a musician, he said, he had avoided much of the hard work in the prison.

By the 1980s, musical talent was still making prison life much easier. David Kimbrough (son of the late Junior Kimbrough), who served time at Parchman, told *Living Blues*: "I got down there and I was out there workin' in the fields, you know, choppin' grass, they had me doin' everything. And so I was singin' and [a guard said], 'You need to get in the Parchman band, man, you don't need to be out here in this field.' . . . Six months later I was in the band. Didn't never have it hard 'cept for the first six months I was there. I was always off the farm there with the band. We was gone every weekend, sometimes whole weeks, you know, livin' in motels . . . You out there workin', you could have your beer or whatever, get you a little sex or whatever you want to do out there, you know."

Kimbrough (then going by the name David Malone) secured a recording contract while he was a prisoner, and recorded a demo at Parchman for his 1994 album *I Got the Dog In Me*. He recorded the released version, however, in an Oxford studio after his parole, with non-inmate musicians.

House in the 1920s, White in the 1930s, and David Kimbrough in the 1980s are the only blues recording artists known to have done felony time in Parchman. Others may have had misdemeanor convictions that landed them there for less than a year.

A song by Mississippi jazz-blues pianist Mose Allison, "Parchman Farm" (covered by British bluesman John Mayall on his 1966 LP *Bluesbreakers with Eric Clapton*) is based on old work-song lyrics:

> *Sittin' over here on Parchman Farm*
> *Ain't ever done no man no harm.*

Allison followed it up with a more sardonic "New Parchman":

> *Sittin' over here on Parchman Farm*
> *The place is loaded with rustic charm*

The late Clarksdale barber-musician Wade Walton, on his out-of-print early-1960s LP *Shake 'Em on Down*, included the talking blues "Parchman Farm." On it, he talks about bringing two white folk-song collectors from California to the prison in 1958. A pistol-packing assistant warden turns them away, addressing Walton:

> *"Boy, you know better than this. If you know like I know*
> *you'd leave here running right now."*
> *[Thrums a chord on the guitar.] That was me, Wade,*
> *running.*
> *[The guitar simulates running.]*

*Oh, Dave and I left Parchman farm. Didn't get no race
relations done. Whoo!*

In 1961, Electro Record Company of Hattiesburg released a
single, the instrumental "Harmonica Boogie," by the Confiners "of
Mississippi State Penitentiary," the label noted. The group's four
members were Parchman prisoners who were let out for public
appearances.

Many nonfamous Parchman inmates undoubtedly sang the
blues. Writer David Cohn collected verses from women inmates in
the 1930s. Most of them were variations on standard blues verses,
but this one gives some insight into the tedium of women prisoners' work:

*You talkin' bout trouble, you don't know what trouble means.
What I call trouble is a Singer sewing machine.*

The 1999 Hollywood film *Life*, directed by Ted Demme, features Eddie Murphy and Martin Lawrence as New York moonshine runners framed for murder while in Mississippi. They are
sentenced to life sentences at Parchman that last from the 1930s to
the 1990s. Although the movie was set in Mississippi, it was filmed
in California. A jook joint scene features songs by Bo Carter and
Casey Bill Weldon in the background. Later in the film there is a
Bukka White song, with modern instrumental backing dubbed in.

Elvis Presley's dad, Vernon, was convicted in 1938 of forging a
check, and was sentenced to three years in Parchman. He served
only eight months. But it affected the three-year-old Elvis, who
cried because he missed his daddy so. Elvis and his mom, Gladys,
often rode the Greyhound, five hours each way, to visit Vernon.

Shelby

To get there: From Highway 61 (which becomes Broadway in Shelby), turn
west onto Second Avenue at the town's main intersection.

Notice the old train depot on your left—it is the Shelby Public Library. Built in 1887, the building functioned as a depot

Club on Second Avenue, Shelby

until the 1960s. It became the town library in 1977. At the architect's insistence, the building was left pretty much in its original state. The original station sign and other artifacts are on display inside.

Continue to the second stop sign, at Second Avenue and Lake Street. There are three jook joints there, all painted in typical funky ways: "Welcome to the People Choice Lounge With Love," "The Windy City Blues House," and "Do Drop Inn, Big E's Place, where the good times are."

Windy City occasionally books touring blues acts—look for posters around town.

On Sundays, the Do Drop Inn has become a fairly reliable place to hear live blues. Little Jeno Tucker, a veteran blues singer based in Clarksdale, was a regular performer there until his death on June 13, 2000. Since then, other acts such as the Billy Smiley Band or the Wesley Jefferson Band have been playing.

This is a big club, with a dance floor and a bandstand, but it is dark and friendly enough to still have real jook joint ambiance. There are murals of city scenes and the Playboy bunny logo. It is open Fridays and Saturdays for dancing to a deejay. The live music is Sundays only, and it begins and ends early—about 6 to 10 P.M. (most of the musicians, young graduates of Clarksdale's Delta Blues Education Program, have to be in school the next morning).

Club on Lake Street, Shelby

• Between Shelby and Winstonville

On the east side of Highway 61, about a half mile north of Winstonville, notice the bottletree near the road, in front of a house. An African American folk tradition, a bottletree is a real or artificial tree with bright-colored bottles slipped over its branches. The pretty bottles are supposed to lure evil spirits, which become trapped inside and thus cannot enter the house. Modern southerners, black and white, who display bottletrees usually do so out of respect for the tradition or because they like the way it looks—not because they really believe in spirit-proofing the house.

Mound Bayou

To get there: The town straddles Highway 61. Turn west at the Walk of Faith Church, a brick building before the U.S. post office, and drive two blocks to see the Bank of Mound Bayou, 201 W. Main St., which was built in 1904 at a cost of five thousand dollars. The bank closed in 1922 and has since been the Circle Inn. Currently it is abandoned and for sale. The city is considering buying it and turning it into a museum. Continue west past the bank building for another two blocks to city hall, which has a display inside of several striking sculptures of musicians, done by an unknown artist who left them there and then disappeared. There also is a small museum of nineteenth-century artifacts such as lamps, weapons, dishes, and photographs.

The outside of the building features a wooden relief sculpture of the faces of African American heroes.

This town was founded in 1887 as an all-black community of independent farmers. It thrived in its early years, with its own bank and an oil mill. But when cotton prices and land values fell in the 1920s, the farmers turned back to tenancy. The town has struggled along ever since.

Despite its all-black population, Mound Bayou has never been known as a big blues town. Bill Patton, Charley's father, saved the money he made farming at Dockery's, bought land near Mound Bayou, and opened a store there, according to one relative. Charley often spent time in the town.

Mound Bayou used to host an annual Heritage Festival on July 4, with national and regional blues and R&B acts, but the festival has been discontinued in recent years.

Merigold

- **Winery Rushing**

  To get there: Turn east on Merigold-Drew Road, an unmarked paved road just south of the Merigold town limits. Drive 2.8 miles east and look to the left. You'll see the sign through the fields, on a building about 200 yards north of the road:

  THE WINERY RUSHING
  Bonded Winery Mississippi No. 1
  Est. 1977

If you want to get close to the abandoned metal building, turn onto the dirt road. The fields by the main road contain the grapevines.

This is the town where Charley Patton encountered Bolivar County Deputy Sheriff Tom Rushing (misspelled in the song title), Merigold Town Marshal Tom Day, and a bootlegger named Halloway. Patton's 1929 "Tom Rushen Blues" tells a rather difficult-to-follow story of his run-in with these real-life characters, in which the narrator goes to bed, "hoping I would have my peace," but is shaken awake by Rushing. Halloway also has gone to bed, but Day takes whiskey "from under Halloway's head"— and maybe brings it to the man in prison who sings

It takes boozy-booze, Lord, to carry me through
But each day seem like years in the jailhouse when there is
no booze.

Patton lived in Merigold from about 1924 to 1929, staying with a woman named Sudy. Rushing, who served as deputy sheriff from 1928 to 1932, later insisted he never arrested Patton, although he did hear him play, since the two men's professions brought them to the same places: "I heard him a good bit around Mound Bayou, Cleveland and Merigold. Being the deputy sheriff, we had to systematically watch those places, and we were welcome at any place to go in if we wanted to. In those days we got by with it. I don't know how we did it, but we never had to have a search warrant. We just went ahead and did things our way. The honky tonk is a big room. It's got a little café in connection with it where they would serve hamburgers and coffee and so forth. Then they had a big area where they could dance, and they had the side rooms for monkey business." Rushing said he was proud that Patton wrote and recorded a song about him.

Rushing's family remained in the area and in 1977 opened the Winery Rushing, making wines from Mississippi's native muscadine grapes. It was an ironic business for the descendants of a man whose job was to break stills and arrest the area's moonshiners and bootleggers. The winery closed in 1990, but the building remains.

• Poor Monkey's Jook Joint
(601) 748-2254

To get there: Driving north on Highway 61, go 1 mile past the Merigold–Mound Bayou turnoff, then turn left onto Pemble Road. Take first left onto the unpaved Poor Monkey Road (although there might not be a sign, because it gets stolen regularly) and follow it about 1.2 miles, until you see the club.

Unfortunately, Poor Monkey's does not feature live music, except for occasional special events. Nevertheless, it ranks high as a must-visit jook joint because of its archetypal out-in-the-country location, cobbled-together wood architecture, fun atmosphere and irrepressible owner.

The deejay spins soul-blues exclusively—Marvin Sease, Tyrone Davis, et al. The no-rap policy ensures a well-dressed, over-thirty-five crowd who come to pack the little dance floor, drink, and have fun. As at any jook worthy of the name, there is a pool table off in one corner. The ceiling is low and the place is subdivided into small rooms, giving it a homey feel. Silver streamers decorate the walls. Food is served.

The joint's owner, Willie Seaberry (aka Poor Monkey), clowns, mugs, sits in women's laps, and dances and struts about, making sure you appreciate his sharp suit of clothes. Twenty minutes later, he is parading about again, wearing a different outfit. He changes clothes at least half a dozen times a night.

Thursday is the big night, although recently the club has also been open on Mondays and occasionally on weekends. The music starts about 9 P.M. There is a cover charge.

Cleveland

- ### Bolivar County Courthouse
  Court St. at Bolivar Ave.

  To get there: From the intersection of highways 61 and 8, go west on Highway 8 (Sunflower Road) and turn south at the third light, onto Sharpe Avenue, then right onto Court Street.

A historic marker notes that W. C. Handy played in this building in about 1905. He also had another blues epiphany here, which affected him at least as much as the one he had in Tutwiler. A courthouse dance would definitely have been for whites. This may have been the site of an event Handy describes in his autobiography:

My own enlightenment came in Cleveland, Mississippi. I was leading the orchestra in a dance program when someone sent up an odd request. Would we play some of our "native music," the note asked. This baffled me. The men in this group could not "fake" and "sell it" like minstrel men. They were all musicians who bowed strictly to the authority of printed notes. So, we played for our anonymous fan an old-time Southern melody, a melody more sophisticated than native. A few moments later a second request came up. Would we object if a local colored band played a few dances?

Object! That was funny. What hornblower would object to a time-out and a smoke—on pay? We eased out gracefully as the newcomers entered. They were led by a long-legged chocolate boy and their band consisted of just three pieces, a battered guitar, a mandolin and a worn-out bass.

The music they made was pretty well in keeping with their looks. They struck up one of those over-and-over strains that seem to have no very clear beginning and certainly no ending at all. The strumming attained a disturbing monotony, but on and on it went, a kind of stuff that has long been associated with cane rows and levee camps. Thump-thump-thump went their feet on the floor. Their eyes rolled. Their shoulders swayed. And through it all that little agonizing strain persisted. It was not really annoying or unpleasant. Perhaps "haunting" is a better word, but I commenced to wonder if anybody besides small town rounders and their running mates would go for it.

The answer was not long in coming. A rain of silver dollars began to fall around the outlandish, stomping feet. The dancers went wild. Dollars, quarters, halves—the shower grew heavier and continued so long I strained my neck to get a better look. There before the boys lay more money than my nine musicians were being paid for the entire engagement. Then I saw the beauty of primitive music. They had the stuff the people wanted. It touched the spot. Their music wanted polishing, but it contained the essence. Folks would pay money for it. The old conventional music was well and good and had its place, no denying that, but there was no virtue in being blind when you had good eyes.

Handy "returned to Clarksdale and began immediately to work on this type of music."

Handy does not identify the trio as bluesmen. But that might be because he had as yet no name for the kind of music they played. His description sounds like how a trained musician would have described his first exposure to the blues (or his second—Handy does not make clear whether this was before or after he heard the Tutwiler guitarist).

Some writers have speculated that Charley Patton and Willie Brown may have been part of the trio that influenced Handy. But Patton and Brown would have been only in their early teens at the time, and even though Handy calls the musicians "boys," he doesn't seem to mean that literally. Also, Patton, who probably would have been the leader, was only five feet seven inches when fully grown, so it is doubtful that anyone would have described him as "long-legged."

Furthermore, the guitar-mandolin-bass instrumentation does not match what we know of Patton and Brown—or of other Delta blues musicians, for that matter. This probably was some kind of African American string band (decades later, the Mississippi Sheiks would become one of the few recorded examples of this type of group).

Regardless of who the musicians were, Handy saw that the blues was not only arresting, as he had learned at Tutwiler, but also lucrative. The scene also shows us how popular blues-type music already was in the Delta—even among whites—years before Handy, "the father of the blues," began writing it in sheet music, and decades before it appeared on records.

This courthouse is also where Charley Patton applied for four marriage licenses: Gertrude Lewis on September 12, 1908, Roxie Morrow on November 12, 1918, Bertha Reed on April 6, 1922, and Mattie Parker on June 7, 1924. Patton family members said the singer had eight wives. Those probably were not all legal marriages, however. Being a popular, charismatic entertainer, Charley Patton had no trouble picking up women, whether for marriage or more temporary arrangements. He reportedly often fought with his women, however, and would whack them with his guitar to end the fight.

- **Blues Masks and Mississippi Delta Blues Hall of Fame**
  In Delta State University's Ewing Hall, first floor; and in the Charles Capps Archive and Museum.

  To get there: From the Bolivar County Courthouse, proceed west on Court Street to its end, at Fifth Avenue, then turn north. The Capps building is on your right.

Sharon McConnell makes "life masks" of blues artists by molding their faces in plaster and then casting them. She donated about sixty of them to Delta State, where they are on exhibit in Ewing Hall. The collection includes Honeyboy Edwards, Hubert Sumlin, Pinetop Perkins, Robert Lockwood, R. L. Burnside, Bo Diddley, and Jessie Mae Hemphill.

The Blues Hall of Fame, for now, is just a "wall of fame" temporarily housed at the Capps building. There are plaques for the honorees of the Peavine Awards: Charley Patton, Willie Brown, Tommy Johnson, Robert Lockwood, Jr., Henry Townsend, Robert Johnson, Son Thomas, Muddy Waters, Little Milton, Robert Nighthawk, Houston Stackhouse, Joe Willie Wilkins, Bukka White, Howlin' Wolf, and Ike Turner.

Plans call for the hall eventually to have its own building, with a Delta blues archive as well. The annual Peavine Awards ceremony includes a blues concert. Proceeds from ticket sales benefit a Robert Johnson Memorial Scholarship Fund, for music students at Delta State University. The date of the event is not fixed—information and details are available from the Cleveland-Bolivar County Chamber of Commerce (662-843-2712).

- **Airport Grocery**
  Highway 8
  (662) 843-4817

  To get there: From the Capps building, head north on Fifth Avenue to its end at Highway 8 (Sunflower Road). Turn west and go 1 mile, just past the airport turnoff at Bishop Road, to a wood building on the north side of the street. It is 2½ miles west of the intersection of highways 61 and 8.

Actually a restaurant, not a grocery, this is where Greenville bluesman Willie Foster recorded his CD *Live at Airport Grocery.* There are signed posters by various blues artists on the walls, and recorded blues is usually on the sound system. Live blues shows are held about four times a year. Call for a schedule of upcoming shows.

Rosedale

To many blues fans, the name of this town immediately recalls the following verse:

> *Lord, I'm going to Rosedale, gon' take my rider by my side*
> *We can still barrelhouse, baby, 'cause it's on the riverside.*

Robert Johnson sang those words in his 1937 "Traveling Riverside Blues." The British blues-rock group Cream included the verse in their 1969 cover of a *different* Robert Johnson song, "Cross Road Blues," which they renamed "Crossroads."

Johnson's original also mentions Vicksburg, Friars Point, and Tennessee. He apparently was truly traveling on or alongside the river, hitting the hot spots. In the 1930s and 1940s, riverside towns tended to be wide open, offering liquor, women, and music to riverboat men and others who passed through. Rosedale, a famed bootlegging center, was no exception.

The welcome signs ignore the town's blues-and-booze heritage and dub Rosedale "the Delta City of Brotherly Love." However, a group of locals has recently formed the Crossroads Blues Society, with an annual one-day Crossroads Blues Festival. They also hope to erect a monument to Robert Johnson (already the most-monumented bluesman, with markers in Hazlehurst, Morgan City, and Quito) in the Rosedale courthouse square.

At least one blues-loving Clarksdale resident has groused about Rosedale's appropriation of the term "crossroads," which many tourists associate with a Clarksdale intersection. Rosedale blues fans reply that they never heard Robert Johnson sing about Clarksdale. And Rosedale at least has the Hollywood version of the crossroads nearby, in Beulah.

Bruce Street is the traditional jook joint street in Rosedale, although most of the old buildings are gone. If Robert Johnson actually visited Rosedale, he probably played on this street. But then, Johnson played in the clubs, streets, depots, and private homes of many, many towns, so if you've been traveling around the Delta you've probably already stood on several places where he played.

- **Great River Road State Park**

    To get there: Go west on Highway 8 to its end, at Highway 1. Go south on Highway 1 and turn east at the park entrance.

This is Mississippi's only state park on the Mississippi River. It offers camping, boating, fishing, a playground, and a tower from which to view the river. It also must be one of the few state parks anywhere equipped with a whiskey still. On exhibit outside the park's visitors center, the still has a sign with a recipe (twenty-five pounds of corn, twenty pounds of sugar, six packs of yeast, ten gallons of water) and directions for making your own.

- **The Blue Levee**

    1310 S. Main St. (Highway 1 at Highway 8)
    (662)759-6333

Formerly Leo's Market, this restaurant is under new management and continues to host live music, usually on Saturdays and sometimes on Fridays. The music is sometimes, but not always, blues.

- **Bug's Place and the Blanche K. Bruce Foundation**

    515 Bruce Street
    (662) 759-0251

Jessie "Junebug" Brown is the friendly and knowledgeable proprietor of this Bruce Street jook, a good place to have a beer and soak up atmosphere, but unfortunately without live music. Brown is one of the principals in the Blanche K. Bruce Foundation, named for Bruce, an ex-slave who became a U.S. senator in 1874, whom this street is named after. The foundation aims to preserve the culture and improve the lot of the poor in this part of the Delta. It puts on the Highway One Blues Festival, a homey affair in Rosedale, Beulah, and other towns in August.

Beulah

• The Crossroads from the Movie *Crossroads*

To get there: From the intersection of highways 8 and 1 in Rosedale, drive 7.4 miles south on Highway 1, through Beulah, to a dirt road on the east side of the highway. It is 2.1 miles south of Beulah's Main Street or 1.6 miles south of the Beulah town limits. Turn onto the road and go over the tracks to the crossroads. There is a small cemetery next to it.

Of all the hundreds of lonely country crossroads in Mississippi, this is the one chosen by the makers of the 1986 movie *Crossroads* for the scenes in which several bluesmen make or break deals with the devil.

This book does not endorse selling one's soul to the devil to achieve blues mastery, either as a historical or a practical matter. Stay home and practice instead, which is really how the great blues artists achieved their powers. However, if you insist on re-creating the apocryphal ritual, this is a perfect place to do it. Not only do you have a real Mississippi Delta dirt-road crossroads, but you also get a cemetery, some burnt old trees, and the remains of a church at the spot. Dogs on surrounding farms tend to howl at night. It is dark except for the moon and stars. And the Mississippi River is close by, adding its power to the place.

Also, since it was really the movie *Crossroads* that popularized the whole crossroads-devil-blues concept, the movie's crossroads could be considered the "real" one.

Dockery

• Dockery Farms

To get there: From the intersection of Highway 61 and Highway 8 in Cleveland, proceed east on Highway 8. After 6 miles you will come to the Dockery community sign, and after another 0.2 mile you will be at Keith Lane, the entrance to the plantation. The street is named after Keith Dockery.

A state historic marker at the road informs you that the plantation was "Established by Will Dockery in 1895 and operated

1937–1982 by Joe Rice Dockery. Included a post office, commissary and cotton gin. The plantation once employed Charley Patton, a legendary blues musician who inspired such greats as Muddy Waters, Robert Johnson, B. B. King and Elvis Presley."

It is nice that the state of Mississippi recognizes the importance of this site. However, that last sentence is not exactly correct. None of those four learned directly from Patton or, except for Johnson, probably ever heard him. Waters's main influences were Son House, an associate of Patton's, and Robert Johnson; Johnson learned directly from House and Willie Brown, another Patton associate; King's and Presley's connections to Patton are much more remote.

A list of well-known musicians who were strongly influenced or inspired by Patton would include Bukka White, John Lee Hooker and, especially, Howlin' Wolf, who learned directly from Patton at Dockery. But they only show traces of Patton's complex, unique style. Like any great artist, Patton is most important for his own work, not for his influence on others.

While many modern blues fans might overlook Patton's incredible music, one must also be wary of an opposite tendency— to deify Patton as the originator of the blues and Dockery as the birthplace of the blues. It is impossible to specify an exact time or place where the blues began—it seems to have appeared throughout the South within a short period around 1900—or to credit any one musician for its creation.

Patton's family moved to Dockery sometime between 1897 and 1904, just a few years after the plantation's 1895 founding. Patton's father, Bill, however, was no ordinary sharecropper. Instead, he rented land from Dockery and sublet it to eight sharecroppers. Bill Patton also owned wagons and horses that he used in a timber-hauling business. And he cooked fish and sold it next to the Dockery store on Saturdays.

Like his dad—but unlike nearly everyone else of their class and era—Charley found ways to earn a living without doing actual farm work. The younger Patton apprenticed to a guitarist at Dockery named Henry Sloan. He soon became a local star. Although he often traveled and moved away several times, Patton lived at Dockery on and off for about thirty years. There were many musicians in the surrounding towns and plantations, and Patton was the center of the whole scene. He made his living

DOCKERY FARMS
EST. 1895 BY
WILL DOCKERY 1865-1936
JOE RICE DOCKERY
1906-1982

Barn at Dockery Farms, Dockery

through his music and with the help of many lady friends, apparently.

Dockery's itself was home to up to four hundred families. Patton would entertain them at occasional outdoor concerts such as the one his nephew Tom Cannon remembered for an interviewer: "Just like on a Saturday a whole bunch would get together, and he'd play at Dockery's at the big store. There used to be a big brick store there at Dockery's. He'd sit out there on the store porch. People all from Lula, Cleveland, everywhere. Just like he plays for one of those places, they would charge so much at the door. They'd have it in one of these big buildings, and they'd charge 'em at the door."

The marvelous music Patton played at Dockery might have been recorded only in sharecroppers' memories had it not been for H. C. Speir, a Jackson music-store owner, who traveled to Dockery (probably following a tip from bluesman Bo Carter) to hear Patton. Speir liked what he heard, and arranged for Patton to record.

Dockery's is mentioned in Patton's 1934 "34 Blues," where he sings, "They run me from Will Dockery's." The song even gives some of the details: "Herman told Papa Charley, 'I don't want you hangin' 'round on my job no more.'" Herman Jett was a white Dockery overseer who ran Patton off, considering him a loafer. He told Patton to quit interfering with people who were trying to work, and to go get a job.

Countless visitors have photographed the Dockery barn, on which the following is painted simply in red and black on white:

DOCKERY FARMS
Est. 1895 by
Will Dockery
1865–1936
Joe Rice Dockery
1906–1982

A subtler place to pose might be by the small Dockery Farms sign on the old filling station near the road, indicating the office. This is a working plantation and private property, so if you stop, respect the place and the privacy of the people living and working there.

The Dockerys paid no attention to the music of Patton and their other sharecroppers. "We were never the type of plantation owners who invited their help to come in and sing for parties," Keith Dockery, widow of Joe Rice Dockery (founder Will's son), told writer Robert Palmer. "I wish we had realized that these people were so important."

Pops Staples, patriarch of the Staples Singers pop-gospel group, also grew up on Dockery. His beautiful guitar playing is based on the downhome Delta blues.

Boyle

- ## Peavine Railroad

    To get there: A few miles south of Cleveland on Highway 61, turn west onto Highway 446. Go 0.4 miles and look for the state blues marker on the right, near City Hall.

The Peavine was a local, narrow-gauge branch of the Yazoo & Mississippi Valley (known in blues as the Yellow Dog) railroad line. The Peavine earned its nickname from its slow, meandering path.

The Peavine was what people used to get around the area. It stopped at towns and plantations: Dockery, Halstead, Boyle, Skene, Victor, Pace, Symonds, Malvina, and Rosedale.

Charley Patton and Dockery's other bluesmen—including Willie Brown and Howlin' Wolf—rode the Peavine regularly, boarding at the Dockery station. Patton sang about its whistle in "Pea Vine Blues":

> *I think I heard the Pea Vine whistle blow*
> *Blowed just like my rider gettin' on board.*

The state blues marker in Boyle marks the spot where the Peavine linked up with the Vicksburg-to-Memphis line of the Yellow Dog. You can see a bit of its narrow-gauge track near the marker. Most of it has been covered over by a walkway through the park.

Some more remnants of the Peavine tracks are visible along the dirt road across from Dockery's entrance. And back in Cleveland, there is a gift shop on Sharpe Avenue (in the commercial area known as Cotton Row) called Pea Vine Station, in tribute to this historic local railway.

Drew

Drew and Ruleville, fourteen miles apart on Highway 49W, were heavy blues territory in the 1920s. Charley Patton, Willie Brown, and the other Dockery-based musicians played often in jooks, at house parties, and on corners in these nearby towns. Tommy Johnson moved to Drew as a young man, in the company of an older woman, and developed his Delta-style music here before returning to the Jackson area. Howlin' Wolf lived in the area, farming and learning music, from 1923 to 1933. David Evans's *Big Road Blues* is a scholarly book that focuses on musicians of this area.

Ruleville

This town is the setting of B. F. Jackson's *Black Hometown Movie,* an amateur documentary that caused a sensation in the blues world in 1997–98, when some people thought that the man playing guitar and rack-mounted harmonica in it was Robert Johnson. Experts analyzed the brief, blurry footage to figure out what chords and tuning the musician was using. A Beale Street merchant tried to market the "original" to foreign collectors.

The excitement subsided quickly when someone noticed a poster for a 1941 film on a wall behind the musician. Johnson died in 1938.

The movie is still interesting, however, as probably the only film of a prewar Delta bluesman (he has not been identified, and is probably not anyone famous), although it is unfortunate that his moment on camera is so brief and blurry. It is also a rare document of an afternoon in the black community of a small Mississippi town in the 1940s. Jackson, who was white, made a film called *White Hometown Movie* the same day on the white side of downtown Ruleville. The films are available for viewing at the Southern Media Archive at the University of Mississippi, Oxford (662-915-5851), and at the Mississippi Department of Archives and History, 100 S. State St., Jackson (601-359-6876).

- **Greasy Street**

    To get there: From Highway 49W, turn west on Floyce Street (following the sign for Ruleville Business District) and continue 0.4 mile into town. Go past Main Street and take the next left onto Front Street.

"Greasy Street" is the local nickname for downtown Front Street, Ruleville's traditional jook joint strip. None of the clubs has live music these days, but deejays at the Top 10 Club and the Black Castle mix in a good deal of soul-blues. The Black Castle is the signless metal building at the south end of the row (the new metal building replaces the old wood building, which burned down recently). Saturdays and Sundays are the big nights at those clubs.

Glendora

To get there: From Ruleville, take Highway 8 east to 49E. Glendora is seven miles north.

Aleck "Rice" Miller, the man the world would know as Sonny Boy Williamson II, was born in Glendora probably in 1912. He left home, probably in his teens, after a fight with his father, and never returned.

The tiny town recognizes Sonny Boy with a large painted sign at its entrance, off Highway 49E. It also has a new B&B named for its favorite son.

On December 5 and 6, 1998 (Sonny Boy's birthday weekend), eighty-seven Glendora children (more than half of all the children in this four-hundred-person town) studied the blues harmonica. They all received harmonicas and two days of instruction by professional harpists including Sugar Blue, Paul deLay, Arthur

Williams, "Jumpin'" Johnny Sansone, and Bruce "Sunpie" Barnes. Some of them thought the blues and the harmonica rather square at first, but by the end of the day they were playing blues riffs, gospel tunes, pop melodies. On the second day, even more children attended, and they were teaching one another techniques. A year later, none of them was still playing. The harmonicas were lost. But everyone in the town had become a little more aware of its most famous son and of the blues. Glendora officials have been talking lately about reviving the harmonica teach-in as an annual event.

- **Sonny Boy's Bed & Breakfast Cyber Café**
  19 Gipson Avenue
  (662)375-7456

There are rooms dedicated to Bobby Rush, Robert Lockwood Jr., Robert Johnson, B. B. King, U.S. Congressman Bennie Thompson for some reason, and Sonny Boy Williamson of course, in this B&B, cyber café and visitor's welcome center that opened in 2008. Each of the six rooms has memorabilia of its namesake. A listening center is planned.

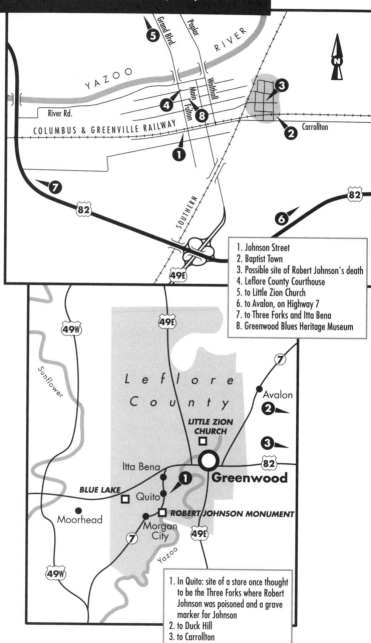

Greenwood & Area

1. Johnson Street
2. Baptist Town
3. Possible site of Robert Johnson's death
4. Leflore County Courthouse
5. to Little Zion Church
6. to Avalon, on Highway 7
7. to Three Forks and Itta Bena
8. Greenwood Blues Heritage Museum

1. In Quito: site of a store once thought to be the Three Forks where Robert Johnson was poisoned and a grave marker for Johnson
2. to Duck Hill
3. to Carrollton

RIVER

Grand Blvd

Poplar

YAZOO

Walthall

Main

Fulton

River Rd.

COLUMBUS & GREENVILLE RAILWAY

Carrollton

SOUTHERN

82

82

49E

N

Leflore County

Sunflower

49W

49E

7

Avalon

2

3

LITTLE ZION CHURCH

Itta Bena

BLUE LAKE

Quito

Moorhead

Morgan City

7

Greenwood

82

ROBERT JOHNSON MONUMENT

49E

Yazoo

49W

chapter 6

THE GREENWOOD AREA

Greenwood

To get there: From Glendora take Highway 49E south to Highway 82.
Greenwood is four miles east.

The welcome signs note that Greenwood is the Cotton Capital
of the World, and a billboard labels the town "Home of Mississippi's most productive workforce." To blues fans, this town of
twenty thousand on the eastern edge of the Delta is where Robert
Johnson sang his last song and died so young.

The Civic Center, Highway 7 at Carrollton Avenue, sometimes
hosts soul-blues concerts, including a Cotton Capitol Blues Festival in October. The River to the Rails festival, held in April or May
in downtown Greenwood, includes blues. The Alluvian Hotel, 318
Howard St., features music regularly in its lobby, and sometimes
it's blues. Webster's, 216 W. Claiborne Ave., also sometimes presents blues. The Blue Parrot Café, 222 Howard St., also presents live
blues regularly.

Radio station WGNC, 104.3 FM, mixes a lot of contemporary
blues into its programming. WVSD, 91.7 FM, the Mississippi Valley State University station, features blues some evenings. WGRM,

High school band marching on Johnson Street, Greenwood

93.9 FM and 1240 AM, is a twenty-four-hour gospel station. WABG, 960 AM, recently was purchased by Greenwood Blues Heritage Museum owner Steve LaVere, who plans to broadcast from the museum and include lots of blues programming.

Bluesman Honeyboy Edwards said he first heard Robert Johnson playing in an alley off **Johnson Street** (which is *not* named after the bluesman, but is a pleasant coincidence), near Main, in the fall of 1937. As Edwards recalls in his autobiography, *The World Don't Owe Me Nothing:* "He was playing the blues so good. One woman, she was full of that old corn whiskey, she said, 'Mister, you play me "Terraplane Blues"!' She didn't know she was talking to the man who made it! She said, 'If you play me "Terraplane Blues" I'll give you a dime!' He said, 'Miss, that's my number.' 'Well, you play it then.' He started playing and they knew who he was then. He was playing and trembling and hollering."

Johnson Street is Greenwood's main black business street. Robert Johnson was not the only bluesman to play on its corners for tips. Sonny Boy Williamson II, Elmore James, and Tommy McClennan were among the many other blues singers who played there while they were living in town or passing through.

Johnson Street turns into Carrollton Avenue at the Southern Railroad tracks. On your left, as you head east and cross the tracks, is **Baptist Town**, a poor residential neighborhood dominated by McKinney Chapel M. B. Church, at Young and Short streets near the tracks. Edwards says Johnson died in a room Johnson was renting in a house at Pelican and Young streets. Others say it is more likely that Johnson died on Star of the West plantation out in the country, however. His death certificate says he died "outside" Greenwood. At any rate, Johnson lived in Baptist Town for his last months on earth, and played the blues like nobody's business on Johnson Street.

On the empty lot at the corner of Young and Pelican streets there is a sign stating that Johnson played music and died at this location—which might be true. For a while a few years ago, there were weekend music celebrations at the site. There also is a blues-related mural at Hoover Store, across from the lot. The store closed after a fire in 2007, however. Owner Sylvester Hoover, who spearheaded the celebrations and also offers Johnson-themed tours, was planning to reopen on Main Street just south of Johnson Street.

Leflore County Courthouse at Market and Fulton is where a judge decided on October 15, 1998, that Crystal Springs truck driver Claud L. Johnson "is the biological son of Robert L. Johnson and under law is the sole heir." On June 15, 2000, the Mississippi Supreme Court upheld the ruling, rejecting an appeal by Annye Anderson and Robert Harris, a half-sister and grandson of Johnson's half-sister Carrie Harris Thompson.

The court records are public. To view them, turn right as you enter the building, and go into the chancery court clerk's office. Ask for case E-380, Estate of Robert L. Johnson, Deceased, vs. Willis B. Brumfield, Administrator. It fills half of a large drawer.

Claud was born to Virgie Jane Smith on December 16, 1931, in Lincoln County. "R. L. Johnson, laborer" was listed on the birth certificate as his father. Smith said, in a 1992 deposition, that the R. L. Johnson was none other than the bluesman. "Going to home parties, I met him," she said. "He would play there." Smith was seventeen; Johnson was nineteen. He was her first lover. She became pregnant. Johnson came by when Claud was five months old and asked Smith to run away to Tennessee with him, she said. She declined to go. He gave her twenty or thirty dollars, and she never saw him again.

Johnson died, penniless, when Claud was six. There was no point in Claud trying to prove who his father was until after the 1990 release of the Columbia CD set *Robert Johnson: The Complete Recordings*, which began putting money in the Johnson estate.

Besides court proceedings, the files have copies of documents including Johnson's two marriage certificates (to Virginia Travis in Penton on February 17, 1929, and to Callie Craft in Hazlehurst on May 4, 1931) and his death certificate.

- ### Three Forks Store
  Northeast side of intersection of highways 82 and 49E west of town—*not* the cloverleaf south of town where the highways also meet

Three Forks is the jook joint where, according to testimony from eyewitness Honeyboy Edwards and hearsay from others, Robert Johnson gave his last performance and then wound up crawling on the floor in agony after drinking a bottle of poisoned whiskey. He died within a few days, or perhaps a few weeks. Although no one was ever prosecuted in the case, it seems that Johnson was murdered by the jook joint's owner, who had learned that Johnson was having an affair with the owner's wife. On the back of Johnson's death certificate, a county registrar wrote that Johnson died of syphilis. That idea apparently came from Luther Wade, the owner of Star of the West, the plantation where Johnson probably died. It is possible that Johnson had syphilis but also was poisoned. Or perhaps it was merely his heavy drinking that night that aggravated the symptoms of the syphilis or helped bring on another condition such as pneumonia. Whether or not Johnson was poisoned, it seems that he did sing his last song at a jook at this site. There is now a church and cemetery here, but they were built after Johnson's death, and after a tornado in the 1940s destroyed the jook where Johnson played. Also, the highway alignments have changed several times since the 1930s, so the intersection was not exactly where it is now.

- ### Greenwood Blues Heritage Museum
  222 Howard St.
  (662) 451-7800

The museum is on the second floor of the Three Deuces building, whose first floor houses the Blue Parrot Café and Veronica's Bakery. A state blues marker in front of the building commemorates WGRM, the radio station that was based in the building in the 1940s (and is soon to move back in). WGRM was never a blues station, but it did present local music acts live on the air—including the Famous St. John's Gospel Singers, whose guitarist was B. B. King.

The museum is open 9 A.M. to 5 P.M. Mondays through Fridays, or by appointment. If the restaurants are closed, climb the outside stairs on the right side of building to get to the museum entrance.

The building and the museum and restaurants are owned by Steve LaVere, who for many years collected royalties from artists who recorded versions of Robert Johnson's songs, and was the main force behind the 1990 CD reissue of Johnson's complete recordings. LaVere continues to own the rights to the photographs of Johnson.

The museum is largely about Johnson, and even more so, about LaVere's relationship with Johnson's legacy. There is a wall of platinum and gold records for Johnson covers by the Red Hot Chili Peppers, Foghat, the Blues Brothers, Lynyrd Skynyrd, Led Zeppelin, and others. There is an R. Crumb depiction of Johnson, which LaVere sued the artist to acquire, according to museum Director George Vasquez. There are official Johnson-related products that were manufactured in recent years—guitar straps, T-shirts, and even a six-pack of Crossroads beer. There are parts from Terraplane automobiles, the model Johnson sang about in "Terraplane Blues." Perhaps most interesting are the 1938 aerial maps of the Greenwood area showing the locations relevant to Johnson's death.

There also is a "Memphis Room" full of posters and photographs from the 1960s and '70s blues shows that LaVere was involved with there. And there are panels of images and information on general blues history. There also are displays about musicians from the Greenwood area.

LaVere recently bought WABG and plans to move it back to its original location in the Three Deuces building and broadcast from there. He also has plans for a nightclub on the building's third floor. In the meantime, there is regular live music, often blues, on weekends at the Blue Parrot downstairs.

• Cottonlandia Museum
1608 Highway 82W
(662) 453-0925

This museum has a nice watercolor of Sam Chatmon on display and prints of it for sale. It also has blues videos for viewing on request. Other than that, there isn't much blues-specific content here. But there is much about the context of the blues: cotton-farming equipment, paintings of sharecropper scenes, a dugout canoe used by moonshiners, etc. It is open 9 A.M. to 5 P.M. weekdays and 2 to 5 P.M. Saturdays and Sundays.

- **Malouf Record Shop**
  712 George St.
  (662) 455-9737

This charming, old-fashioned record store in a tin building south of downtown seems like a relic of a bygone era. It sells soulblues tapes and CDs, local concert tickets, and recorded sermons by Greenwood preachers.

North of Greenwood

- **Robert Johnson's Grave**

  To get there: From Fulton Street in downtown Greenwood, drive north, over a bridge that takes you out of downtown. The street name becomes Grand Boulevard. Continue north, through residential neighborhoods, until you cross a second bridge that takes you over the Tallahatchie River and out of town. From that bridge, continue north 2.3 miles to Little Zion M.B. Church, on the left. There is a Johnson marker in the cemetery next to it, under the big tree toward the back.

Although this was the third place marked as Robert Johnson's grave (see Quito and Morgan City entries in this chapter for the other two), this seems to be the correct one, as there is an eyewitness who confirms the burial.

Rosie Eskridge was twenty-two when her husband, Tom, dug Robert Johnson's grave in the cemetery of this church, to which Eskridge still belongs. She does not remember the exact spot, but she knows it is near the big tree, which the casket sat under while the hole was being dug. Eskridge has never been a fan of Johnson's music or of blues in general, but she knew who the locally prominent singer was. She has not attempted to make money on her story and does not especially relish talking about it, so there is no reason to think she is making it up. Until someone comes forward with other evidence, it seems safe to call this cemetery—although probably not the exact spot where the marker is—Johnson's grave.

Eskridge's story jibes with the now-accepted location of the Three Forks jook joint where Johnson played his final gig, at highways 82 and 49 just outside of Greenwood, instead of in Quito as

The third and latest Robert Johnson grave, near Greenwood

had been believed earlier. It also jibes with the statement on Johnson's death certificate that he was buried at "Zion Church," although that also can be said of the Morgan City location. There
are many churches with "Zion" in their names. Since speaking
with Eskridge, Steve LaVere decided this was the correct location
of Johnson's grave, and he paid for the marker placed on the site
in 2002. LaVere, a longtime Johnson researcher who used to con-
trol the rights to Johnson's songs, had identified the Morgan City
site as Johnson's grave in the 1980s. (To see a map delineating the
geography of the events of Johnson's poisoning, death, and burial,
visit LaVere's Greenwood Blues Heritage Museum.)

The stone's inscription includes a reproduction of a Bible-
themed note supposedly written by Johnson, along with a quote
from his "From Four Until Late" and much commentary.

Given the struggles to correctly identify his grave and the mul-
tiple markers, another Johnson quote might be relevant here. In
"Me and the Devil Blues," between repetitions of "You may bury
my body down by the highway side," the great bluesman inserts a
spoken aside: "Babe, I don't care where you bury my body when
I'm dead and gone."

If sleeping near Robert Johnson's ghost appeals to you, check
out Tallahatchie Flats, 58458 CR 518, a few hundred yards north
of Little Zion cemetery, (662)453-1854 or (877)453-1854. Surrounded by a cottonfield, it offers refurbished shacks for rent,

similar to the Shack-Up Inn at Hopson Plantation in Clarksdale. It is another enterprise of Greenwood Blues Heritage Museum owner Steve LaVere (see museum entry above).

Avalon

To get there: On Highway 7 at the intersection with County Road 41, halfway between Holcomb and Greenwood—about 11 miles to either of those towns.

> *Avalon's my hometown, always on my mind*
> *Pretty mamas in Avalon want me there all the time.*
> *—opening verse of Mississippi John Hurt's "Avalon Blues"*

It was a tiny town to begin with, and Avalon's population had declined so much by the 1960s it was left off of most maps. Therefore, 1960s fans of Mississippi John Hurt thought that Hurt's 1928 "Avalon Blues" might refer to an Avalon in a different state. When they failed to find any trace of him at other real Avalons, they decided it might be a mythical place. But finally someone consulted an old map, found Avalon, Mississippi, went there, and found Hurt.

Born in nearby Teoc, Hurt moved to Avalon with his family as a child. He made his living mainly as a farmer and bootlegger, but he also was locally renowned as a musician, playing at parties and dances. About 1923 Hurt played a square dance with the white country fiddler Willie Narmour, filling in for Narmour's regular guitarist, Shell Smith. After Narmour and Smith garnered a record contract a few years later, they recommended Hurt to the record company. Hurt traveled to Memphis and New York to record in 1928. The records did not sell well.

But he continued to play and was still playing, very well, when "rediscovered" in 1963. And he quickly agreed to move to Washington, D.C., and begin a new career as a full-time musician. For three years, Hurt was a hit on the college, coffeehouse, and festival circuit. He also made plenty of new recordings. Then he moved back to Mississippi and died in 1966. Although some sources state he bought a house with his earnings from those three years in music, that is untrue. Whatever money Hurt generated in that period did not do anything for his standard of living. He died in a rental house he could barely afford to live in, according to his family.

Avalon's population has continued to decline, and it hardly ex-

Mississippi John Hurt's grave, Avalon

ists as a town. But there are some things to see. On Highway 7 there is a state historic marker—a green sign, predating the blue blues markers—commemorating Hurt and his connection to the town. It reads:

"Mississippi" John Hurt/John S. Hurt (1893–1966) was a pioneer blues and folk guitarist. Self-taught, Hurt rarely left his home at Avalon where he worked as a farmer. Although he recorded several songs in 1928, including "Avalon Blues" and "Frankie," he lived in relative obscurity before he was "rediscovered" in the blues revival of the 1960s

West of Highway 7 you can find some old buildings (many are current residences, so please respect people's privacy) including the depot where Hurt caught the train to begin his trips to Memphis and New York to record in 1928—perhaps his only trips away from Avalon until his move to Washington at age seventy-one.

Driving east on County Road 41 toward the grave and museum, notice the small white church on the right. That is St. James Church #2, the Hurt family church and the site of his funeral.

- **Mississippi John Hurt's Grave**

To get there: Do this trip by daylight. From Highway 7, turn east (the only way it goes) onto County Road 41, which has a large sign that says "Auto Electric Rebuilders." After 3.3 miles the road changes from paved to gravel. Continue another 0.4 miles and then turn sharp left at the New Highlandale Stables sign, onto an uphill, unpaved road. Continue past the house on left and the stables on the right, through the woods on a dirt road. The road is rutted but drivable by ordinary sedan—as long as it is dry. Do not stop to ask for directions, as some of the residents have been openly hostile to what they consider intrusions on their private road (it actually is a logging road, open to the public). Drive 1 mile, looking carefully (or having your passenger look, as the road is narrow and dangerous) into the woods on the left to spot the graves. There might be some flowers or other decorations there. A huge old oak tree is across the road from the cemetery. Do not block the road or anyone's driveway when you park. Do wear bright clothes, as there may be hunters about. Walk up the path and into the lovely grove that contains the Hurt family cemetery. There are maps to the grave and museum at Auto Electric Rebuilders on Highway 7 in Avalon, at Cottonlandia Museum in Greenwood, and at Upchurch Store in Teoc.

The Hurt family cemetery is in this remote location because St. James Church was up here, before it was replaced by St. James Church #2, which you passed on County Road 41. Hurt attended school at the hilltop church.

Mississippi John Hurt's grave is way in the back. The stone reads, simply:

> *John S Hurt*
> Born Mar 8 1892
> Died Nov 2 1966

Recently, someone outlined the actual grave with railroad ties, to clarify on which side of the marker Hurt's body lies.

There is another stone nearby that you might mistake for Hurt's, but it is that of his son. It reads:

> *Mr. J.C. Hurt*
> Born: June 12, 1917
> Died: October 12, 1996

Another marker is for Gertrude Conley-Hurt, June 25, 1890 to April 26, 2002. She was Hurt's first wife, to whom he was still legally married all his life, although he may not have realized it. They lived together four years and had two children together. The story is that Hurt told his boss he had to leave work one day to go to the county clerk to get a divorce. The boss told him, "Keep working, I"ll get it for you." Hurt gave him $10 but the boss failed to carry out the errand and never told Hurt that he hadn't.

Jessie, the common-law-wife Hurt lived with for most of his life and at the time of his death, is buried right behind Gertrude, an unmarked slab over her grave. Among the other Hurts buried here is John's brother Henis Hurt, 1887–1968.

Valley

- ## Mississippi John Hurt Museum
  (662) 455-3958 (This is the home number of curator Art Browning; there is no phone at the museum.)

  To get there: From John Hurt's grave, drive back down the hill, past the mailboxes, and turn left on the main road, continuing in the direction away from Highway 7. Go through a clump of buildings, the Valley community. The road becomes paved as you pass through the town. At the far edge of Valley, note Christ Advent Church on the right, and take the left onto the dirt road opposite. From that road, take the first left onto County Road 109. When that road forks, bear to the left, continuing on 109. When you come to a clearing, you will see the museum in the field on your left, before you get to the first house. (There are maps to the museum and grave at Auto Electric Rebuilders on Highway 7 in Avalon, at Cottonlandia Museum in Greenwood, and at Upchurch Store in Teoc.)

Housed in the little shotgun shack that Hurt lived in, this museum contains photos, record jackets, and articles about Hurt, as well as artifacts from his era, including a table that he made. Part of its charm is its remoteness. The house has been moved from its original location a few miles away. Driving to it gives you a feel for the land that produced John Hurt and his music—the Carroll County hills—and might stimulate some ideas about why Hurt's music sounds so different from that of the musicians of the nearby Delta flatlands.

Hurt's granddaughter Mary Frances Hurt Wright, a Chicago schoolteacher, saved his old house from demolition, moved it, and restored it. It opened July 4, 2002, with a dedication ceremony that included a surprise performance by 1960s music star John Sebastian of the Lovin' Spoonful, a group that took its name from a Hurt song. A John Hurt Festival takes place at the site every year on July 4.

Before Hurt Wright moved it, Hurt's house stood on the property where Mailbox 42849 is, in the Valley community. (That is private property, so please observe it from the road and do not trespass.) Hurt often sat and played under the magnolia tree near the road. He lived there from sometime in the 1940s through 1963, when he moved to Washington.

Carrollton

In the county seat, many people are proud that Mississippi John Hurt was from Carroll County and spent his last days in Carrollton.

Carroll County Market, 607 Lexington St. (662-237-1133), is a folksy restaurant that brings in local, regional, and national acts, usually playing blues or other roots-type music. It also hosts an open mic on Fridays, beginning at 7 P.M., often bringing out performers with a strong Hurt influence.

An annual John Hurt Fundraising Gala is held in February (around his birthday) at Carrollton Community House, a 1936 log structure.

Duck Hill

- **The Grass Roots Blues Festival**
  (662)565-2478

  To get there: Just off Route 404 about 4 mi east of Interstate 55. In case of rain it moves to the Duck Hill gymnasium.

Held in early July, this festival has proven to be an excellent one. It has a woodsy outdoor site and a lineup that crosses race, age, and subgenre boundaries. Organizers subtitle it "a family affair" and created it to teach youth about blues, but grownups have a great time too. Duck Hill's own Little Willie Farmer, who rarely plays outside the area, always is part of the bill.

Itta Bena

- **Ralph Lembo's Store**
  114 Humphreys St.

  To get there: Go west from Greenwood on Highway 82 to Highway 7. Turn south onto Highway 7, which becomes Main Street in Itta Bena. Humphreys is the northernmost of the two streets that border the grassy strip in the middle of town. Turn east on Humphreys. Lembo's store is on the north side of the street, next to Fred's Express. Recently it was vacant and had a "Mattie's Upholstery" sign above the front window.

The Sicilian-born Ralph Lembo, who lived from 1896 to 1960, peddled dry goods from a cart in Itta Bena before opening this store. Like Jackson's H. C. Speir, Lembo was another white furniture-and-record-store owner who scouted for bluesmen on the side. But while Speir traveled around the state looking for artists, Lembo stayed home in Itta Bena. Probably for that reason, he was not nearly as successful as Speir at finding artists. Lembo did score two big finds: Rubin Lacy and Bukka White, who both auditioned at the store. White described his 1930 audition to an interviewer:

> I went on up there and Ralph give me a big glass half full of bonded whiskey. I don't believe I ever had tasted a bonded whiskey. It taste just like syrup to me, it was so good. And I drank the last of it and he caught me licking the glass, just holding it up getting the last drop. And I could feel it commencing building me up. I played "Downtown Women Sic 'Em Dogs On You" and he just had a fit. He said, "Can you stand another half a glass?" I said, "You can fill it up; it ain't gonna hurt." Well, I had sense enough to didn't drink it, I just sipped a little on it 'til I got through, then I killed it. Ooooo, I was the happiest soul going down that highway. You be hearing my foots hitting them rocks like somebody had a sledgehammer hitting on the rock. Man, I was feeling good.

Before Speir tracked down Charley Patton and got him to record, Lembo had talked to Patton, but couldn't make a deal with him.

Lembo also brought Blind Lemon Jefferson, who was already a blues star, to Itta Bena for a performance at Lembo's store in about 1927. Lembo paid Jefferson's train fare from Chicago, and charged people twenty-five cents to attend the Saturday afternoon show. He also booked Jefferson to play at a local high school on the same trip. Both performances were financial failures. And Lembo's attempt to get Jefferson to record while he was in town also fell through.

In about 1930, Lembo heard Walter Vincson and Lonnie Chatmon, who were in Itta Bena to play a white dance. Lembo sent them to Shreveport, Louisiana, to record for Polk Brockman of Okeh Records. At that session they came up with their name—the Mississippi Sheiks.

Vincson said he wrote the Sheiks' big hit, "Sitting on Top of the World," while he and Chatmon were sitting on the street in Itta Bena, rehearsing for a dance—probably on the same visit when Lembo heard them, since they recorded the song at their first session. Chatmon commented, "What kind of song is that?" when he first heard it. But they knew they were onto something good when their tip bucket filled up as they were still working on the song.

Honeyboy Edwards says he lived in the area for a while and sometimes swept Lembo's floor, in hopes of getting a chance to record. The ploy did not work.

Blue Lake

To get there: From downtown Itta Bena, go a few blocks north on Main Street (Highway 7) to an old Gulf gas station on the west side of the street. Turn west there, onto Fitzhugh Street. Follow that street as it goes around a large cotton-gin complex. It becomes gravel for a bit, but stay on it as it becomes paved again and goes through a residential area. After 3.6 miles you will come to a stop sign, just past a cemetery on the right. Turn left and then right at the next street, so you are continuing west. Go 2 miles to a bridge on your left. Drive over the bridge and park.

B. B. King is sometimes said to be from Itta Bena. He actually was born a few miles out of town, on the shore of Blue Lake, near the tiny community called Berclair. At any rate, he stayed in this immediate area only until he was about five. King considers Indianola, where he lived from age thirteen on, his hometown. He plays an annual homecoming concert in Indianola, but he has not forgotten Itta Bena, either. He recently has contributed to the capital campaign at Itta Bena's Mississippi Valley State University, with both cash and a benefit performance.

Blue Lake is a lovely and popular fishing spot. A few houses stand on its banks, but the house King was born in, on the south bank, is no longer there.

Quito

- ## Three Forks Store

To get there: From Highway 82, take Highway 7 south through Itta Bena, following the signs as the highway zigzags to the right and back to the left. After the second zigzag, continue 2.6 miles south on Highway 7. On the east side of the highway, at the last corner north of the bridge, is a house said to be the building that once was the original Three Forks Store. Since it is now someone's home, respect the privacy of the residents.

Until it fell down a few years ago, this is where a house stood that previously had been a store called "Three Forks." Robert Johnson played his final performance, and was poisoned, in a jook joint called "Three Forks." However, this is not the same "Three Forks." That name is a common one, attached to many places where three roads come together.

This Three Forks store, when it was operating, was at a different location. It was later moved to this spot and turned into a residence. To get to what is said to be its original location: Turn east onto the road just north of this spot, then turn right onto the first

Marker at what might be Robert Johnson's grave, Payne Chapel
M. B. Church, Quito

gravel road. This intersection was called Three Forks, and there
was a store and jook joint here. It is possible that Johnson played
here sometime in his life. But it does not seem to be the place
where he played his final gig.

After the building was moved, the *business* also was relocated,
to another building that has burned down. The Delta Blues Museum in Clarksdale has the "Three Forks" sign from that burned-
down building—not from the Three Forks in Greenwood, which
is now believed to be the site where Johnson last sang.

- **Robert Johnson's Grave Marker**

    To get there: From the Three Forks house, continue south on Highway 7 for
    0.2 mile, over the bridge and into Quito (there is no sign for the town). Just
    past the bridge, turn west onto a dirt road across from the big cotton gin with
    a "HE Hardwick-Etter Ginning Systems" sign. Drive in a block, to the church
    on the right. Park and walk into the cemetery. Marked with a flat stone, John-
    son's grave is in the back, away from the road, near the woods.

In its November–December 1990 issue devoted to Robert
Johnson, *Living Blues* magazine identified the cemetery of Payne
Chapel M. B. Church, Quito, as Johnson's resting place. The issue
even included a photo of the unmarked patch of land, next to a
stump, that was supposed to be the grave. The information had
come from one of Johnson's ex-girlfriends, who insisted he was in
Hell and wouldn't appreciate flowers, much less a tombstone. But

a Georgia rock band, the Tombstones, disregarded that advice and showed up soon afterward to place a marker there.

This flat marker is much smaller than the ones at Johnson's other marked graves. It draws its share of offerings, however—especially guitar picks. It is inscribed with a guitar and a treble clef, and reads:

> *Robert Johnson*
> May 8, 1911
> Aug. 16, 1938
> Resting in the blues

The evidence now points to the grave on Money Road, north of Greenwood, as the correct one.

Morgan City

• Another Robert Johnson Grave Marker

To get there: From the Quito grave marker, get back onto Highway 7 and head 3.7 miles south. At a sign on the right that reads "Matthew's Brake Wildlife Preserve," turn east and go to the cemetery by the white church ahead on the left.

After Johnson researcher Steve LaVere found a Three Forks store in Quito, he asked about a "Zion Church"—since that is where Johnson's death certificate says he is buried—and found this one, Mount Zion Missionary Baptist. Going by LaVere's pointer, with financing from Sony Records, which issued the fabulously successful Johnson reissue CD set, a new organization called the Mount Zion Fund erected this marker. The fund has since gone on to coordinate the erection of markers for many other blues artists.

This church was founded in 1909 (although the building was rebuilt in 1983), so it existed during Johnson's day. However, this is not where Johnson is buried. LaVere has admitted that he identified it erroneously and now believes that Johnson is buried at Little Zion Church north of Greenwood.

Even when it was believed that Johnson was buried in this cemetery, no one knew the exact spot. So the monument was placed near the road to fulfill Johnson's line from "Me and the Devil Blues":

> *You may bury my body down by the highway side*
> *So my old evil spirit can catch a Greyhound bus and ride.*

The largest of Johnson's three grave markers, this is an impressive obelisk, lengthily inscribed on all four sides:

1. Born in Hazlehurst, Copiah County, the recording career and brief transit of Robert Johnson left an enormous legacy to American music. Preserved for the ages by Columbia Recording Company, the body of his work is considered to be among the most powerful of its kind, a haunting and lyrical portrait of the human spirit.

2. [The familiar dimestore photo of Johnson, cigarette in mouth, has been replaced on this side after being stolen.] Robert Johnson "King of the Delta Blues Singers." His music struck a chord that continues to resonate. His blues addressed generations he would never know and made poetry of his visions and fears.

Monument at a cemetery where Robert Johnson once was thought to be buried, Mount Zion M. B. Church, Morgan City

3. "You may bury my body down by the highway side" . . . This monument erected April 20, 1991 through the generosity of people across America, with profound respect and appreciation for the people and culture of the Mississippi Delta.

4. [A list of all of Johnson's songs.]

Johnson has two or three more grave markers than any other blues artist, and many more words inscribed on the stones. He also gets more gifts left at his graves. Sonny Boy Williamson II's marker, which comes in second, usually has a harmonica or two and some coins. Johnson's draws jewelry, notes scrawled on food-stamp tickets or other kinds of paper, CDs by obscure artists (perhaps left by the artists themselves, hoping that some of Johnson's spirit will penetrate their music), pencils, cigarettes, flowers, beer cans, pretty stones, and of course guitar picks.

Moorhead

- ### Where the Southern Cross the Dog

  To get there: From Robert Johnson's graves, head back north on Highway 7 to Highway 82. Turn west and go 13 miles to Highway 3. Turn south into Moorhead. "Home of Grand Ole Opry star Johnny Russell," the signs proclaim. You'll be on Olive Street. At Olive and Southern Avenue, there is a railroad crossing sign. Turn right onto Southern, past the closed-up Yellow Dog Store, and see the railroad crossing. There is a state historic marker at the site.

The intersection of the Southern and the Dog is a perfectly perpendicular crossing, due north-south and east-west. And it sits in a handsome spot. A wood pavilion suitable for picnicking is off to the side. Trees and grass are plentiful. There is a U.S. post office right near the crossing and an old water tower nearby. Unfortunately the Yellow Dog Store, an archetypal Southern general store, recently closed.

The line "I'm going where the Southern cross the Dog," repeated over and over, baffled W. C. Handy when he heard it at the Tutwiler train station in 1903. Many sources infer that the Tutwiler singer was headed for Moorhead. However, that may already have been just a standard blues line. He might actually have been going somewhere else or just hanging out at the depot.

At any rate, some blues singer once coined a line about heading to this spot—the intersection of the Southern (which is still active) and the Yazoo and Mississippi Valley (whose tracks are now part of the Columbus and Greenville line, or C&G). The Yazoo and Mississippi Valley was also known as the Yazoo Delta, and "Yellow Dog" was apparently a reinterpretation of the initials "YD." Writer Paul Oliver talked to some people, however, who maintained that the line was named after an actual yellow dog that used to stand along the track and bark and to others who said it was so named by employees of rival lines, deriding it as a "short dog" or minor line.

Handy used the line in his 1914 composition "Yellow Dog Rag," which he would later rename "Yellow Dog Blues." "My song was made around the line (but not the music) I had heard the guitar player, impassive, sing that night at Tutwiler," Handy explained in his autobiography. Handy's lyrics paint a picture of a happy Southland:

> *Money don't zactly grow on trees*
> *On cotton stalks it grows with ease.*

Charley Patton also sings "I'm goin' where the Southern cross the Dog" in his "Green River Blues." Patton, like the Tutwiler singer, sings the same line three times, without a rhyming answer line. Some people conjecture that Patton *was* the singer Handy heard at Tutwiler. But since Patton probably was born in 1891, he would have been twelve years old when Handy heard the singer, and Handy didn't say it was a boy he heard.

Big Bill Broonzy also sang about the spot in his 1935 "The Southern Blues," which includes a train whistle. Broonzy first wonders aloud whether his baby caught the Southern or the Dog. Then he considers getting a job on the Southern line, to make the money to send for her. Finally he announces:

> *Said Southern cross the Dog at Moorhead, mama, Lord, and*
> *she keeps on through*
> *I say my baby's gone to Georgia, I believe I'll go to*
> *Georgia too.*

Broonzy's song helps explain *why* someone would be determined to get to Moorhead: to get a railroad job or to leave the state.

Greenville & Area

1. The Levee
2. Nelson Street
3. The Flowing Fountain/Nelson Street
4. Walnut Street
5. to Delta Blues Festival site
6. Eugene Powell's grave
7. to Leland
8. Jigger & Jug Package Store,
   1304 Highway 82

N

Township Line

Broadway

Old Leland Rd.

LAKE FERGUSON

Nelson St.

Main St.

Washington Ave.

82

82

7

1

6

4

2

3

8

1

5

1

82

1

61

River

Greenville

Holly Ridge

Indianola

82

LILLO'S

Leland

SON THOMAS' GRAVE

49W

454

DELTA BLUES FESTIVAL

Bourbon

82

River

Washington County

Mississippi

Hollandale

Murphy

12

61

Sunflower

1

Rolling Fork

chapter 7

GREENVILLE TO VICKSBURG

Greenville

The Delta's largest city, Greenville has a long blues heritage centered on its infamous Nelson Street. It also hosts the region's biggest and oldest blues festival. In recent years, spurred by the development of waterfront casinos, Greenville nightlife has heated up. The music scene has moved, however, from authentic-but-decaying Nelson to the newly redeveloped Walnut Street, closer to the casinos.

Among the must-see Greenville-area blues musicians is Eddie Cusic of Leland, who took a young Little Milton into his band in the 1950s, then later set down his electric guitar to become a powerful solo acoustic singer-guitarist. Electric guitarist T-Model Ford is often on tour but plays his stripped-down, good-times boogies at local clubs and festivals when he is in the area. Guitarist Little Bill Wallace, a semiretired Greenville blues artist, is definitely worth hearing if you get the chance. Guitarist John Horton is a flashy dresser who plays Albert King-style lead with his own group or with others. Then there's Mississippi Slim, an even flashier dresser, sometimes

Greenville singer-guitarist "Little" Dave Thompson in recording studio, October 1999, Greenville

coloring his hair to match his bright red or blue suits. Catch him singing outside on Walnut Street or at a festival.

Radio station WBAD, 94.3 FM, is the one to listen to in Greenville. It plays some contemporary blues and gospel, mixed in with R&B and oldies.

• The Levee

To get there: Driving west on Highway 82, cross Highway 1 and take a right on Washington Ave. Washington turns back to the left and ends at the levee. Take a left on Walnut St and go one block; you can drive up on the levee.

Downtown Greenville (like downtown Helena and many other spots) is a fine place to walk along the levee. The Mississippi River levee, the wall of earth that holds the river in its banks, is the world's largest human creation. A few years ago, a northern newspaper described the levee at Helena as a "natural amphitheater" for the audience at a blues festival. However, the levee is not natural at all. Men and mules built it over more than a century of hard work, moving the dirt wheelbarrow by wheelbarrow. The levee-camp hollers the workers sang were a predecessor of the blues.

Later on, levee camps attracted blues singers. On the days when the levee workers were paid, as Honeyboy Edwards explains, "[T]here's prostitutes coming out and whiskey flowing, and I'm right there playing my harp and guitar. I'm going to make enough money to stake a gamble with . . . I knew the paydays, when they paid off up and down them levees, up and down the Mississippi clean to Vicksburg. I didn't work but I knew when they got paid off. I kept that in my book."

There had been small levees along the Mississippi since the 1720s, and the complete, federally funded levee was in place by 1912. The river has overflowed or broken through numerous times, however, with disastrous results. As Kansas Joe and Memphis Minnie sang in their 1929 "When the Levee Breaks" (later covered by the rock group Led Zeppelin):

> *If it keeps on raining, levee's going to break*
> *And all these people have no place to stay.*

The Mississippi River flood of 1927, the worst disaster in U.S. history, happened after the levee burst near Greenville. Floodwater covered twenty-six thousand square miles of the Delta, killing hundreds of people and driving hundreds of thousands from home. Greenville was hit the worst. Many whites, especially the elderly, women, and children, were evacuated. Planters fearful of permanently losing their labor forced the blacks to stay. Thousands camped on the levee, which was the only high ground.

Bessie Smith's "Back Water Blues" was a big hit at the time of the flood. Bessie had somehow had the intuition to write and record it three months *before* the big flood hit. She was inspired by lesser flooding on the Ohio River she had seen while on tour:

> *Then I went and stood upon some high old lonesome hill.*
> *Then I looked down on the house where I used to live.*
>
> *Back water blues done caused me to pack my things and go*
> *'Cause my house fell down and I can't live there no more.*

A much less famous blues singer, Alice Pearson of Greenville, cut a locally relevant "Greenville Levee Blues":

> *Living on the levee, sleeping on the ground*
> *I will tell everybody that Greenville's a good old town.*

The epic blues about the flood was Charley Patton's 1929 "High Water Everywhere," parts 1 and 2, which covered both sides of a 78. Patton sings and plays at his most impassioned, and reports on a dozen places all over the Delta:

> *Looky here, boys, around Leland tell me river is raging*
>   *high—boy, it's rising over there! Yeah.*
> *I'm going to move over to Greenville, bought our tickets,*
>   *goodbye.*
> *Looky here, the water dug out, Lordy, levee broke, rolled*
>   *most everywhere.*
> *The water at Greenville and Leland, Lord, it done rose*
>   *everywhere.*
> *I would go down to Rosedale, but they tell me there's*
>   *water there.*

The flood formed Lake Ferguson, an oxbow that now separates the city from the river itself. Still, the memory of the flood and a history of riverboat traffic give Greenville a strong connection to the Mississippi. The river's silt even finds its way into Greenville tap water. Its brown color is shocking, but the water won't hurt you. Cheers!

• Jigger & Jug Package Store
1304 Highway 82 (north side of street, just east of Highway 1)

National Prohibition in the United States ended in 1933. Care to guess when it ended in Mississippi? Would you believe 1966?

Actually Prohibition has not yet ended in all of Mississippi, since there are still some dry counties. But most of the state, including the Delta, is wet. And yes, it wasn't until 1966 that Mississippi allowed the manufacture and sale of alcohol and Jigger & Jug Package Store—Mississippi's first legal liquor store since 1907—opened. Prohibition started early and ended very late here.

Not that Mississippians refrained from drinking for sixty years, of course. In fact, booze's illegality is what forced it into the jook joints, barrelhouses, and house parties that were central to blues culture. So the legalization of liquor in 1966 can be seen as another historical change—like the mechanization of cotton picking—that may have made life more pleasant for many people, but helped ruin the blues.

Let's raise a glass to the Mississippi Department of Archives and History for placing a state historic marker (not a blues marker) at this site. There is still a liquor store here, although it is under different ownership from when it opened on August 6, 1966. The original owner, Joe Azar, has a connection to music: he is the father of country singer-songwriter Steve Azar, a Greenville native. Steve Azar says he learned to play from 1930s bluesmen Sam Chatmon and Eugene "Sonny Boy Nelson" Powell, who were still active in the 1960s and would come play outside the liquor store.

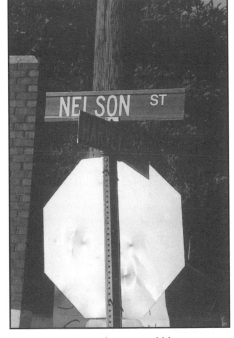

Mississippi's most infamous and blues-drenched street: Nelson Street, Greenville

• **Nelson Street**

Friends back home may have thought you were crazy for wanting to visit Mississippi blues sites, and warned you of dangers they imagine here. But even in Mississippi, even in Greenville, people will warn you not to go to Nelson Street. Even longtime residents of Greenville, even some blues musicians, might caution you against it.

Well, after all those warnings, how could you *not* want to visit Nelson Street? This onetime prime commercial street of Greenville's black community certainly is long past its heyday. And it has not yet entered the rehab stage that community and city officials have been talking about for a long time. Many of its businesses are abandoned, and not much live blues has been heard there lately.

There is life, though. Taverns with colorfully painted fronts house jukeboxes and pool tables. Aspiring boxers duke it out in a ring clearly visible through a big glass window. Murals on Nelson and its side streets commemorate local people or make antidrug statements. On Saturday nights Nelson becomes a cruising street for young motorists. A barbecue vendor is usually cooking and selling his wares from a smoke-chugging stand. A shoeshine ven-

Mural on Nelson Street, Greenville

dor might be ready for business—or for a beer, if you have one to spare. People, alone or in little groups, are just hanging out. And at any time Nelson Street tends to have plenty of cops driving to and from the street's police substation.

Nelson Street is worth a visit so that you can look at the buildings and try to imagine what the street was like from the mid-1940s through the 1970s, when Little Milton, Eddie Cusic, Charley Booker, Willie Love, Little Bill Wallace, T-Model Ford, and a host of other top-notch local blues artists, as well as big-name touring acts, played in its clubs. Like Jackson's Farish Street and Clarksdale's Fourth Street, this is one of the places where the postwar blues thrived and developed. Willie Love and His Three Aces, featuring Little Milton on guitar, celebrated the street in their 1951 "Nelson Street Blues" (a hit on Jackson-based Trumpet Records):

> *Boy, if you ever go to Greenville, please go down on Nelson Street*
> *Yeah, walk on the levee and have a lot of fun with most everybody you meet.*

The song goes on to suggest that you stop at various Nelson Street businesses—Tails and Tie Shoeshine Parlor, Deluxe Barbershop, Sharp Shop ("for a sharp suit of clothes"), Snow White Laun-

Greenville singer Mamie "Galore" Davis, a former Ikette, singing with guitarist John Horton and trumpeter Robert Williams at the 1999 Little Wynn Nelson Street Festival, Greenville

dry, and, finally, the Silver Dollar Cafe, "that's right on the corner. You can stop in there now and have just as much fun as you want to."

If you feel safer in crowds, visit during the annual **Little Wynn Nelson Street Festival**, held on the day before the annual Delta Blues Festival (which is on the third Saturday of September). The free festival affords a rare opportunity to see Nelson Street lively and crowded with people walking around, shopping, eating, and listening to music. Fine local blues acts and a headliner play on a stage at one end of the street, while gospel groups play at the other end. Vendors sell hamburgers, fried catfish, and barbecue, as well as yo-yos, shoes, and other goods. Unfortunately, most Nelson Street bars lack live music even at festival time.

Southern Whispers, 756 Nelson St. (662-335-1477), is one club that has been presenting live music lately. The state blues marker for Nelson Street is in front of Southern Whispers.

- **Perry's Flowing Fountain**
  816 Nelson St.

Perry's flowed on for awhile after original owner Perry Payton died on May 3, 2000, but then it closed for good. Payton, who worked as a mortician by day, had been connected to blues

The late Perry Payton in front of the Flowing Fountain, 816 Nelson Street, Greenville

history since his youth, when he helped his dad, also a mortician, deal with the hundreds of dead from the Natchez Rhythm Club fire. He opened the Flowing Fountain in the 1970s.

The club's largest room was named Annie Mae's Café. That also is the name of Little Milton's 1985 hit, which goes:

*Annie Mae's Café, you can
find one in every town
I go there after hours and
drink a little whiskey,
before long somebody's
acting a clown.*

Was the Flowing Fountain the original Annie Mae's Café that inspired the song? Payton said so. And as Milton starts his guitar solo, he clearly speaks, "In my hometown they call it the Flowing Fountain." However, in his liner notes to *Greatest Hits,* Milton explains that it's generic: "People always ask, 'Is there such a place?' And I tell them, 'Everywhere I go there's always one.' And that's the truth. The point is, it's a club that stays open late, good food still served and liquor available."

Milton did not write the song, however. That credit goes to George Jackson and Larry Addison. And Jackson told writer Rob Bowman he based the song on an actual Annie Mae's Café where he used to hang out in *Memphis*. At any rate, thanks to Milton's improvised line and the sign on the wall inside, the Flowing Fountain became the real Annie Mae's Café.

Roosevelt "Booba" Barnes, king of Greenville blues in the 1980s, worked as a bartender and regular performer at Perry's Flowing Fountain before opening his own club.

• **Playboy Club**
928 Nelson St.

This club, then owned by the late Booba Barnes, appears in the movie *Deep Blues*. Although he doesn't look too pleased or comfortable, Greenville's mayor at the time, Frank Self, shakes the hand of wild jook-joint owner/musician Barnes and commends him for what he has done for the festival and the town. Narrator Robert Palmer asks Self if the town appreciates Nelson Street's blues history, and the mayor assures him that it does. "We're starting, very busy, to clean up Nelson Street, make it a tourist attraction," he tells Palmer.

After his little chat with the mayor, Barnes launches into his burning signature song, "Heartbroken Man." He wears a red suit and big gold chains. As always, he bugs out his eyes and plays with an intense, nervous sound. He slows the tempo down for the next number but keeps up the intensity, playing with his teeth.

In that song, Booba pays tribute to his city: "In my hometown, where I live—the name of the town, they call it Greenville— it ain't no pity, ain't no shame. My baby left me, I'm a heartbroken man."

A furniture store before it was a nightclub, Barnes's Playboy Club has since become a church, The Vessels of Mercy. It has a bright blue exterior that might seem flashy for a church elsewhere but, amid the gaudy storefronts and murals of Nelson Street, looks austere. The club opened in about 1982 and closed in about 1992 when Barnes, riding a wave of national renown after the movie's release, decided he was a professional and moved to Chicago. Sadly, he didn't get to enjoy his success for long. Barnes died of lung cancer on April 3, 1996, at age fifty-nine.

• **Walnut Street**

Right downtown, near the waterfront and the casinos, Walnut Street has in the past few years become the place to hear live music in Greenville. Because of the street's convenient location and because it does not have a seedy reputation, upstart Walnut has bypassed traditional Nelson in quantity and variety of live music.

The Walnut Street Blues Bar, 128 Walnut St. (662-378-2254); Club 129, 129 Walnut St. (662-335-7888); and Beady's Bar & Grill (which has a blues wall inside), 139 Walnut St. (662-335-3334) feature live music regularly. Blues is often, but not always, the genre—rock groups also play at these clubs, so call ahead or just walk around until you hear what you're seeking.

Besides providing live music, Walnut Street Blues Bar also functions as a museum of sorts. It has a long wall covered with Greenville blues-related photos, posters, articles, and a few instruments.

Emulating Beale Street (which in turn was emulating Hollywood Boulevard), Walnut Street has begun to feature bronze plaques in the sidewalk in recognition of prominent entertainers with local connections. B. B. King and Boogaloo Ames were the first two so honored, and there are plans for Sam Chatmon and others. Greenville artist Alan Orlicek creates the plaques.

- **The Meeting Place**
  247 South 6th St.
  (662) 335-9123

This friendly neighborhood bar, away from Nelson and Walnut streets, has been featuring live blues on Sunday nights.

- **The Mississippi Delta Blues & Heritage Festival**

This festival began in 1977, operated by Mississippi Action for Community Education (119 Theobald St., 662-335-3523), a nonprofit community-development corporation that dates from 1967 and lists among its founders the civil rights leader Fannie Lou Hamer.

Dubbed "the Big One" by its organizers, this is the biggest blues festival in the Delta and one of the biggest and oldest in the country. Besides the main stage, there is a smaller "jukehouse" stage for local acts, as well as a gospel tent. It lasts from noon to 11 P.M. one day, the third Saturday of September; the festival site is at Highway 1 at Route 454, six miles south of Highway 82.

Held in a big grassy field, this is the kind of festival where people come in groups and set up camp, bringing chairs, blankets, and awnings and feasting on their own food and drink. In the festival's early years, attendees would bring in the equipment and supplies to do their own barbecuing at the site. Grills have been prohibited, but coolers are still allowed. If you want to travel light, plenty of barbecue is available for purchase. Bring repellent for

Eugene "Sonny Boy Nelson" Powell's grave, Metcalfe

the mosquitoes, and beware of the fire ants when staking out your turf. Make sure to walk around and check out all three stages.

Metcalfe

- ## Eugene "Sonny Boy Nelson" Powell's Grave

  To get there: Head north out of Greenville on Highway 1. Right after a sign that says "Metcalfe 1½ mi.," the road forks. Take the right fork, Broadway Road Extension. Proceed 1 mile to another fork, and again take the right fork, onto an unmarked paved road. Go 1.1 mile, then turn left onto a dirt road that crosses a little bridge and leads into a cemetery. The headstones are flat, so it is difficult to notice Powell's stone until you are right in front of it. From the road that leads in, about 90 feet before the two scraggly trees, walk to the left, into the cemetery, for about 90 feet.

The flat stone includes an etched drawing of Powell by Alan Orlicek. It reads:

BLUES AIN'T NOTHIN' BUT A WORRY ON YOUR MIND
[A LINE FROM A FAVORITE SONG]
Play it a long time 'cause a short while is gonna make me mad
[a quote from him]
A guitar virtuoso his music touched people the world over
Eugene Powell
"Sonny Boy Nelson"
Dec. 23, 1908
Nov. 4, 1998

Eugene Powell, who used to play for Parchman inmates as a boy and recorded in 1936 as Sonny Boy Nelson, was one of the last surviving artists from the original blues recording era. After his one recording session, he married Mississippi Matilda—who also cut a few tunes at that session—and led a quiet life, working at John Deere in Hollandale for decades. But in the 1970s, Powell's old friend, bluesman Sam Chatmon, helped him get festival gigs, and the two of them became beloved elder statesmen of the Mississippi blues. Keb'Mo, Lonnie Pitchford, and Alvin "Youngblood" Hart were among the young musicians who stopped by Eugene Powell's for lessons in the 1990s.

Leland

I said Greenville's smokin', baby, and Leland's burnin',
   Leland's burnin' down
Well, I believe I'll retrieve my woman out of Greenville town.

So sang local bluesman Charley Booker in his 1952 recording "No Ridin' Blues." The words proved strangely prophetic (much as Bessie Smith's "Back Water Blues" predicted the 1927 flood). A month *after* "No Ridin' Blues" was issued, a whole block of downtown Leland was destroyed in a blaze that could be seen from miles away and threatened to spread.

Leland's downtown is north of Highway 82. Broad Street takes you into town. There is a jook joint on Main Street called Boss Hall that occasionally features live music.

A state blues marker at 3rd and Main streets marks the intersection of highways 10 and 61. Highway 82, now the Delta's main east-west thoroughfare, was completed in 1936. It replaced the old Highway 10, which meandered through all the towns and plantations.

- **Lillo's Italian Restaurant**
  Highway 82 near the intersection of Highway 61
  (662) 686-4401

A plain, dependable old Italian-American restaurant, this may seem an unlikely place to hear the blues. But for many years, until his death February 4, 2002, Lillo's presented Abie "Boogaloo" Ames, a pianist dubbed the "Mozart of the Delta," every Thursday. Backed by a dance band, Boogaloo wore a suit and a bowler hat, sipped whiskey and stroked the keys on standards, swing tunes, boogie-woogie, deep blues, or whatever struck his fancy. He and his disciple, Eden Brent, are the subjects of an award-winning 1999 TV documentary, *Boogaloo and Eden: Sustaining the Sound*. Brent carries on her master's tradition at local festivals and clubs. Lillo's continues to host live music on Thursdays, although rarely blues.

• Leland Blues Murals

At Fourth and Main streets, at Third and Main streets, on Main near Third, and on Deer Creek Road between Main and North Broad St.

There are four murals within a few blocks of one another in downtown Leland. The Highway 61 Blues Museum offers a map, but you probably can find them by walking around.

In 2000, local artists Cristen Barnard and Jay Kirgis and a bunch of volunteers pitched in to paint a mural of blues singers born within twenty-five miles of Leland. The long list of local talent includes such stars as Jimmy Reed and Little Milton along with local favorites such as Eddie Cusic, Willie Foster, and James "Son" Thomas. Among the group are the pale-skinned bluesrockers Johnny and Edgar Winter. The Winter brothers grew up in Beaumont, Texas, but actually were born in Leland, where their father, John Dawson Winter Jr., once served as mayor. Johnny Winter included his own "Leland Mississippi Blues" on his 1969 debut album.

That first mural on Fourth Street has been joined by three others: one all about B. B. King (from nearby Indianola) on Third Street, one for Jimmy Reed (who grew up on Collier Plantation in Dunleith) on Deer Creek Road, and one on Main Street celebrating "Delta Dancing" at Leland's Lillo's Restaurant.

• Highway 61 Blues Museum

307 N. Broad Street
(662) 686-7646

The museum is open 10 A.M. to 4 P.M. Mondays through Saturdays. There is an admission fee.

This museum does not try to tell the whole story of blues in the Delta, or even of the whole length of Highway 61. It focuses on artists from the area within 50 miles of Leland—which turns out to be a remarkable cast of characters. Little Milton, Charley Patton, Jimmy Reed, B. B. King, Albert King, and Johnny Winter are some of them, alongside local favorites Willie Foster, Son Thomas, Abie "Boogaloo" Ames, and others famous and obscure, living and dead. The museum also contains farm implements that city dwellers might have heard of in blues songs but never seen: a crosscut saw and a singletree.

The museum's director, Billy Johnson, presents an annual **Highway 61 Blues Festival** in mid-June, again spotlighting some of the many blues artists with local connections.

• James "Son" Thomas's Grave

To get there: About one mile east of Leland on Highway 82, turn south onto an unmarked road across from a large Phillips 66 gas station. Go ½ mile to the first left, Old Tribbett Road, turn left and go another ½ mile to the intersection with Mark Road, where there is a graveyard in front of a small, new brick church set way back from the road, Greater St. Matthew M. B. Church. Turn into the driveway and look to the left. Thomas's grave is near the front, facing the driveway.

The front of the stone reads:

James "Son" Thomas
Oct. 14, 1926–
June 26, 1993
World renowned Sculptor and Recording Artist,
beloved father, grandfather and friend.

The back of the stone quotes from Thomas's "Beefsteak Blues":

Give me beefsteak when I'm hungry,
Whiskey when I'm dry,
Pretty women when I'm living,
Heaven when I die.

Thomas, a gravedigger by trade, was a charismatic local bluesman with a high-pitched voice and an unusual guitar style. He was also a gifted sculptor who specialized in clay skulls. Hailing from Yazoo County, Thomas moved to Leland in 1961, at age forty. A few years later he met the anthropology student William Ferris, from Vicksburg. In film, photography, and words, Ferris documented the blues house parties of Thomas, Poppa Jazz, and other Delta bluesmen in an era when many people thought the blues was already dead. Thomas and Ferris helped each other in their careers: Thomas's music and art gained international renown (he performed for the Reagans at the White House, and appeared on Charles Kuralt's *On the Road*), while Ferris became author of the well respected *Blues from the Delta* and a professor at the University of Mississippi and founder of the Center for the Study of Southern Culture there (he later served as director of the National Endowment for the Humanities).

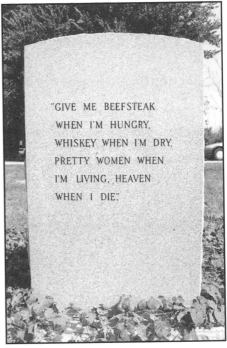

"GIVE ME BEEFSTEAK WHEN I'M HUNGRY, WHISKEY WHEN I'M DRY, PRETTY WOMEN WHEN I'M LIVING, HEAVEN WHEN I DIE."

Back side of James "Son" Thomas's grave, near Leland

Thomas died June 26, 1993, at age sixty-six. One of his sons, Pat Thomas, has vowed to carry on his dad's musical legacy. Although he has not yet caught up to that level of virtuosity (as he readily admits), Pat manages to capture some of the feel, and has inherited the vocal quality. Pat Thomas lives in Leland but performs only occasionally. He usually appears on the acoustic stage of the annual Sunflower Blues Festival in Clarksdale.

Bourbon

A town called Bourbon ought to have a place to get a drink, and this one does. The Bourbon Mall, 105 Dean Road (662-686-4389) is not a shopping mall, but a roadhouse-style restaurant that specializes in steaks and features live music nightly. Often the music is rock or country, but it is blues at least once a week. When you call to check on who is playing, you can also hire a limo from the restaurant's fleet to come and pick you up, which might be a good idea, since it's a remote location—fifteen miles southeast of Leland off Tribbett Road South.

Holly Ridge

- ### Graves of Charley Patton, Willie Foster, and Asie Payton

  To get there: From Highway 82 between Leland and Indianola, take the Holly Ridge turnoff, which is to the north. The town is a mile from the highway. Turn left onto Main Street and look for New Jerusalem M. B. Church, 0.2 mile down on the left. Patton reportedly used to sing at the church. The graveyard is another 0.2 mile past the church, just past Holly Ridge Gin.

Near the road, on the right, is the grave of Asie Reed Payton. An obscure performer, he is one of the few whose headstone (another modern one, financed by his record company) reads "bluesman." A Holly Ridge tractor driver who lived from April 12, 1937, to May 19, 1997, Payton also sang and played the blues. His one and only recording is a posthumous one, the 1999 Fat Possum release *Worried*. It was recorded in two sessions intended as demos in 1994—one live at Junior Kimbrough's jook, the other at a studio.

Charley Patton's grave marker is near the back of the cemetery and on the far left, near the gin. His remains are probably not right at the marker, however—some sources say he lies underneath the gin building. The stone reads:

> *Charley Patton*
> April 1891–April 28, 1934
> "The Voice of the Delta"
> The foremost performer of early Mississippi blues
> whose songs became cornerstones of American music.

Charley Patton is buried in the town where he and Bertha Lee lived for most of the last two years of his life, 1933 and 1934. They performed at jooks in the area, and especially in the back of a white-owned store in Holly Ridge, which also was Patton's last residence. The white store owner sometimes accompanied him on fiddle. The store probably was on one of the corners of the main intersection in Holly Ridge.

Near—but not too near—a church and right next to a gin, this seems an appropriate resting place for the great Delta bluesman and sometime gospel singer. The cemetery contains a lot of hand-engraved stones, although Patton's, erected in 1991 (and financed largely by blues-influenced rock musician John Fogerty), is modern and professionally done.

A niece told interviewers that a representative of Vocalion records had come to the site shortly after Patton's death and put up a tombstone. That stone apparently has vanished, however.

Near Patton's is the grave of Greenville-based singer-band-leader-harmonica player Willie Foster, identifying him curiously as a "harmonica parader."

Foster was literally born on a cotton sack when his mother, working in the fields near Leland, lay down to give birth to him on September 19, 1921. Foster bought his first harmonica at the Rexall (now Fred's Xpress) in Leland, paying for the twenty-five-cent instrument gradually over a period of weeks. After serving in the military in World War II, Foster lived and played in various Midwestern cities but found his greatest success after about 1990, when he was living back in the Delta and playing locally, regionally, and sometimes internationally. The loss of first one leg, then the other, did not slow down his musical career. Foster continued to sing, blow harp, and lead the band masterfully from his wheelchair. He had just finished a private-party gig the night he died, May 20, 2001.

Indianola

"Welcome to Indianola, Home of B. B. King," this town's signs proclaim. They feature a picture of King, a cotton boll, and a factory. There is a B. B. King Road west of downtown, on one side of a big cotton gin.

King was born September 16, 1925, on the bank of Blue Lake near Berclair, outside of Itta Bena. When he was about five years old, he moved with his mother to Kilmichael, in the hill country east of the Delta. In 1935, after his mother's death, his dad took him south to Lexington, on the edge of the Delta. In the fall of 1938, young B. B. got on his bicycle and rode back to the Delta, to Indianola, to live with relatives and work in the cottonfields. He has claimed the town as his home ever since, and the town has returned the favor, considering him its son. He titled a 1970 album *Indianola Mississippi Seeds.*

Club Chicago, Church Street, Indianola

Indianola has connections to other blues greats: according to his death certificate, Charley Patton died on April 28, 1934, at 350 Heathman Street (a house that is no longer standing), and master string bender Albert King (no relation to B. B.), was born April 25, 1923, in Indianola, but moved to Forrest City, Arkansas, as a child.

From Highway 82, Catchings Street takes you south into downtown Indianola. The black section is south of that, across the tracks. Church Street is the street for little jooks, liquor stores, and a few downhome restaurants. There are some colorful buildings and some colorful characters hanging out and drinking in front of them. But there has not been any live music on Church Street recently. Even Mary Price's famous Keyhole Club—a green building without a sign—has dropped its live music lately.

Church Street's clubs once presented acts such as Louis Jordan, Count Basie, Pete Johnson, Jay McShann's band featuring Charlie Parker, and Sonny Boy Williamson II. As a teenager, B. B. King would lurk outside the clubs to get a listen and a peek inside. After a while, he got the idea to bring his guitar along and sit on a curb singing gospel music for tips. "I was this skinny kid with his own corner on Church Street in Indianola, my hopes in the hat by my side," he wrote.

- **B. B. King's Footprints, Handprints, and Signature**

B. B. King used to sing for tips at this spot, on the east side of Church Street just south of Second Street, as a teenager. He started off singing church songs and received smiles and blessings from passers-by. When he tried the blues, however, people responded with cash. He noted the difference and decided to focus on the blues.

On June 5, 1986, King placed his footprints, handprints, and signature in the sidewalk where he used to sing. Recently, a large photo of King has been added to the site along with a historical marker. There also is painting of King's guitar, Lucille, by Indianola musician Bobby Whalen at the site. And there is a state blues marker. On a wall a block west of this corner there is a King mural by Lawrence Quinn of Jackson.

- **Club Ebony**
  404 Hanna Ave.
  (662) 887-2264

The Ebony is not a little jook joint, but a large, well-kept-up nightclub/restaurant in a residential area. It has been in business since 1948. Mary Shepard bought it in 1974 from B. B. King's former mother-in-law, Ruby Edwards (King met his second wife, Sue Carol Hall, at the club). King completed the circle by buying the club from Shepard in 2008. He is not actively involved in its management. King still plays at the Ebony once a year, right after his free outdoor homecoming concert.

Besides the annual B. B. King performance, the Ebony presents occasional shows by big-name soul-blues acts such as Denise LaSalle, Little Milton, or Willie Clayton. There is live music from local bands on Sunday nights.

- **B. B. King Museum**
  2nd and Sunflower streets
  (662)887-3009

Years in the planning, and with government agencies and private corporations contributing funds, this museum promises to be a fine one, although it had not yet opened as of press time. The museum campus includes a cotton gin where King once worked, along with a newly constructed main building. King is cooperating fully with the museum and donating guitars, awards, journals of his life on the road, and odd items he collects such as globes, clocks, and battery-operated dolls.

- ### B. B. King Homecoming

King comes back to Indianola to play a free outdoor concert each year on the first Friday in June (unless June 1 is a Saturday, in which case the concert is May 31) at B. B. King Park on Roosevelt Street. He has done that since 1968, in memory of the slain civil rights leader Medgar Evers. "It helps heal some hurt," King wrote. "It helps to see thousands of little black and white kids playing together, to see the big crowds so happy to hear blues that feels good to everyone."

When King skipped the homecoming for two years, Club Ebony owner Mary Shepard set him straight. "I said, 'Mr. King, this is your home. You need to come back home,'" she says.

- ### 308 Blues Club and Café
  308 Depot Ave.
  (662) 887-7800

The 308 is a large club that opened in November 2003. It presents live blues on Fridays and Saturdays, by blues acts from throughout the Delta. It also serves downhome food such as barbecue, catfish, plate lunches, and salmon-and-rice breakfasts.

- ### Gin Mill Galleries
  109 Pershing St.
  (662) 887-3209

Housed in an old cotton gin, this business started as an art gallery and furniture studio but now also includes a bar and restaurant. It offers live music, often blues, on weekends. The décor is faux-folk, with fried-bologna sandwiches and Cool Moon (warm Moon Pie with ice cream) among the menu offerings. There are blues photos, posters, and guitars on display. Open nightly except Tuesdays and Wednesdays, and for lunch.

Belzoni

To get there: From Indianola, go south on Highway 49W. Belzoni is 23 miles from Indianola.

Belzoni is the town where Lillian McMurry tracked down Sonny Boy Williamson II, who was living in a shack here, and asked him to record for her Trumpet label. When a teenage Elmore James moved to Belzoni in the 1930s with his parents, Sonny Boy and Robert Johnson both were prominent local musicians, and both influenced James's music. Sonny Boy and Elmore were still in town around 1947, doing radio advertising (the Talaho Show) for a local drugstore and playing in the area, sometimes with Arthur "Big Boy" Crudup, who also lived around here. Sonny Boy met his wife, Mattie Gordon, while living in Belzoni.

The late bluesman Paul "Wine" Jones also hailed from Belzoni, where he worked as a welder at a catfish farm.

Center of the state's catfish industry, Belzoni embraces the delicious, wily fish as its icon. There are artist-decorated catfish sculptures all over downtown. Catfish Capitol, 111 Magnolia St. (800-408-4838) is a small museum at the renovated train depot, with more catfish art outside and in.

• The Old Jailhouse

To get there: Go south of downtown on Hayden Street. It is in the 100 block, past the courthouse (which has a new jail behind it) and just before the library, on the left.

No longer in use, the old county jailhouse Charley Patton sang about is still standing (although it is condemned and falling apart). Patton was familiar with the inside of this building. He sang about it in his 1934 "High Sheriff Blues":

> *Get in trouble in Belzoni, ain't no use to screamin' and cryin'*
> *Mr. Webb will take you back to Belzoni jailhouse flyin'.*

This song has the same tune and accompaniment as Patton's 1929 "Tom Rushen Blues," which describes a jailing in Merigold. However, "High Sheriff" is more autobiographical. Patton really was jailed in Belzoni. An Officer Webb arrested both Patton and his wife, Bertha Lee, in a disturbance at a house party where they were playing. W. R. Calaway of American Record Company bailed them out and brought them to New York to record for what would be the last time. "High Sheriff Blues" is one of the songs Patton recorded at that final session.

• Catfish and Buffalo Fish Festivals

Mississippi's two favorite fishes are both honored with annual festivals on the first Saturday of April (unless Easter falls in the first weekend of April, in which case the festivals are moved to the second Saturday).

The World Catfish Festival, which started in 1976, is a mass corporate-sponsored event that includes the crowning of the Catfish Queen and a catfish-eating contest. The 2000 festival included entertainment from Greenville's Willie Foster—the first time blues was on the program. Since then, blues has been part of every year's entertainment lineup.

The African-American Heritage Buffalo Fish Festival, which debuted in 1996, is a much smaller, more downhome event. It usually features a performance by soul-blues star Denise LaSalle, who is a Belzoni native.

Hollandale

To get there: From Belzoni, take Highway 12 west. Hollandale is 21 miles at the intersection of Highway 12 and Highway 61.

This town had a lively blues scene around 1936, including Bo Carter, who that year organized a group of musicians—Eugene "Sonny Boy Nelson" Powell, Mississippi Matilda, and Robert Hill—to go record in New Orleans. Hacksaw Harney and Willie "Brother" Harris also lived in town, as well as others who never recorded.

"Bo Chatmon put me on to the first record I ever made, in 1936," Powell told an interviewer decades later. "He said I wasn't doing nothing but wasting music, said, 'I'm gonna put you on record.' That was Bo Carter, Sam Chatmon's brother. So them were the first ones I ever made in my whole life. Sonny Boy Nelson with Mississippi Matilda and Robert Hill in 1936. It was down in New Orleans. I liked it down there, you know, country boy, had my wife with me, nothing to worry about, was giving her a good time, I felt good. I thought I was something, doing something I hadn't never done—I thought I was more than I was! I put out three records for ninety dollars, and that was some money then."

Sexy Lady Club, Blue Front, Hollandale

Houston Stackhouse told an interviewer he remembered a day in Hollandale about 1930 when Robert Nighthawk, with another guitarist and a pianist, was playing at a black-oriented drugstore while Bo Carter and Lonnie Chatmon played at a white drugstore.

Summerfest is a wonderful free blues festival, held the Friday and Saturday before Memorial Day at Hollandale City Park. Information on it is available by calling 662-827-5545.

The **Rainbow Inn,** 310 East Avenue South (Old Highway 61) at Goldstein Street, is a clean and friendly jook joint but does not have live music. It has a soul-blues deejay Thursdays through Sundays after 9 P.M., who draws an older crowd. It is worth stopping to see the wild décor inside and out and to meet sharp-dressed owner L. C. Hutchins.

• Blue Front

Highway 12 becomes Washington Street. Take that across the tracks to a row of dilapidated storefronts along the track, on South

Rainbow Inn jook joint, Hollandale

Simmons Street. Known as Blue Front, this was the black entertainment and dining district for decades. Some jooks still operate there, although none has live music.

- ## Sam Chatmon's Grave

  To get there: From Highway 61, turn west on Highway 12 into Hollandale. At the stop sign, turn right onto East Avenue South. At the four-way stop, turn left onto East Washington and then right on Morgan. Follow Morgan as it zigzags, across Dr. Martin Luther King Jr. Drive, and ends at Sanders Memorial Garden. Turn right into the cemetery. The grave is on the left, at the third tree.

The stone reads:

SITTING ON TOP OF
THE WORLD
Sam Chatmon
Jan. 10, 1899
Feb. 2, 1983
Considered to be among the most important
figures in American music,
his contribution helped create the lyrical art form of the blues.
Performed with the Mississippi Sheiks and the Chatmon Brothers.
A beloved friend and true gentleman.

Across the drive from the fourth tree is the grave of Chatmon's wife, Elma Lue Chatmon, April 10, 1911, to March 18, 1996.

Leland bluesman Eddie Cusic playing in front of drawings of Sam Chatmon, at the dedication of Chatmon's grave marker, March 1998, Hollandale

Born in Bolton, Sam Chatmon lived in Hollandale from the 1940s on. He was an active musician in the 1930s, pretty much retired from music in the forties and fifties, then became active again from the 1960s on, probably reaching his greatest glory in his old age.

His tombstone proclaims him "among the most important figures in American music." But in his youth, Sam Chatmon was not even the most illustrious musician in his own family. Of ex-slave fiddler Henderson Chatmon's thirteen children, the big names were Bo Carter, a blues star of the 1930s with such hits as "Please Warm My Weiner," and Lonnie Chatmon, violinist with the Mississippi Sheiks of "Sitting On Top of the World" fame.

Sam Chatmon played on only a few recordings of the immensely popular Sheiks, who were mainly a duo composed of Lonnie and singer-guitarist Walter Vincson. However, he probably often joined in on their live performances. Chatmon distinguished himself from his musical siblings by outliving all of them and bringing traces of the old black-string-band and smutty-blues traditions into the late twentieth century. He was a funny entertainer and fine musician who played at festivals and clubs across the country in his later years.

Sam Chatmon worked in the **cotton compress** that is part of the complex of buildings around the cotton gin on Morgan Street near Washington. He lived at **818 Sherman Street**, which is still standing. Respect the privacy of the house's current tenants if you go to look at it.

Murphy

For real fans of the movie *Crossroads*: Take Highway 12 east from Hollandale and go ten miles to Sunflower Road, which is just before a bridge across the Sunflower River. Turn right on Sunflower and go about five miles south to Murphy Road (noting Torrey Wood & Son, a rare surviving wood cotton gin that just happens to be named "Wood," on the left on your way). At the intersection there is an abandoned white building with a wooden porch. In the 1986 Walter Hill film *Crossroads,* this is the building where Willie Brown (played by Joe Seneca) and young hotshot Eugene Martone (Ralph Macchio) escape from the rain and meet the runaway girl Frances (Jami Gertz).

Panther Burn

To get there: Panther Burn is 8 miles south of Hollandale on Highway 61.

A scene in the movie *Blues Brothers 2000* is set in Panther Burn, although obviously it was not filmed there. The movie shows Spanish moss hanging from all the trees along the highway, something you don't see in this nontropical Delta town.

The real Panther Burn does have a Ray Charles Road, however.

Rolling Fork

To get there: From Panther Burn go south on Highway 61 for 13 miles.

Muddy Waters was born in this town on April 4, 1915, but moved to his grandmother's house near Clarksdale when he was three. Still, Rolling Fork is proud of its native bluesman. A monument stands on the south side of the courthouse square, on China Street by the gazebo. It reads:

IN HONOR OF MUDDY WATERS

Muddy Waters, master of the blues, was born McKinley Morganfield in 1915 near Rolling Fork. His special technique and interpretation powerfully influenced the development of Delta blues music.

There are Muddy-themed murals on a building across from the monument and another at 176 Walnut St. You also will see sculptures and murals of bears and President Teddy Roosevelt around town. Those commemorate Roosevelt's 1902 bear hunt, in which he declined to kill a tied-up bear, thus spawning the Teddy Bear craze. The hunt actually happened at Onward, about 20 miles south of Rolling Fork at the intersection of Highways 61 and 1. Rolling Fork has two annual festivals: the Deep Blues Festival, in May, and the Great Delta Bear Affair, in October. Both include good regional blues.

There are Muddy Waters T-shirts for sale at the town's branch of Sharkey-Issaquena library, which also has a small blues section.

For a while, the town also had signs on Highway 61 welcoming visitors to the home of Muddy Waters. Some visitors stole the signs, however, and there are no plans to replace them.

Waters sang about his hometown in his 1953 cover of Big Joe Williams's 1935 "Baby, Please Don't Go":

> *You got me way down here*
> *Down by Rolling Fork*
> *You treat me like a dog*
> *Baby, please don't go*

Vicksburg

To get there: Go south on Highway 61.

Second only to Gettysburg as a major Civil War site (the battlefield is preserved as Vicksburg National Military Park, 3201 Clay St., 601-636-0583), this charming river town also figures in blues history. By the traditional definition, Vicksburg is the southern tip of the Delta, as Memphis is the northern tip. Songwriter-bassist Willie Dixon was born and raised here. Like many others, Dixon fell under the spell of Little Brother Montgomery.

"Vicksburg—where I run upon Little Brother," Skip James says in his introduction to his own version of "Vicksburg Blues," on his 1965 recording *Skip's Piano Blues*. Montgomery, perhaps the greatest of all blues pianists, made his lovely tribute to Vicksburg his signature tune:

> *I got the Vicksburg blues and I'll sing 'em anywhere I please*
> *Now the reason I sing 'em—to give my poor heart some ease.*

A slow-slow blues with a slip-sliding bass line, Montgomery's "Vicksburg Blues" quickly became a piece every Delta blues pianist was required to play. Guitarists, too, developed versions of it—including Howlin' Wolf's "44 Blues" and Skip James's "Special Rider Blues."

A Louisiana native, Montgomery was a regular in Vicksburg joints in the 1920s, relocated to Jackson in the 1930s, and then became part of the electric Chicago blues scene in the 1950s.

• Catfish Row Art Park and Floodwall Murals

To get there: Take Clay Street all the way to the river.

"The Mississippi Delta begins in the lobby of the Peabody Hotel in Memphis and ends on Catfish Row in Vicksburg," David Cohn wrote in 1935. He was not only defining the Delta's geographic limits, but also contrasting the lifestyles of those who sell the cotton and those who work in the fields.

Unlike the Peabody lobby, Cohn continued, on Catfish Row there "are no marble fountains, no orchestras playing at dinner, no movement of bell-boys in bright uniforms. Tumble-down shacks lean crazily over the Mississippi River far below. Inside them are dice games and 'Georgia skin'; the music of guitars, the aroma of love, and the soul-satisfying scent of catfish frying to luscious golden-brown in sizzling skillets."

It isn't clear exactly where Catfish Row was, except that it was on a bluff high over the river—quite a ways south of where Catfish Row Art Park now is, perhaps about where the Ameristar Casino sits.

The new Catfish Row appropriates the name, moves it near downtown, and turns it into a public space with a riverfront walk with public art by children and adults and floodwall murals sponsored by local organizations and businesses. Except for one abstract by Vicksburg artist Martha Ferris, the others are all by Robert Dafford of Lafayette, Louisiana. Dafford's are all realistic depictions of local events, with an explanatory plaque on each.

There is one about Willie Dixon, showing him playing at the Blue Room, a beloved old lounge where touring artists performed for decades. He is surrounded by sheet music of some of his many classic compositions. Among the other murals are depictions of the 1902 Roosevelt bear hunt, the first bottling of Coca-Cola (that happened in Vicksburg in 1899), the Sultana steamboat disaster of 1865, and the 1974 burning of the Sprague towboat (some remnants of the Sprague are part of a children's play structure at the park).

- ## LD's Restaurant and Lounge
  111 Mulberry (right by the Catfish Row Art Park)
  (601)636-9838 or (601)631-0800

You *can* get catfish on Vicksburg's new Catfish Row—at this downhome restaurant right next to the park. LD's serves soul-food lunches that are good, although pricey—but it is a prime location, after all. Chitterlings, a labor-intensive Southern delicacy, are for sale on Saturdays from 11 A.M. until they run out an hour or two later. Evenings, LD's becomes a lounge for drinking and dancing—to a soul-blues deejay Thursdays through Saturdays and to a bluesy jukebox the rest of the week. The Vicksburg Blues Society meets in the lounge every second Tuesday at 7 P.M. and brings in a blues act followed by a jam session.

- ## Bottleneck Blues Bar
  Ameristar Casino
  4646 Washington St.
  (800) 700-7770

Yes, it's a casino bar with slot machines, big-screen TVs, and all. But it's decorated jook-joint style and often features good blues or R&B acts.

- ## Slipper's Inn
  2416 Pearl St.

Slipper's Inn, a thirty-year-old jook, was the set of the jook joint in "Warming by the Devil's Fire," director Charles Burnett's segment of the 2003 PBS *The Blues* series. Other scenes from that film also were shot in Vicksburg.

- **Willie Dixon Way**
  This small street connects South and Veto streets between Washington and Mulberry streets. It is near the Vicksburg Convention Center, 1600 Mulberry St.

This street was dedicated in 2002 to Willie Dixon, blues composer extraordinaire, who also produced, arranged, sang, and played bass. Born in 1915 in Vicksburg, Dixon was already selling songs to local bands in his teens, besides singing in a gospel group, working as a carpenter, and boxing. By the late 1930s, he had moved to Chicago. He began working with the Chess brothers in the late 1940s and soon became their mainstay songwriter/arranger/producer/bassist. Dixon worked on sessions with Muddy Waters, Howlin' Wolf, Little Walter, Chuck Berry, Robert Nighthawk, Lowell Fulsom, Bo Diddley, Otis Rush, and others. Among his hundreds of compositions are the classics "Hoochie Coochie Man," "I Just Want to Make Love to You," "Spoonful," "Back Door Man," "Little Red Rooster," "My Babe," "Bring It On Home," "Evil," "I Ain't Superstitious," "Mellow Down Easy," "The Seventh Son," "You Shook Me," "Pretty Thing," "I Can't Quit You Baby," "You Need Love" (covered by Led Zeppelin as "Whole Lotta Love"), and "Wang Dang Doodle."

This short, insignificant street had no particular connection to Dixon's life. His childhood home is miles away, at 1631 Crawford St. That address is now an empty lot, although the neighborhood still shows the poverty and type of housing he emerged from to become one of the world's most successful songwriters.

Dixon died in 1992 in Chicago and is buried there.

- **Highway 61 Coffeehouse and Attic Gallery**
  1101 Washington St.
  601-638-922

This coffeehouse has nice music-themed décor and an authentic location (Old Highway 61 becomes Washington Street in town) but its Thursday-evening live music is rarely blues. Art-loving blues fans—and just about anyone else—might find something interesting in the gallery upstairs. It is incredibly packed with art of all kinds, and lots of it. There is plenty of Southern folk art and faux folk art, including blues-themed items.

Margaret's Grocery, Vicksburg

- **Margaret's Grocery and Market**
  4535 N. Washington St.
  (601) 638-1163

Margaret's Grocery and Market is a handbuilt religious shrine. Although not directly related to the blues, this is a fantastic work of African American folk architecture.

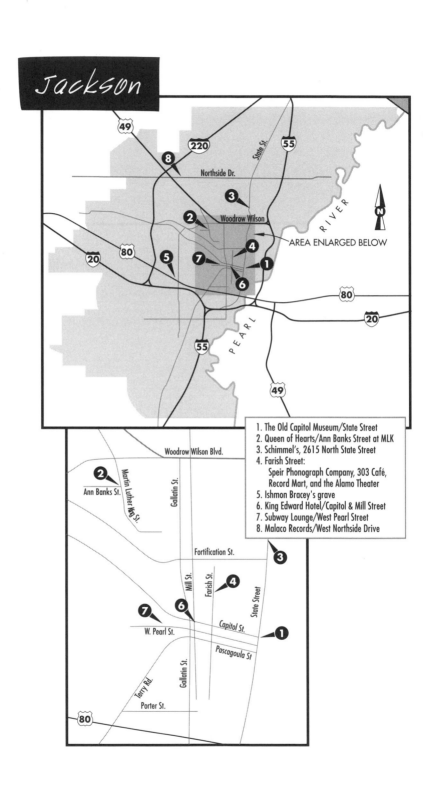

Jackson

1. The Old Capitol Museum/State Street
2. Queen of Hearts/Ann Banks Street at MLK
3. Schimmel's, 2615 North State Street
4. Farish Street:
    Speir Phonograph Company, 303 Café,
    Record Mart, and the Alamo Theater
5. Ishmon Bracey's grave
6. King Edward Hotel/Capitol & Mill Street
7. Subway Lounge/West Pearl Street
8. Malaco Records/West Northside Drive

AREA ENLARGED BELOW

Woodrow Wilson Blvd.

Ann Banks St.

Martin Luther King St.

Gallatin St.

Fortification St.

Mill St.

Farish St.

State Street

Capitol St.

W. Pearl St.

Pascagoula St

Gallatin St.

Terry Rd.

Porter St.

Northside Dr.

Woodrow Wilson

State St.

R I V E R

P E A R L

chapter 8

THE JACKSON AREA

Jackson

I liked Jackson better than I did either Memphis or New Orleans. Blues was more popular. Anytime you go to Jackson, they's be telling us, "Put me down there where they chunkin' tin cans." They mean just play 'em as low as you can get to 'em, then. Where they going to chunk tin cans, that's in the alley. You don't find no tin cans in the street. "Put 'em in the alley," that's what they holler for.

—Sam Chatmon

The state capital, being outside the Delta, does not conjure up "blues" in the popular imagination the way other Mississippi locations do. Even those on the Library of Congress field-recording trips largely ignored Jackson, presuming that it was too urban to have real folk singers.

But, as Sam Chatmon observed, the town actually has a strong blues tradition, one that goes back a long way and continues today. Being a big city, it has always attracted musicians. Chatmon reported seeing Memphis Minnie playing on the streets of Jackson in about 1910, when she was in her early teens and already a hot guitarist. Skip James met Lightnin' Hopkins, a

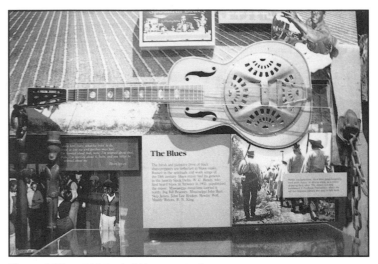

Blues exhibit at Old Capitol Museum, Jackson

Texan whose fame would not come until after the war, in Jackson in 1930. James said Hopkins, then a teenager, spent a week in Jackson, during which time the two mainly gambled, but James also gave Hopkins a few guitar pointers.

Jackson radio station WMPR, FM 90.1, plays soul-blues much of the time, with some gospel programming. The Jubilee! Jam (601-969-2008), held in mid-May on outdoor stages downtown, features various music and arts, including the blues.

- **Old Capitol Museum**
  State Street at Capitol Street
  (601) 576-6920

The museum is open 8 A.M. to 5 P.M. Mondays through Fridays, 9:30 A.M. to 4:30 P.M. Saturdays, and 12:30 to 4:30 P.M. Sundays. Admission is free.

This three-floor museum of Mississippi history contains only a small blues exhibit, in the twentieth-century room on the first floor. Besides a resonator guitar and photographs, the exhibit includes some unique artifacts: a record cutter and label-printing block from Trumpet Records, along with a microphone of the type Trumpet used. There also are copies of some Trumpet hits:

Elmore James's 78 "Dust My Broom" and Willie Love and his Three Aces' 45 "Nelson Street Blues."

Near the blues exhibit are other items that might be of interest to blues fans. One is a model of the first mechanical cotton picker, with a 1936 *New York Times* article explaining that the machine, invented by Texan brothers John and Mack Rust, would deprive nine million people of work (the brothers planned to devote the profits to the rehabilitation of those displaced workers). And a railroad exhibit has a photo of blues-yodeling country singer Jimmie Rodgers and a piece of Yazoo and Mississippi Valley (aka Yellow Dog) track.

King Edward Hotel, where the Mississippi Sheiks, Bo Carter, and other "race record" artists recorded in 1930, Pearl and Mill streets, Jackson

- **King Edward Hotel**
  Pearl St. and Mill St.

The King Edward is long abandoned but continues to tower over downtown Jackson, its original sign still on top. Like the Peabody in Memphis and other grand downtown hotels in southern cities, the King Edward was the site of field-recording trips by northern record companies.

The Okeh label set up a studio at the King Edward December 15–19, 1930, and recorded the Mississippi Sheiks, the Mississippi Mud Steppers (Walter Vincson of the Mississippi Sheiks, with Charlie McCoy—among their recordings is an instrumental "Jackson Stomp"), Bo Carter, Walter Jacobs (Vincson again, in an alias), Charlie McCoy, Slim Duckett and Pig Norwood, Elder

Curry, Caldwell Bracey, the Campbell College Quartet, and Elder Charlie Beck.

Decades later, blind and impoverished, Bo Carter was living in a Memphis roominghouse when he recalled that session at the King Edward for British writer Paul Oliver: "Tell ya, we was the Mississippi Sheiks and when we went to make the records in Jackson, Mississippi, the feller wanted to show us how to stop and start the records. Try to tell us when we got to begin and how we got to end. And you know, I started not to make 'em! I started not to make 'em 'cause he wasn't no musicianer, so how could he tell me how to stop and start the song? We was the Sheiks, the Mississippi Sheiks, and you know we was famous."

There are tentative plans to restore the King Edward as a hotel and telecommunications center. In the meantime, it is an illegal haven for homeless people and a party site for college students.

• Pascagoula Street

This is the street where bluesman Bo Carter reportedly lived in the 1920s. A native of Bolton, twenty miles to the east, Carter became a national blues star in the 1930s with such songs as "Banana in Your Fruit Basket" and "My Pencil Won't Write No More."

Carter was a central figure in the Jackson blues scene of the 1920s and early 1930s, which also included his brothers Sam, Harry, and Lonnie Chatmon; Walter Vincson (Lonnie's partner in the Mississippi Sheiks); and brothers Charlie and Joe McCoy (Joe became "Kansas Joe" when he recorded with his wife, Memphis Minnie). All these musicians collaborated occasionally on recordings and probably more often in live performances. Some of them also worked with Tommy Johnson, who was living in the city.

Pascagoula Street is one block south of Pearl Street, which is the traditional border between black neighborhoods and white ones. The part of Pascagoula west of Terry Road, near Varnado Alley, is a poor neighborhood with character that may date from the 1920s.

Although the nonpoetic word "Pascagoula" didn't make it into any of his songs, Carter did sing an "East Jackson Blues" in 1928:

> When you come to East Jackson, man, and don't find me there
> You can bet your bottom dollar that I'm walking the road
> somewhere.

- **Former Residence of Tommy Johnson, Skip James, Elmore James, and Other Bluesmen**
  905 Ann Banks St.

Tommy Johnson was born in Terry, a town about fifteen miles south of Jackson, in about 1896. He moved to Drew, in the Delta, as a young man and learned from Charley Patton and his associates at Dockery. But he developed a style that differed from theirs: a delicate, precise guitar-picking to back up his vibrato-filled, yodel-like vocals that delighted audiences throughout the state.

Johnson continued to travel to the Delta during picking season but was based in Jackson or Crystal Springs for the rest of his life—a startlingly long life, considering his taste for "canned heat" (Sterno), shoe polish, or anything else that would get him high, as well as plenty of regular whiskey when he could get it. Johnson's drinking was legendary even among blues singers, who are not known as a teetotaling bunch. He immortalized his own habits in the song "Canned Heat Blues" (a 1960s blues-rock group took the title for its name):

> *Crying mama, mama, mama, crying, canned heat is*
> *killing me*
> *Believe to my soul, Lord, it's going kill me dead.*

The house at 905 Ann Banks is where Tommy Johnson stayed when he was in town. It was the longtime home of Johnny Temple, who lived there until his death in 1968. Other blues artists who stayed at the house include Joe and Charlie McCoy, Skip James, and Elmore James, who was rooming there with Temple just before James's death in 1963.

After that dizzying lineup of blues-star residents, the house is vacant as of this writing but still in fairly good shape. And it remains in earshot of the blues—one empty lot separates it from a great jook joint, the Queen of Hearts.

- **Queen of Hearts**
  2243 Martin Luther King, Jr., Dr. (at Ann Banks St.)
  (601) 352-5730

The club is open nightly; live music is generally on Sundays only. The building dates from about 1900, and people have been playing the blues in it at least since 1972. "Big Bad Smitty and I

Owner Chellie B. Lewis (left) and drummer Charlie Jenkins outside the Queen of Hearts jook joint, 2243 Martin Luther King, Jr., Drive, Jackson

started the blues in Jackson," says club owner Chellie B. Lewis. "The blues had gone." The Queen of Hearts also hosted Jackson's first blues festival, in 1978, according to Lewis.

"This club is for you, but if you came to clown you can just turn around," reads the inscription on the mirror behind the club's tiny stage. Singer-harpist Sam Myers, who later left Jackson to join Dallas-based Anson Funderburgh and the Rockets, used to play regularly at the Queen of Hearts. So did Big Bad Smitty, who moved to St. Louis and then died in 2002.

The energetic King Edward, who wears a bowler hat and sometimes plays guitar with it, has been playing at the Queen of Hearts since its early days, and still does. He puts on a fierce performance whether there are five or fifty people in the club. Other singers stop in to sing a few or just to socialize. The music usually doesn't start until after midnight—and sometimes not at all. Relax, have a drink, and be patient, or take up a collection to motivate the band.

• Farish Street

The traditional black business street, Farish Street is to Jackson what Beale Street is to Memphis and Nelson Street is to Greenville. As centers of black commerce and activity, these streets also naturally became focal points for the blues. In the 1950s, Willie Love told Lillian McMurry, Farish Street had a church with moonshine stored under it and a restaurant with liquor flowing from a water faucet.

Farish has fallen into decline and decay. However, it is supposed to be on the verge of rejuvenation. The city has declared the area a historic district, purchased about half the buildings in the 200 and 300 blocks, and hired Performa Inc.—the same company that restored Memphis's Beale Street—to turn it into an entertainment district. A large banner at Amite and Farish announces that the Farish Street music, culture, food, and history are "coming soon." But after several years, a street-resurfacing is the only thing new. In the meantime, there are some old businesses that have managed to survive among the abandoned buildings—restaurants, bars, a barbershop, a shoe and hat store, a funeral home, and an upholstery shop.

The Louisiana-born piano great Little Brother Montgomery, who spent a lot of time in Jackson, recorded "Farish Street Jive," a spirited instrumental, in 1936. (Montgomery apparently liked place-name songs. He also cut "Vicksburg Blues" and "Shreveport Farewell.") "Farish Street Rag," another instrumental, was recorded by the New Orleans Nehi Boys.

The **Farish Street Festival** (601-960-2383), held on a Saturday in September, presents music on outdoor stages on the street. It features big-name soul-blues acts.

- ### Speir Phonograph Co.
  225 N. Farish St.

  The building has been demolished. It was just south of the alley and across the street from number 230. Speir later moved his business to 111 and 118 N. Farish, buildings that also have been demolished and replaced by the McCoy Federal Building.

Henry C. Speir, a white store owner, was one of the most influential nonmusicians in blues history. Besides running his store in Jackson, Speir traveled the South as a talent scout from the mid-1920s to the mid-1930s, finding blues artists for record companies. He would drive hundreds of miles to hear a singer he had heard about, then ask him to play. As Speir told writer Gayle Dean Wardlow, if he liked an artist he would say, "You sound pretty good. You know, I make records; if you will keep practicing and get your songs together real good and come to Jackson in a few days, I see that you get on records." An artist who took him up on the offer received travel reimbursement and spending money, along with fifty dollars per recorded side. Speir reportedly received a hundred and fifty dollars from the record company for each session of at least four songs.

Charley Patton, Skip James, and Willie Brown were among Speir's discoveries and the ones he considered the finest musicians. Among the other blues artists he worked with were the Mississippi Sheiks, Bo Carter, Son House, Will Shade, Robert Wilkins, Tommy Johnson, William Harris, the Mississippi Jook Band, Ishmon Bracey, Kokomo Arnold, Jim Jackson, Blind Joe Reynolds, Geechie Wiley, Elvie Thomas, and Isaiah Nettles. He also discovered and recorded many jazz, sacred, and hillbilly artists.

To pass the audition, an artist had to have at least four original songs. One whom Speir rejected was the bluesy hillbilly singer Jimmie Rodgers. Speir told Rodgers to go back home to Meridian and work up some more material.

Speir established his music store in 1925, specifically to sell records to the black community. He used talent scouting as a way to increase the store's business. There was a small recording machine upstairs for auditions and for vanity recordings, which anyone could make for five dollars.

By 1929 Speir had moved the store to 111 N. Farish, where an often-reproduced photograph was taken of him, another man, and a young woman standing in the narrow store. Among the artists who auditioned there was Robert Johnson, in 1936. Speir passed Johnson's name on to Ernie Oertle, an ARC records salesman, who took Johnson to San Antonio to record.

In 1930, according to Wardlow, Speir was offered the whole Paramount Record Company for twenty-five thousand dollars, including the costs of moving it from Grafton, Wisconsin, to Jackson. Speir turned down the offer because he did not have the money and was unable to raise it through the chamber of commerce.

About 1937, Speir left Farish Street and moved his business to West Capitol Street. In 1944, in the wake of a nationwide musicians' strike, Speir decided the record business was dead. He closed his music store and opened a furniture store in a white neighborhood in northern Jackson. Speir died in 1972.

- **Ace Records**
  241 N. Farish

  To get there: Ace Records is two buildings north of Speir Phonograph (Ross Furniture is between the two). The last door before the corner was the entrance to Ace.

Producer Johnny Vincent started Ace in 1955 to record New Orleans artists Earl King, Huey "Piano" Smith, and Bobby Marchan. King's "Those Lonely, Lonely Nights" was the label's first big hit, recorded at the Trumpet studio on Farish Street. "The piano was a little bit out of tune" for the "Lonely Nights" session, King told an interviewer. "But the guitar was out of tune and we had better takes than [the one] that was in tune." Blues artists Johnny Littlejohn and Willie Clayton also recorded here.

In the 1990s, Vincent relocated to Pearl, a Jackson suburb, where he operated the pop-blues label Avanti (135 Fairmont Plaza, 601-939-6868). Avanti artist Rue Davis recorded "Farish Street Blues," a tribute to the street's beloved businesses, but it remains unreleased. Vincent died on February 4, 2000, at age seventy-four.

- **303 Café**
  303 N. Farish St.
  (601)717-0856

Originally a gas station, this sturdy building was a beloved watering hole called Frank Jones' Corner in the 1960s, and then Fields' Café, which hosted blues into the 1990s. New owner Princess Smith saved it from demolition and reopened it as a nightclub. She hosts a deejay on Saturdays and plans to have live blues on Mondays. There is jukebox music on other nights.

- **Record Mart (and Trumpet Record Company and Diamond Recording Studio)**
  309 N. Farish St.

  To get there: The bricked-up middle door of this building, which also includes Big Al's Recovery Room, was the entrance to Record Mart. There is a state blues marker in front of the building.

This building was once a furniture store; its function began to change in 1949 when the owner's wife, Lillian McMurry, found Wynonie Harris's "All She Wants to Do Is Rock" in the store and put it on the turntable. "It was the most unusual, sincere and solid sound I'd ever heard. I'd never heard anything with such rhythm and freedom," McMurry, who was white, recalled later. It was her first exposure to black music.

McMurry started ordering blues and gospel records and selling them from her husband's store. She put speakers outside to attract customers. She sponsored a blues radio show and sold records by mail order. The record department soon took over the store. She founded the Trumpet label and began recording music—gospel groups at first. After hearing about the live radio broadcasts done by Sonny Boy Williamson II, McMurry tracked him down and persuaded him to make his first recordings. Sonny Boy brought in Joe Willie Wilkins, Elmore James, and Willie Love for his January 4, 1951, session, which included "Eyesight to the Blind," Trumpet's first hit. The recording studio for those songs and many other early Trumpet records was at **Scott Radio Service**, 128 N. Gallatin St. That building has been demolished and replaced by a parking lot.

Williamson remained close to McMurry throughout his life. She produced most of his hits, bailed him out of jail, and paid for his tombstone after he died. On one occasion, McMurry allegedly ran Williamson out of her studio at gunpoint—using his gun, which she had made him turn over when he entered—for cursing. He returned and apologized a few weeks later.

In 1953, Williamson recorded "309"—the street address of his record company. A kind of musical calling card, it also includes two phone numbers for McMurry:

> *To get in touch with my manager, please call 5-4121*
> *She can always tell you that Sonny Boy is out on the run.*

Besides playing with Williamson, Elmore James made his first recording under his own name, "Dust My Broom," for McMurry, then left her label.

Big Joe Williams, the Crawford-born country bluesman who had been recording since 1935, showed up at Trumpet in 1951 and recorded for McMurry. An even older bluesman—Bo Carter, who had recorded more than a hundred sides for other labels between 1928 and 1941—also sought to revive his career at Trumpet

Records, but was turned away. As McMurry told an interviewer: "He was friends of Sonny Boy, Willie Love, and Joe Willie Wilkins and a nice old fellow, light-skinned like [his brother] Sam Chatmon . . . Anyway, Bo Carter couldn't sing anymore; Bo was half blind, his voice broken completely. I'd audition him and tried to be kind and turn him down gently. Sonny Boy and Willie always helped get Bo gone without hurting his feelings. Today, some of those auditions would be collectors' items for just the blues collectors but Diamond Record Co. could not sell them then."

Trumpet folded in 1954, and McMurry's next label, Globe Records, didn't make out. But McMurry continued to make sure her artists got their royalties when other labels rereleased their material. She died March 28, 1999, at age seventy-seven, in Jackson.

McMurry installed a recording studio in the building in 1953, calling it Diamond Recording Studio. Sonny Boy and Jerry "Boogie" McCain both recorded at the studio here at 309. Earlier recordings were made at other Jackson locations or out of town—Williamson's "309," for example, was recorded in Houston.

Later, this building served as the offices of the *Jackson Advocate*, an outspoken African American newspaper. The paper moved its offices one street west to 438 Mill Street after the Farish Street building was firebombed in 1997.

There might be some recording going on again at 309 soon. Princess Smith, new owner of the 303 Café next door, also has bought the 309 building. She plans to renovate it and put in a recording studio.

- **Peaches Café**
  327 N. Farish St.
  (601) 354-9267

This locally beloved soul food restaurant has been open since 1961 and is still owned and operated by its founder, Willora "Peaches" Ephram, with help from her son Roderick. On Thursdays, veteran blues guitarist Jesse Robinson plays for lunchtime diners, 11 A.M. to 2 P.M. On weekend nights Peaches becomes a jook joint–like neighborhood hangout with grooving to the blues from the jukebox and, occasionally, live music. Beer is served weekend nights (BYOB liquor).

The Alamo Theater and other buildings on Farish Street, Jackson

Alamo Theater
333 N. Farish St.
(601) 352-3365

This is a grand old theater that once hosted movies, vaudeville shows, touring jazz acts, and a weekly talent contest. Pianist Otis Spann, a Belzoni native who moved to Jackson at an early age, won the Alamo's talent contest at age eight, in 1938, and became a regular part of the stage show. Dorothy Moore of "Misty Blue" fame, a native Jacksonian, also was a frequent winner of the contests.

The current Alamo was built in the 1950s (replacing an earlier Alamo) and restored in 1996, with support from the city and various agencies. Its façade and sign have been returned to their original glory, but the interior is simple and modern. People have not yet started flocking to the post-restoration Alamo's occasional shows, which feature blues, jazz, classical music, or plays. A plan to bring back the talent contests has not yet been realized.

• Big Apple Inn
509 N. Farish St.
(601) 354-9371

Sonny Boy Williamson II and his wife, Mattie, lived in the upstairs apartment in this building during the years he was recording at Trumpet. Their address was 507½ N. Farish. Williamson associates such as Willie Love and Elmore James also stayed in the apartment. Gene Lee, owner of the restaurant downstairs, used to go fishing with Sonny Boy. "We'd get on our bicycles and ride to the Pearl River, push our bicycles over the tracks," Lee says. "With our cane poles. We never caught any fish. It was relaxation for him, after playing all night."

Later, that apartment became the state NAACP headquarters, and civil rights leader Medgar Evers worked there as state field secretary. He was murdered in 1963 at age thirty-six.

The Big Apple is known to regulars as Big John's, after original owner Juan "Big John" Mora, Lee's grandfather. And it is famous for a downhome dish that Big John invented: pig-ear sandwiches. The ears are boiled and served on a biscuit-size roll, dressed with coleslaw, mustard, and hot sauce. Whenever he's in town, B. B. King is among the musicians, politicians, and regular folks who stop by for a bagful. Bobby "Blue" Bland, who also enjoys them, calls them "listener sandwiches." Smoke-sausage, hamburger, hot dog, and bologna sandwiches also are available, as well as hot tamales.

- **Birdland**
  538 Farish St.
  (601) 352-5124

This bar was once the Crystal Palace, which brought in touring jazz and R&B acts. The old name is still visible in fading paint on the brick wall on the building's south side.

- **Edward Lee Hotel**
  144 Church St. (in the first block west of Farish St.)

This was the hotel where touring black musicians usually stayed when they came to Jackson for gigs at the Alamo or Crystal Palace. Framed by empty lots, the large brick building is abandoned and falling down. Unfortunately, its sign has recently disappeared.

North of Church on Farish is a row of old **shotgun houses** recently purchased by the city, restored and repainted. Long before the restoration, bluesman Willie Love lived in one of these homes. Bluesman Hacksaw Harney lived at 722 Farish and posed in front of his home for a photo by Steve LaVere that has become a postcard.

- ## Ishmon Bracey's Grave

To get there: Heading west on Highway 80 between Terry Road and Ellis Avenue, turn right at the Jim Hill High School sign, onto the frontage road. Continue west on the frontage road, around Wright Music Company and past the school. You will wind up heading north on Hattiesburg Street. The large cemetery occupies both sides of the street. Take the northernmost entrance into the part on the east side of the street.

Bracey's grave is about halfway back, in the middle of a row. It is one of the few cross-shaped stones in the cemetery. It reads:

REST IN PEACE
Rev. Ishmon Bracey
Born Jan. 9th, 1901
Died Feb. 12, 1970

Born in Byram, Ishmon (sometimes spelled "Ishman") Bracey lived in Jackson from the 1920s on, singing and playing guitar in a simple, straightforward style. H. C. Speir approached him while he was playing on Mill Street in Jackson in 1927 ("I thought he was the law," Bracey recalled of that encounter). Bracey recorded a few sides for Speir but never reached the legendary status of some of his peers. One distinctive aspect of his recordings is the addition of a pianist and clarinetist, along with Bracey's voice and guitar—unusual instrumentation for a Mississippi blues record of the 1920s.

Bracey played the blues until he turned to religion in 1951. He still didn't mind talking about the blues after that, telling interviewers about his old pal Tommy Johnson.

Bracey's grave is interesting because the stone is a fairly old one erected by his family soon after his death, rather than a large new one provided by fans or a record company, as are many blues artists' stones. The site is easily accessible and right in the city.

- ## Subway Lounge

Basement of the Summers Hotel, 619 W. Pearl St. (near Minerva St.) There is a state blues marker at the site.

The Summers Hotel was, for decades, one of the few hotels in Jackson open to blacks. Retired schoolteacher and part-time singer Jimmy King opened the Subway Lounge in the old hotel's basement in 1966, running it first as a jazz club and switching to blues around 1986.

It was a classic after-hours, literally underground nightspot. The place didn't even open until after midnight, and the live music went on until at least 4 A.M. After the bar closed at 1 A.M., you could go buy beer and, if you were hungry, "blues dogs" from the house next door. Many musicians stopped by after gigs to hang out or sit in.

The Subway and its musicians were celebrated in the 2003 Starz! TV documentary *Last of the Mississippi Jukes*. The film also deals with the history of the building and the efforts to save the building from demolition or collapse.

But alas, even a movie was not enough to save the Subway. It closed later the same year, after flood damage and controversies on the committee that was supposed to save it. It was demolished in 2004. There has been talk of erecting an amphitheater at the site.

King continues the Subway tradition by hosting music nights at Schimmel's (see entry below).

- **Poindexter Park Inn**
  803 Deer Park Street
  (601) 944-1392

This bed-and-breakfast is run by former city councilwoman Marcia Weaver, a blues enthusiast and manager of Jackson singer Dorothy Moore of "Misty Blue" fame. Weaver is familiar with the history and current state of blues in her city, and has a small library of blues-related books at the inn.

- **930 Blues Café**
  930 N. Congress St.
  (601) 948-3344

This cozy nightclub is up a narrow flight of stairs in a historic house and is decorated jook-joint style. It offers live blues nightly, generally of the high-energy electric variety (although unfortunately the place is too small to allow much dance space). There are house bands during the week and regional or national acts on Fridays and Saturdays. The downstairs is a restaurant that serves hearty lunches with a limited menu available at night.

- **Schimmel's**
  2615 North State St
  (601)981-7077

This upscale restaurant is a far cry, both in neighborhood and atmosphere, from the down-and-dirty Subway Lounge. Yet it continues the tradition with Saturday Subway Blues Nights and Friday Jazz Nights, both hosted by Subway owner Jimmy King, who also sings on Fridays.

The Saturday Subway Blues Nights start late, as at the old Subway, and the tables are rearranged into long rows to re-create the seating arrangement, if not the entire feel. The Houserockers, house band from Subway and from the documentary about it, are on hand. King is at the door taking the cover charge.

Schimmel's also presents acoustic blues from Ben Payton on Thursdays. And there are photographs of jazz and blues musicians on the walls.

- **Hal & Mal's Restaurant and Brewery**
  200 S. Commerce St.
  (601) 948-0888

Monday night is blues night at this downtown restaurant/ brewpub/nightclub, which features other styles of music the rest of the week. The wall decorations include signed photos of various artists, including Albert King. Jack Owens's mailbox and the sunglasses Elvis Presley wore in the Rose Bowl parade are also on the premises. The women's bathroom has a Ma Rainey theme, while the men's is devoted to Elvis.

- **George Street Grocery**
  416 George St.
  (601) 969-3753

This is another downtown club that sometimes offers blues, but also presents rock and other genres. George Street is where Texas-based Anson Funderburgh and the Rockets were playing in 1982 when Jackson singer-harpist Sam Myers sat in with them for the first time. Myers became a full-time member of the group a few years later. A blues jam begins at 9 P.M. on Tuesdays. Check the listings in Thursday's *Clarion-Ledger* for the week's blues offerings at this and other Jackson clubs.

- ## Malaco Records
  3023 W. Northside Drive
  (601) 982-4522

Tommy Couch and Wolf Stephenson got into the music business by booking bands for fraternity parties when both were pharmacy students at the University of Mississippi in the early 1960s. After graduating, they moved to Jackson and continued booking bands and promoting concerts, using an office they rented from Ace Records.

Soon they tried their hands at recording. Johnny Vincent of Ace told them about the Northside Drive building, part of which he was renting as a warehouse. They rented the other half as a studio, and they are still there.

Fred McDowell's 1967 album *I Do Not Play No Rock 'n' Roll* was recorded at Malaco and released on Capitol. Besides that one venture into deep blues, and a few experiments with disco, funk, pop, and country, Malaco has focused on soul, soul-blues, and, in recent years, gospel. Denise LaSalle, Shirley Brown, Latimore, and Bobby Rush are among the company's soul-blues mainstays.

Two Malaco releases are the blues anthems that rekindled blues interest among black listeners in the 1980s: Z. Z. Hill's 1982 "Down Home Blues" and Little Milton's 1984 "The Blues Is All Right." The company also has had three top ten pop hits, all recorded here: King Floyd's "Groove Me" in 1970–71, Jean Knight's "Mr. Big Stuff" in 1971, and Dorothy Moore's "Misty Blue" in 1976.

Malaco gives tours by appointment only.

- ## Red Hot & Blue
  1625 E. County Line Rd.
  (601) 956-3313 (and a branch at 5530 Highway 80, Pearl, 601-664-0098)

This suburban strip-mall barbecue restaurant was founded by Malaco Records co-owner Tommy Couch, who has since sold it. Its walls are covered with signed posters, photos, and other memorabilia from blues artists, and not only from Malaco artists. On display is a giant multimedia painting of bluesman "Son" Thomas by Patterson-Barnes. There are blues jams Monday nights, blues acts on weekends, and recorded blues on the stereo every day.

Ebenezer

- **Graves of Elmore James and Lonnie Pitchford**

  To get there: From Highway 55, take exit 146 (Highway 14, Goodman, Ebenezer). Take Highway 14 west for 1.3 miles, until it makes a T intersection with Highway 17. That T is in the town of Richland, where Elmore James was born (he was not born in the larger Richland just south of Jackson). Head north on Highway 17 for 2.6 miles, to Newport Road. Turn left on Newport Road and drive 3.9 miles to New Port M.B. Church, a red brick building on your left.

Park at the church and walk behind and to the right of it, into the cemetery. Elmore James is buried about a hundred feet back, midway between the church and the right-hand edge of the cemetery. His stone is striking. It is black, with a three-dimensional metal sculpture of him coming from the front of it. The front reads:

Elmore James
"King of the Slide Guitar"
January 27, 1918
May 24, 1963

The reverse says:

Born in Holmes County, Mississippi, Elmore James electrified the rural Delta blues with his unique slide guitar style. Creating a powerful legacy that will remain forever in American music. "The sky is crying . . . look at the tears roll down the street."

Lonnie Pitchford's grave is about thirty feet farther back. His gravestone has built-in pegs for a playable string, although the string is usually missing.

The legend on Elmore James's headstone is no exaggeration. He really is responsible for the electric slide-guitar sound, which has become familiar in blues, rock, even pop and country. Apparently being the brother of a radio technician gave James the idea and the know-how to amplify his acoustic guitar. He also is the songwriter of such classics as "It Hurts Me, Too," "Shake Your Moneymaker" and "The Sky Is Crying," a line from which is on his tombstone.

A native of nearby Lexington, Lonnie Pitchford was born on

Detail from Elmore James's grave marker, Ebenezer

October 8, 1955, and died on November 8, 1998. He was, for his age, startlingly well versed in the blues of earlier eras. He was also a remarkably good musician, regardless of age. Pitchford first gained fame as a master of the one-string guitar, which he would build onstage and then play. He also was a master of the six-string guitar in its acoustic and electric versions, and was an especially adept interpreter of Robert Johnson material (which he learned directly from Robert Lockwood, Jr., who was Johnson's only pupil). Pitchford made only one full album, *All Around Man*, during his too-short life. He also appears in the documentary *Deep Blues* and on its soundtrack, on a few concert compilations, and on a John Mellencamp album.

Bentonia

The tiny town of Bentonia (population 518) looms disproportionately large in blues history and legend. It is the hometown of Skip James, who recorded such classics as "Devil Got My Woman," "I'm So Glad," and "22-20 Blues" in 1930. It is hard to avoid the word "haunting" when discussing James's music, which features his falsetto singing and minor-key guitar playing or quirky piano. After a long period away from music, James did some more recording and performing during the 1960s blues-folk revival. He died on October 3, 1969, and is buried in Philadelphia, Pennsylvania.

Skip James had seemed to be a unique artist, but it turned out there was another Bentonia man, Jack Owens, about the same age who played in the same style. It is unclear which of the two originated the style, or whether they are part of a Bentonia "school" that predates them. Although Owens did not record until the 1960s, he had been playing at house parties and jooks in his area for many years. In his last decades he recorded several albums, appeared in the movie *Deep Blues*, and performed at festivals, always accompanied by Bentonia harpist Bud Spires.

Bentonia's blues tradition lives on: In the mid-2000s, Blue Front Café owner Jimmy "Duck" Holmes released two critically acclaimed CDs of himself playing in the style he learned directly from Owens, with accompaniment from Spires on some tracks.

• Blue Front Cafe

108 E. Railroad Ave.
(601) 755-2278

To get there: From Highway 49, take either Bentonia exit and head into town. Cross the tracks and look for the Blue Front Cafe, which has a big sign, next to a ramshackle old grocery building. There is a state blues marker in front of the building.

The Blue Front is a picture-perfect jook joint, as authentic as they come. Musician Jimmy "Duck" Holmes has run it since 1970, taking over from his parents who opened the place in 1948. Skip James, Jack Owens, Henry Stuckey, Sonny Boy Williamson, and "Son" Thomas are among the many musicians who played there, and Holmes carries on the tradition of live blues.

The Blue Front opens at 10 A.M. daily, with Holmes coming in about 3:30 P.M., after he finishes at his other job as a school truant officer. There are crate-type stools at the bar, seven tables with metal chairs, bare lightbulbs overhead, and a woodstove for heat in the winter. "Time did that," Holmes says, laughing at the idea of creating jook-joint decor as some bars do. "I didn't have to make it look old."

The regulars come in in the early evening to talk, flirt, drink, and listen to the jukebox. "They don't call this going out," Holmes notes. "This is like a family room, a sitting room. They come here to decide where they're going to go out."

Sometimes there is live music from Holmes and other local musicians. There is no cover charge. Pickled pigs feet, Spam, Cheetos, and Vanilla Wafers are available, but customers often bring in their own meals. Microwave. Beer and sodas are the only drinks served.

The Blue Front hosts a **Bentonia Blues Fest** on the third Saturday of June.

• Jack Owens's Grave

To get there: From downtown Bentonia, take Cannon Road (Highway 433) northeast for 4.4 miles, then turn right at Scotland Road (there is a sign pointing you toward Scotland). You will go past Old Liberty M. B. Church, where Owens's funeral was held. Continue to the cemetery, up a dirt drive into the woods on the right, 3.0 miles from the turn onto Scotland Road. There is a small "Day Cemetery" sign. Park at the end of the drive and walk in toward the right and almost to the back.

The grave is marked by a double stone for Owens and his wife, Mrs. Mable Owens. A guitar is inscribed between them. His half reads:

Mr. L. F. Nelson
(Jack Owens)
Sunrise Nov. 17, 1904
Sunset Feb. 9, 1997

Owens's sister, Marie Owens, is buried nearby.

Jack Owens was a farmer who for a while ran a jook house as a side business; music was never the main thing in his life. But after folklorists David Evans and Alan Lomax discovered and documented his music, Owens's reputation expanded beyond the Bentonia area, where he lived all of his life. He played at festivals, did a few tours, and appeared in the documentaries *Land Where the Blues Began* and *Deep Blues* along with harpist Bud Spires.

"The Devil" or "Must Have Been the Devil" was Owens's signature tune, one he would play for a long time. Skip James called his version "Devil Got My Woman." This piece crops up in the repertoires of singers from outside Bentonia: Robert Johnson's "Hellhound on My Trail" and Bo Carter's "Old Devil" are both related to it.

Yazoo City

This town has lent its euphonious name to Yazoo Records, a reissue company that has brought the music of old blues 78s to new generations via LPs and then CDs. The Yazoo River forms the east border of the Delta, as the Mississippi does the west. (The name "Yazoo" comes from an extinct Indian tribe).

There is a blues exhibit inside the Triangle Cultural Center, 332 N. Main St., 662-746-2273. For a while the town put on an annual Yazoo Blues Festival in June, but that has been abandoned lately as the nearby Bentonia Blues Fest has grown in popularity.

Crystal Springs

Tommy Johnson, the crooning singer of such blues masterpieces as "Cool Drink of Water," "Canned Heat Blues," and the much-covered "Big Road Blues," was born in nearby Terry and grew up in Crystal Springs. Johnson lived from 1896 to 1956 but recorded only a handful of songs, in about 1929. He lived in Jackson for his last few decades, and often returned to Crystal Springs to play at parties and jooks. He is buried on private property in Crystal Springs.

There is a state blues marker for Tommy Johnson at Georgetown and Railroad streets, by the tracks.

There is a grave marker for Johnson inside the **Crystal Springs Public Library**, 200 S. Jackson St., 601-892-3205. The library is open 9 A.M. to 5 P.M. Mondays through Saturdays. Efforts are ongoing to allow public access to the abandoned cemetery where Johnson is buried and to place the marker there.

With his brothers LeDell and Mager, Tommy Johnson used to play in front of **Thaxton's** drugstore, 112 E. Georgetown St., in the mid-1920s. The building is still there, now occupied by Chopsticks Restaurant. Look up to find the "Thaxton's" in raised brick on the front of the building.

- **Robert Johnson Blues Foundation Headquarters and Museum**
  218 E Marion Ave.
  (866)402-5837

Open 9 A.M. to 5 P.M. Mondays, Tuesdays, Thursdays, and Fridays; 9 A.M. to noon Wednesdays; and by appointment.

Robert Johnson's grandson, Steven Johnson, at the Robert Johnson Blues Foundation Headquarters and Museum, Crystal Springs

This small, folksy museum has some big things going for it: actual living descendants of Robert Johnson. The great bluesman's grandson, Steven, runs the place. Steven's dad, Claud—Robert Johnson's only known child—sometimes stops in, too.

The museum also contains an instrument Robert Johnson supposedly used to play. And—surprise!—it's a piano, which the museum got from a local joint where, they say, Johnson played piano as one of the Freetown Boys, a trio that also included Tommy Johnson and James Adams.

And there are guitars donated by Robert Lockwood Jr. (who learned music directly from Johnson as a child), Rory Block (who recently played at the Robert Johnson Blues Jam and collaborated with Steven Johnson's church choir), Allen Collins of Lynyrd Skynyrd, and others famous and unknown. It also has exhibits on local history, stately paintings of Lockwood and Honeyboy Edwards by Vicksburg artist Tony Davenport, and other art and artifacts.

The museum hosts an annual **Robert Johnson Blues Jam** festival around the bluesman's birthday (May 8).

Hazlehurst

Robert Johnson, "the King of the Delta Blues Singers," was born outside the Delta, in this town on Highway 51 south of Jackson, on

May 8, 1911. He left Hazlehurst when he was a baby, being taken first to Memphis and then to Robinsonville, where he spent his childhood and teen years and began playing music.

But Hazlehurst was still to play a role in Johnson's personal and musical life. Around 1930, he came back to look for his real father, Noah Johnson. It is unknown whether that search was successful. But Robert Johnson, a young widower, got remarried in Hazlehurst, to an older woman named Calletta Craft. He also apprenticed with an unrecorded bluesman named Ike Zinnerman. And he practiced a lot. When Johnson returned to the Delta a few years later, the improvement in his playing astounded everyone to the point that some wondered if he had made a deal with the devil.

• Robert Johnson's Birthplace

Robert Johnson was born on a farm just north of Hazlehurst. The spot is where Interstate 55 and Highway 28 intersect today, making it the easiest blues-heritage spot to visit—driving north on I-55 you go across Johnson's front yard. The actual house he was born in has been moved to a secret location, local sources say. The house might eventually be restored as a Johnson museum.

• Robert Johnson Monument

Hazlehurst's town square is loaded with markers and monuments. One historical marker commemorates Mrs. Annie Coleman Peyton, a Hazlehurst citizen who led the effort to establish Mississippi State College for Women (now Mississippi University for Women), the country's first state-supported college for women, in 1884. A small stone monument acknowledges the Illinois Central Railroad. There are monuments to the veterans of several wars and a marker for the town itself, which was named for the chief engineer of the first railway connecting Jackson and New Orleans, the last spike of which was driven in Hazlehurst in 1858. And the newest monument, tombstone-like, recognizes the town's most famous citizen, Robert Johnson. The inscription is taken verbatim from the Johnson memorial in Morgan City. Memorial bricks in front of the monument include one for H. C. Speir, the Jackson record store owner and talent scout who recommended Johnson to Vocalion Records.

That big building on the square is the **Copiah County Court-house**, where Johnson married Calletta Craft on May 4, 1931. Johnson used to play on the courthouse steps on Saturday afternoons.

- **Hazlehurst Depot Museum**
  138 N. Ragsdale Ave.
  (601) 894-3752

Robert Johnson undoubtedly passed through this 1925 passenger depot, and played at it, on his trips through town. It has been restored as a museum, which includes a Robert Johnson exhibit, and the offices of the Hazlehurst Chamber of Commerce. There is a state blues marker for Johnson in front of the building.

Renfroe Valley

- **J. B. Lenoir's Grave**
  To get there: From the intersection of highways 84 and 27 in Monticello, head south on Highway 27 for 15 miles to Price Road. Price is on the left only; Dummy Line Road is opposite it. There is a sign reading "Sauls Valley Baptist Church, 5 mi." at the intersection, on the left. Turn left, onto Price Road, and drive 1.7 miles to Salem M.B. Church, on the left. The Lenoir grave is near the middle of the small cemetery.

J. B. Lenoir (pronounced "Lenore") was part of the Chicago blues scene of the 1950s–'60s. Although he never made it big or even was able to support himself through music, he had a distinctive style that touched many who heard it. Many of Lenoir's songs are overtly political, although his best-known number is the nonpolitical "Talk to Your Daughter." He sang in a high, womanly voice, accompanying himself with infectious rhythms on the acoustic guitar.

In the early 1960s Lenoir traveled to England as part of the American Folk Blues Festival. He befriended and impressed British bluesman John Mayall, who wrote two songs about him, "The Death of J. B. Lenoir" and "I'm Gonna Fight for You J. B." Lenoir died in 1967, at age thirty-eight, due to injuries from a car accident.

Lenoir is the subject of a film made by Steve and Ronnog Seaberg, intended for Swedish television. It didn't air, however, until 2003, as part of Wim Wenders's "The Soul of a Man" episode on PBS's *The Blues* series. Wenders had become a fan of Lenoir's after hearing Mayall's songs.

Lenoir is buried in the community where he was born. The grave has a double stone for J. B. and his wife Ella L. Craft, identified as "father" and "mother." It bears a photo of J. B. in his trademark zebra-striped coat. There are an engraved guitar and some musical notes and the inscription, "Let the works we've done speak for us."

Varnado, La.

- ## Birdie's Roadhouse
  26646 Highway 21
  (985) 732-4032

  To get there: From J. B. Lenoir's grave, take Highway 27 north back to Monticello, then Highway 587 south. Highway 587 will become Highway 35 and then, at the Louisiana border, will become Highway 21. The club is on the right, about 7 miles south of the state border.

This club is a little off the blues path, but if you are visiting J. B. Lenoir's grave late on a Friday or Saturday afternoon, you might want to swing down to Birdie's—about an hour's drive. It is also about an hour from New Orleans; about 2½ hours from Jackson.

Birdie's looks as if it's been there forever, the proverbial little shack out in the sticks, near the prison. But it just opened in 2000, in a 1936 double-shotgun house that was moved to the site and renovated as a jook joint-ish club. It has a great blues jukebox (J. B. Lenoir, Frank Frost, Robert Nighthawk), live music 10 P.M. to 2 A.M. Fridays and 8 P.M. to midnight Saturdays. Thursday is open-mike night. Beer only is served, BYOB liquor (there are compartments in the wall where regulars lock up their bottles).

Port Gibson

- ## F. S. Wolcott's Rabbit Foot Minstrel Show Headquarters
  Carroll St. and Market St.

  To get there: From Highway 61, continue south into town and turn right at the stoplight where the Exxon station is (Carroll Street, although there is no street sign). Go two blocks to the corner of Market Street (again unmarked). Titles for Cash is the business occupying the building that Wolcott once owned and used as headquarters for the minstrel show. The performers sometimes rehearsed on the field in front of the building.

From about 1900 to the 1940s, the Rabbit Foot Minstrels were one of the country's two most popular minstrel shows (the other was Silas Green from New Orleans). Wolcott, a white man, ran the black entertainment revue from his hometown of Port Gibson. Touring nationally by train (and later by bus), a minstrel show would come to town and perform under a large tent. The show featured comedians, wrestlers, jugglers, animal acts—and blues singers.

Among the many singers who toured with Rabbit Foot are Ma Rainey, Bertha "Chippie" Hill, Bessie Smith, Jim Jackson, Big Joe Williams, Louis Jordan, Jim Seals (father of Son Seals), Maxwell Street Jimmy Davis, Rufus Thomas, Chico Chism, Diamond Teeth Mary, and Brownie McGhee.

It was while touring with Rabbit Foot in 1902 that Ma Rainey heard a young Missouri woman singing a "strange and poignant" song that awakened Rainey to the blues—an experience similar to W. C. Handy's blues awakening in Mississippi a few years later. It was also while she was with Rabbit Foot, in 1914, that Rainey met and coached the young Bessie Smith, who joined the troupe that year.

Natchez

Jackson on a high hill, Natchez just below
I ever get back home, I won't be back no more.
—Charley Patton, "Screamin' and Hollerin' the Blues"

Before the Civil War, Natchez and Vicksburg were the state's only towns with sidewalks, brick buildings, or paved streets. Natchez, the oldest settlement on the Mississippi River and the first cotton capital, was once home to half of America's millionaires. It still has hundreds of antebellum structures, which it shows off during fall and spring pilgrimages. Like Charleston, South Carolina, or Savannah, Georgia, Natchez is an Old South town.

It also shows some New Orleans flavor in its architecture, atmosphere, and music. One unusual Natchez blues band, Hezekiah and the House Rockers, included a trombonist. That band has

Natchez bluesman Little Poochie performing in 1999, downtown Natchez

broken up, but its leader, singer-harpist-drummer Hezekiah Early, still lives in the area, often playing and recording with slide guitarist Elmo Williams.

Bluff City Blues, a three-piece band featuring the great Little Poochie on vocals and guitar, is a more orthodox Natchez blues act.

The town's annual **Blues on the Bluff Festival** (601-446-9351) takes place in mid-April in Natchez Memorial Park.

A historical marker notes the site of **Forks of the Road** slave market, on the left as you come into town from the north on Highway 61. This was the South's second-largest slave market in the nineteenth century.

- ### Site of the Natchez Rhythm Club Fire

  To get there: Highway 61 becomes St. Catherine Street. Just north of Martin Luther King Street, past the large brick Holy Family Church on the left, there is a fork in the road and a barnlike, signless car wash on the right, which is where the Natchez Rhythm Club stood.

The Natchez Rhythm Club burned to the ground on April 23, 1940, killing two hundred sixty of the five hundred people inside. The death rate was so high because the windows had been boarded up to prevent people outside from enjoying the show without paying the cover. That left only one exit. Among the dead were Walter Barnes and most of his orchestra, a popular jazz group who were playing that night. To deal with the bodies, African American morticians were called in from miles around, including a young Perry Payton of Greenville, who was helping his mortician father. Payton later established his own funeral home business and the Flowing Fountain nightclub in Greenville.

In the immediate wake of the fire, blues singers Gene Gilmore and Leonard "Baby Doo" Caston recorded songs about it, which were released back-to-back on one single. Caston played piano on both tracks, and Robert Lee McCoy accompanied both on harmonica. Caston's "The Death of Walter Barnes" included these lines:

> *Now, it was just about midnight, just about twelve o'clock*
> *Poor Walter played his theme song, the dance hall began*
>   *to rock.*

> *The peoples all was dancin', enjoyin' their lives so high*
> *Just in a short while, the dance hall was full of fire.*

Gilmore's "The Natchez Fire" was equally somber:

> *Lord, it was late one Tuesday night, people had come from*
>   *miles around*
> *They was enjoying their lives when that Rhythm Club*
>   *went down.*

> *Lord, it was sad and misery when the hearses began to roll*
> *It was over two hundred dead and gone, Lord, and they can't*
>   *come here no more.*

Sixteen years after the fire, Howlin' Wolf recorded his tribute, "The Natchez Burning." A slow, spooky number that is different from anything else he recorded, the song personalizes the tragedy:

> *Did you ever hear about the burning that happened way*
>   *down in Natchez Mississippi town?*
> *The whole building got to burning, there was my baby lay-*
>   *ing on the ground.*

- ## Monuments to the Rhythm Club Dead and to Richard Wright

Although there is no marker at the site of the tragedy, there is a monument to the Rhythm Club dead at the riverfront, Broadway and State Street. Donated by the Natchez Social and Civic Club of Chicago, the monument lists the names of those who lost their lives in the fire.

About a hundred feet north of that monument is a historical

marker for novelist Richard Wright, who was born in Natchez in 1908. Wright wrote the introduction to *Blues Fell This Morning: Meaning in the Blues*, the 1960 book by British writer Paul Oliver.

- **Biscuits and Blues**
  315 Main St.
  (601) 446-9922

This restaurant-nightclub has blues acts most Sunday nights. It is part of a small chain that also has restaurants in San Francisco, California, and St. Paul, Minnesota.

chapter 9

EAST MISSISSIPPI

Although it is on the opposite side of the state, the area between Meridian and Tupelo resembles the Delta in some places, with soybeans and sometimes cotton growing on flat prairies. A handful of great musicians come from this region. And the residents of this area seem to recognize their musicians as heroes, with monuments and other tributes. (Refer to map in Chapter 1.)

Mississippi State University's WMSV, 91.1 FM Starkville, broadcasts the blues 6 to midnight on Sundays.

Meridian

This rough, funky old town has railroad tracks everywhere and a cool-looking (but not lively) art deco downtown. Although it is the third-largest city in Mississippi, Meridian has never had much of a blues scene. It is, however, the hometown of a major figure in American music—Jimmie Rodgers, the Singing Brakeman, the Blue Yodeler, the Father of Country Music. (This is not the same person as Jimmy Rogers, the Delta-born blues guitarist who worked with Muddy Waters in Chicago.)

Meridian also was home base of blues researcher/writer Gayle

Dean Wardlow while he was working on the books *King of the Delta Blues* and *Chasin' that Devil Music* and his many articles. Wardlow has moved to Mississippi's Gulf Coast.

Singing Brakeman Park, downtown at 1901 Front St., next to Union Station, is named after Rodgers. There is a state blues marker for Rodgers at the park.

A **Jimmie Rodgers Memorial Festival** happens every spring at the park. It includes a gospel concert, a barbecue cookoff, a country talent competition, and other events, although usually no blues.

• Jimmie Rodgers Museum

1725 Jimmie Rodgers Dr.
(601) 485-1808

To get there: Enter Highland Park at 39th Avenue and 16th Street and follow the signs around to the museum. Look for the full-size train outside the building.

Like Elvis Presley, Jimmie Rodgers is one of the few white singers regularly identified as a blues singer by black blues singers and blues fans. And this for a man who is also credited as being the father of country music! If there is any doubt, Rodgers's music proves that, from the beginning, country-western itself was based strongly on the blues.

Rodgers, who recorded in the late 1920s and early 1930s, was a contemporary of the first generation of recorded bluesmen. He certainly met and heard blues singers in his work and travels on the railroad. Rodgers used stock blues verses and chord progressions in his songs, many of which have "blue" or "blues" in their titles. Even his trademark yodel may have been influenced by African American field hollers.

In his autobiography, B. B. King lists as one of his early influences Rodgers, "a yodeler who happened to be white, but who sang songs like 'Blues, How Do You Do?' They called him the Singing Brakeman and I sang along with him." Howlin' Wolf admired Rodgers, and may have based his wolf howl on Rodgers's yodel. Leadbelly liked to sing Rodgers songs, including the yodels. Even Robert Johnson would play a Jimmie Rodgers tune when requested, according to his pal and fellow bluesman Johnny Shines, who did the same.

The Rodgers museum is supposed to move soon into the com-

plex of buildings around the refurbished Union Station downtown. Besides being more centrally located, that site will be appropriate for a museum dedicated to a man who worked on the
railroads for years. In the meantime, it is in a replica of a depot
building in a city park, with an old train next to it.

The museum contains Rodgers's awards (including a Handy
Award and places in the Rock 'n' Roll Hall of Fame and the
Nashville Songwriters Hall of Fame), letters, and records. Also on
display are musical instruments, including the Martin guitar with
his name inlaid in the fretboard and "Thanks" on the back, which
Rodgers holds in his best-known "thumbs-up" photo; a denim
jacket worn by Rodgers and a dress worn by Mrs. Rodgers; handwritten sheet music by Elsie McWilliams, Rodgers's sister-in-law
and cowriter; and a 1920 windup Victrola that record company
executive Ralph Peer gave McWilliams.

- **Jimmie Rodgers's Grave**
  Oak Grove Cemetery

  To get there: From Interstate 20, take exit 154A (Butler-South). Turn left at the
  first light, then right at the first road, behind the McDonald's. You will be on
  Azalea Drive. Turn left on Oak Grove Drive. The cemetery is on the right, just
  past Oak Grove Baptist Church. From the cemetery entrance road, Rodgers's
  grave is to the left, two rows from the road.

Several members of the extended Rodgers family are buried in
the same broad gravel-filled plot. A large stone is inscribed simply
"Rodgers" on one side, with "Carrie" and "Jimmie" on the other.
Rodgers and his second wife, Carrie, also have small individual
markers. His reads:

"JIMMIE"
James Charles Rodgers
Sept. 8, 1897
May 26. 1933
America's blue yodeler

The one next to him reads:

Carrie Cecil Williamson
Wife of
Jimmie Rodgers
Aug. 8, 1902
Nov. 28, 1967
First lady of country music

Their daughters, Carrie Anita Rodgers Court and June Rebecca, also are buried here. So are Elsie W. McWilliams and her husband, Edwin R. "Dick" McWilliams.

- **Peavey Visitors Center**
  Montgomery Industrial Park, Marion-Russell Road off Highway 45 bypass
  (601) 483-5365
  To get there: From the exit, turn right and go 1 mile to the visitors' center.

The center is open 10 A.M.–4 P.M. weekdays, 1–4 P.M. weekends. Admission is free.

This company was started in 1965 by Hartley Peavey, a Meridian youth who liked to tinker with old radio and TV parts in his parents' basement. It grew phenomenally, and now employs two thousand people in two dozen buildings around Meridian and a few more elsewhere.

Aaron Neville and Steve Cropper are the only blues-related artists (among the rock and country-western players) showcased as Peavey instrument users in the visitors' center. But many lesser-known blues players use equipment, especially amps and PA systems, made by Peavey, which is the world's largest amp manufacturer.

The visitors' center is a museum that tells the company's story with replicas of the workbenches Peavey himself used over the years, equipment he or the company built, and artifacts and photos from various events, including President George Bush's visit to Peavey in 1990.

Thanks to an employee who is a blues fan, there is a small exhibit of 78s by Muddy Waters, Howlin' Wolf, Fats Domino, T-Bone Walker, and John Lee Hooker, along with B. B. King posters.

The fun part is the music room, where visitors of any age or musical inclination may wail away on microphones, drums, guitar, bass, or keyboards, amplified as loud as you please. In case you don't want to accompany yourself, there's even a karaoke machine.

Crawford

- **Welcome Sign**

Big Joe Williams's hometown honors him as a "blues legend" on its welcome signs on Highway 45A, although he shares the sign with

Jook joint, Crawford

two other Crawford natives—NFL star Jerry Rice and NBA star Clarence Weatherspoon.

• Big Joe Williams's Grave

To get there: From Highway 45 Alt heading south into Crawford, go under the underpass and take the first right onto Main Street. Stay on that street for 4.4 miles, going past a group of brick buildings, including the Silver Fox Lounge. Farther up, on the left, you will pass city hall. Continue through town to Bethesda Road, where the Bethesda Baptist Church sign is. Turn left onto Bethesda, a gravel road. Continue straight, past the church, and bear to the right at the fork. Keep driving through the pastures and past a few houses. The grave is 1.6 miles from the turn onto Bethesda, on the right, across from house number 3162. It is near the road, in a pasture that does not look like a cemetery (although there are a few more graves farther back from the road), behind a barbed-wire fence.

The marker reads:

> *Joe Lee "Big Joe" Williams*
> 1903–1982
> "King of the Nine-String Guitar"
> Big Joe sustained the longest recording career of any Mississippi
> bluesman, spanning seven decades (1929–1982). He was a true
> American Original.

Big Joe probably deserves the award for longest *continuous* blues career. Other blues artists of the 1920s and 1930s were "rediscovered" and began performing and recording again in the 1960s. But there was no need to rediscover Williams. He began playing and rambling at about age twelve and just kept on playing, touring, and recording until he died in 1982. He was part of the prewar blues era, the postwar era, the blues revival, and all the slack periods around those. (Despite what it says on his tombstone, however, experts believe that Williams's recording career began in 1935—even though he said that he had played on some earlier recordings.)

Williams was a thirty-four-year-old, seasoned musician on May 5, 1937, when he teamed up with Sonny Boy Williamson I and Robert Nighthawk for the session that launched the recording careers of Williamson and Nighthawk. Such Williams records as "Baby Please Don't Go" and "49 Highway Blues" directly influenced Muddy Waters and Howlin' Wolf. In the 1960s, living in the basement of a Chicago record store, Williams became a mentor to young white bluesmen including Charlie Musselwhite and Mike Bloomfield.

Another remarkable aspect of Williams's career is his invention and use of the nine-string guitar, which he made by installing three extra tuning pegs across the top of the headstock of a six-string and doubling three strings.

In his last years, Williams returned to Crawford and lived in a trailer, although he continued to tour or record when someone made him an offer. He died in a hospital in nearby Macon, Mississippi.

West Point

This town claims Howlin' Wolf as a native son, although he actually was born a ways out in the country, in a community called White Station or simply Whites. Wolf spent a lot of time in this larger town, however. He played in its jook joints and on its downtown streets.

In his teens, Wolf left this area and moved to the Delta. If he was looking for blues teachers, he went to the right place: he learned guitar from Charley Patton and harmonica from Sonny Boy Williamson II. Although he sang and played all of his life, Wolf would not make his name or his living as an artist until he was over forty, beginning in 1951, when he walked into Sam Phillips's recording studio in Memphis.

But even in the 1960s, when he was an established blues star living in Chicago, Howlin' Wolf would come back to the West Point area twice a year or so to hunt, a hobby that some say was more important to him than music.

- **Howlin' Wolf Statue**

To get there: Coming into town from the north on Highway 45 Alt, follow the signs into downtown, turning east on West Main (Highway 50). Just past the downtown area, turn right toward the park. Look for the windmill. The statue is next to it. There is a state blues marker near the statue.

Howlin' Wolf statue, West Point

Wolf's likeness stands in a park near the center of town. Made of black granite, it's a flat statue, like a cutout cookie, with the details etched in. It reads:

A memorial to the blues legend
HOWLIN' WOLF
Chester A. Burnett
June 10, 1910–January 10, 1976
Native of White Station, Clay County, MS
Rock and Roll Hall of Fame, Blues Hall of Fame, West Point, Miss.,
Hall of Fame
Given by Howlin' Wolf Blues Society of West Point MS Inc.
August 29, 1997

Erected during the 1997 Howlin' Wolf Blues Festival, the statue is based on a photo by Memphis photographer Ernest Withers,

Memorabilia at Howlin' Wolf Blues Museum, West Point

which was donated by Wolf's widow, Lillian. It was also Lillian's idea to place a bench next to the statue, so that she and others could sit and admire the statue and the sunset. There is a marker honoring her near the bench.

- ### Howlin' Wolf Blues Museum
  307 W. Westbrook
  (662)494-2921
  Open by appointment

Richard Ramsey, a rabid Wolf fan, operates this one-room museum. Ramsey gives a personal tour of the museum, will direct you or maybe accompany you around town to places connected to Wolf, and will happily talk for as long as you care to about all things Wolf-related.

The museum contains some unpublished photos of Wolf, bricks and siding from his childhood home in White Station, guitars and other items donated by Wolf sidemen Hubert Sumlin and Jody Williams, a chunk of railroad track from White Station (the track that may have inspired "Smokestack Lightning"), posters from European tours and a Fillmore East concert with Big Brother and the Holding Company, and some superb Wolf-inspired artwork donated by various artist-fans.

- ### Howlin' Wolf Memorial Blues Festival

The town's blues society presents this annual one-day, single-stage festival on the Friday of Labor Day weekend, the day before the town's Prairie Arts Festival. It is held indoors at the Civic, Sixth Street near Main.

Its out-of-the-way location has kept this festival from developing into the big draw that Delta festivals have become. West Point residents don't seem to care, and turn out to have a great time at their festival. Each year's headliner must have a connection to Howlin' Wolf. (More information is available at 662-494-2921.)

- **Anthony's**
  116 Main St.
  (662) 494-0316

This big restaurant is decorated faux-jook-joint style. It features blues on the first Saturday night of each month.

- **Chef David's BBQ**
  608 W. Main St.
  (662)494-5944

This restaurant is decorated in tribute to Wolf and plays his music constantly. It occasionally hosts live blues performances.

- **Wolf's Juke at Waverly Waters**
  2700 Old Waverly Road
  (662)494-1800

This "juke" is actually an elegant outdoor patio at a fishing lodge on the outskirts of town. Blues nights have been going on there monthly, with extra events around the Howlin' Wolf Blues Festival. Waverly Waters also offers rustic cabins and a group lodge for rent.

- **Cottrell Street**

Across the tracks from downtown, Cottrell Street is West Point's traditional black business street. It includes several old jooks where Wolf and other blues artists used to play. None of them remains open, but the Howlin' Wolf Blues Society has persuaded the city to buy them and delay demolition, with the idea that they might someday be restored or at least left as monuments in ruin.

Ferdinand Sykes's Rainbow Café, 318 Cottrell; the Melody Club, the gray building across the street; and Annie Garth's, a two-story building down the block on that side, all were popular jooks through at least the 1960s, and Wolf played at all three.

- **Murals**

On the side of Lyon Insurance Agency, 325 Commerce St. (at Westbrook St.), a mural depicts the history of West Point. Painted by visiting Italian artist Joe Vitrano and local artist Terry Craig during the 1998 festival, it includes an image of Howlin' Wolf playing guitar.

Another mural at High and Main streets has the words "Murff Row," the name of that neighborhood. Painted by high-school students, it includes a depiction of Wolf and other scenes of local history and geography, including a spooky blue picture of "the bottoms" that inspired his song.

Whites (White Station)

> To get there: From downtown West Point, go east on East Main, then left on Eshman Avenue. Go about three miles, then right on Hazelwood Road, then half a mile to White Station Road. Turn left and into the community.

This community, where Wolf actually grew up, is a few miles outside West Point. There isn't really anything to see, but some houses date from the days when Wolf—"Bigfoot Chester"—was a child. The house he lived in with his family is long gone; it stood on the now-wooded lot just before the store and barbecue pit. Many years later, Wolf still came back to White Station annually to visit relatives and friends and to hunt and fish.

"He used to sit and play on the porch while I was cooking biscuits," said Miss Annie Eggerson, the widow of Wolf's first cousin. "He sure could eat some chicken."

Aberdeen

Bluesman Booker T. Washington "Bukka" White was born in Houston, Mississippi, and grew up in the Delta. But he also lived for a while in Aberdeen, just thirty miles from his hometown. He apparently got involved there in the shooting that landed him in Parchman for almost three years. Upon his release, White went to Chicago and recorded twelve songs, including "Aberdeen Mississippi Blues," which contains this verse:

Aberdeen's my home but the mens don't want me around
They know I'll take these women, take them out of town

White settled in Memphis after the recording session. But he still had a relative working in the Aberdeen post office in 1963, when a letter arrived there addressed to "Bukka White, Old Blues Singer, c/o General Delivery, Aberdeen, Miss." The letter was from California blues fans John Fahey and Ed Denson, who took the song as a clue to White's whereabouts. The relative forwarded the letter to White, who responded to Fahey and Denson, leading to White's "rediscovery" and a new performing and recording career that lasted until his death in 1977.

Tupelo

All right, so Elvis Presley was not a bluesman. He was blues-drenched, however, not only in his choice of material (Big Mama Thornton's "Hound Dog," Arthur Crudup's "That's All Right," and Junior Parker's "Mystery Train," for example) but in his style of singing, acting, and dressing (before Elvis started shopping there, Lansky's in Memphis catered almost strictly to hip-dressed blacks). His music and style, in turn, immensely affected dozens of other performers and millions of regular folks, helping bring the blues lifestyle out into mainstream America.

Also, Elvis Presley—or Jimmie Rodgers, depending on the person's age—is often the only white singer mentioned by black blues singers as one of the blues singers they admire. Yes, real blues singers often consider the King of Rock 'n' Roll and the Father of Country Music *blues* singers. It is interesting that both Presley and Rodgers were from Mississippi.

- ### Elvis Presley's Birthplace
  306 Elvis Presley Dr.
  (662) 841-1245

At a total cost of $180, Vernon Presley built a two-room shotgun shack next to his parents' house to prepare for the birth of his only child. Vernon and Gladys Presley moved into it in December 1934, and Elvis was born January 8, 1935. The bank that had lent

Tupelo Hardware Company, the store where Elvis Presley bought his first guitar, Tupelo

Vernon the $180 soon repossessed the house. The Presleys lived in several other houses in Tupelo until 1948, when the family moved to Memphis. Most of their other Tupelo residences were near the birthplace; it is a neighborhood where you still see people sitting on the front porches of simple wooden houses.

The birthplace house is furnished in period goods that are *not* originals from when the Presleys lived there, such as a washboard and tub, pots, and framed pictures. The roof and ceiling have been replaced. The fireplace is original. It costs a dollar to enter the house and takes about a minute to see it.

On the birthplace grounds there is a small museum/gift shop, with an additional admission fee.

One building on the grounds that can be entered free of charge is the Elvis Presley Memorial Chapel, built in 1979 from fans' donations. It includes a pulpit from the First Assembly of God Church, which the Presleys attended in Elvis's early childhood, and a Bible that belonged to Elvis.

• Tupelo Fairgrounds

To get there: The fairgrounds are just off East Main Street, near Highway 45.

At age ten, Elvis gave what was probably his first performance in front of an audience. He sang (unaccompanied and into a microphone) "Old Shep" to several hundred people at the annual

Mississippi-Alabama Fair and Dairy Show at the Tupelo fair-grounds. It was a contest sponsored by a radio station on Children's Day at the fair, October 3, 1945. Elvis did not win.

• Tupelo Hardware Company
114 W. Main St.
(662) 842-4637

Charming inside and out, Tupelo Hardware Company is where Elvis Presley bought his first guitar. An old-fashioned, three-story hardware store right on Main Street, it still carries cast-iron cookware, knives, and other such non-hardware items. It no longer stocks guitars or guns, but it did in January 1946 when Elvis and his mother came in to buy one or the other. Fortunately, they decided on the guitar.

Forrest L. Bobo, the clerk who sold them the guitar for $7.75, wrote a letter about the transaction in 1979. The letter is on display along with an old guitar case and a few Elvis-related books. You can buy a yardstick with the name of the store and the words "Where Elvis bought his first guitar," a plastic guitar keychain with the same legend, or a T-shirt. Other than that, it's just a regular and very complete hardware store, with high wood shelves, a tin ceiling and other features that haven't changed since that fateful day. It's open 7 A.M. to 5:30 P.M. weekdays and 7 A.M. to noon Saturdays.

• McDonald's
372 S. Gloster St. (just south of Main St.)
(662) 844-5505

Fit for a king, this restaurant looks from the outside like an ordinary McDonald's but is full of Elvisiana. There are etchings of Elvis in the glass wall behind the ordering area and a case full of record albums, books, mugs, and knickknacks. The walls are covered with framed photos, articles, quotations, and other interesting writings.

North Mississippi Hills

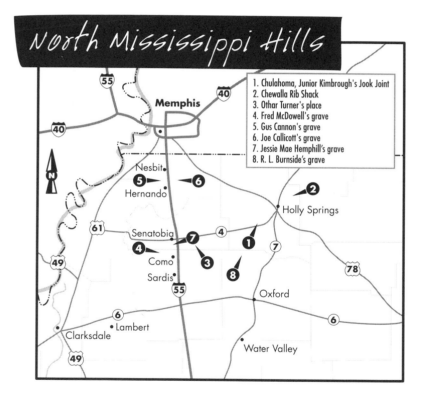

1. Chulahoma, Junior Kimbrough's Jook Joint
2. Chewalla Rib Shack
3. Othar Turner's place
4. Fred McDowell's grave
5. Gus Cannon's grave
6. Joe Callicott's grave
7. Jessie Mae Hemphill's grave
8. R. L. Burnside's grave

Memphis

Nesbit
Hernando

Holly Springs

Senatobia

Como

Sardis

Oxford

Lambert

Clarksdale

Water Valley

chapter 10

NORTH MISSISSIPPI HILL COUNTRY

The great folklorist Alan Lomax described what he heard in North Mississippi in the 1940s and 1950s as "an early phase of African-American music—not only that, but a clear revival of African tradition, kept alive in the Mississippi backwoods . . . we have found instruments, musical styles, and dancing that link the black South to the black Caribbean and, no question of it, to the dance of Africa as well."

In the hills, Lomax found such oddities as panpipes (also known as quills), fife-and-drum bands that used handmade cane fifes, and wall-mounted one-string guitars made from broom wire and played with a slide. He also found a hypnotic, grooving type of blues epitomized by Mississippi Fred McDowell.

The North Mississippi Hill Country sound lives on in Robert "Wolfman" Belfour and the many children, grandchildren and musical offspring of R. L. Burnside and Junior Kimbrough. The late music journalist Robert Palmer referred to this sound as "North Mississippi slash-and-drone trance-blues." Veteran jook joint musicians Kimbrough and Burnside, both of whom learned from McDowell in their youth, enjoyed international popularity in the wake of the 1990 documentary *Deep Blues* and

their successful (in blues terms, anyway) recordings on the Fat
Possum label based in Oxford, Mississippi.

Oxford

Although it is close to both the Delta and the hill country, Oxford does not have much of a local blues heritage. But the presence
of the University of Mississippi makes Oxford more inclined toward the study and commercialization of the blues than other
Mississippi communities.

WMAV, 90.3 FM, hosts a blues program from 10 P.M. to midnight Saturdays that is also broadcast by other NPR affiliates
throughout the state.

- ## University of Mississippi
  (662) 915-7211

Known locally as "Ole Miss," this campus is where thousands
of armed whites fought to try to keep out the first black student,
James Meredith, in 1962. The mob killed two journalists and
wounded dozens of U.S. marshals. President John F. Kennedy sent
in federal troops to secure Meredith's education and maintain the
peace. Nina Simone and Bob Dylan both wrote protest songs
about the incident. Bluesman J. B. Lenoir made a 1966 recording,
"Shot on James Meredith," about the later, nonfatal, shooting of
Meredith in a protest march away from the campus. One of the
few politically outspoken blues singers, Lenoir also had written
and recorded the 1965 "Down in Mississippi" (later covered by
Pops Staples).

Meredith himself is a blues fan who fondly describes a Jackson
jook joint performance by "Elmo"—Elmore James—in his mem-
oir, *Three Years in Mississippi*. And Meredith opened a 1998 lecture
at the university by dancing to James recordings. He explained
that he had listened to the blues for hours every day during his
struggle to enter the university, and that the music gave him the
strength to continue.

B. B. King, who also donated his records to the university's
Blues Archive, recorded a 1980 album here, *Live "Now Appearing"
at Ole Miss*.

The University of Mississippi has an indirect connection to the blues dating from 1885, when Will Dockery graduated from it. Ten years later, Dockery would found the Delta plantation where Charley Patton developed his music.

The university radio station, WUMS, 92.1 FM (662-915-5395), sometimes hosts blues programs, most often on Sundays.

- **The University of Mississippi Blues Archive**
  In Department of Archives and Special Collections, third floor of
  J. D. Williams Library
  (662) 915-7753

The room is open from 8 A.M. to 5 P.M. Mondays through Fridays.

At first glance, the Blues Archive looks disappointingly dull. One small display case, an array of posters, and a small rack of records are the only obvious things to look at. But its main functions are preservation and research. The joys of this room go not to the casual looker but to the person who, having obtained the staff's help in gathering items, takes at least a few hours to sit and listen to recordings, read books and magazines, watch videos, or flip through photographs.

Since most of the collection is locked up and the catalog is incomplete, one should ask for staff help immediately upon entering. Nearly any blues-related item you might want is here—if they can find it! Patience and perseverance will pay off.

Among the archive's thirty-three thousand recordings is a complete set of Document reissues—which means that every prewar blues recording is available. The postwar holdings are not so complete. B. B. King donated his collection of seven thousand records in 1982. That list itself is interesting to browse through for clues about influences on him. The video holdings include documentaries like *Deep Blues* and *The Land Where the Blues Began*, as well as privately made tapes of Mississippi artists and some curiosities like Othar Turner and Jessie Mae Hemphill's appearance on *Mister Rogers' Neighborhood*.

- ***Living Blues* Offices**
  Third floor, Hill Hall, University of Mississippi
  (662) 232-5742

As its name implies, *Living Blues* looks not just at old blues records but also at the living practitioners of the form. Another of its policies, which has sparked some controversy, is to write features only about African American artists (although it reviews records by blues-related artists of any color). A third important part of its philosophy is that an artist's musical quality is what matters, not how many records he or she sells.

Those policies distinguish *Living Blues* from other blues magazines and make it important to serious fans, scholars, and artists. Its consistently good writing, photography, and editing also help that image.

Jim O'Neal and Amy van Singel started the magazine in Chicago in 1970. They moved part of its operations to Oxford in 1983 and had sold it entirely by 1986. It is now part of the university's Center for the Study of Southern Culture.

The magazine's small staff works in a worn-out old building in an out-of-the-way corner of the campus. There isn't much to see there, but no one minds if you stop by for a quick visit. Subscriptions, T-shirts, and some back issues are available for purchase. If you want to read old issues, visit the Blues Archive.

- **University Museums**
  University Avenue at Fifth Street
  (662) 232-7673

The museum is open 10 A.M.–4:30 P.M. Tuesdays through Saturdays and 1–4 P.M. Sundays. Admission is free. Its folk art room, past the main exhibit area, contains four clay sculptures of animals by James "Son" Thomas of Leland, a bluesman who was also highly regarded as a folk artist. William Ferris, author of *Blues from the Delta*, donated the sculptures while he was professor of southern studies and anthropology at the university.

- **Nightclubs**

Half of Oxford's twenty thousand residents are college students, so there are several nightclubs that cater to them. **Parish Baker Pub**, 1101 Jackson Ave. (662-281-3325), **Two Stick**, 1107 Jackson Ave. (662-236-6639), and **Proud Larry's** (211 S. Lamar Blvd., 662-236-0050), all close to the town square, mix blues acts into their schedules. Check the weekly *Oxford Town* for listings of who is playing where.

Water Valley

- ## Fat Possum Records
  904 N. Main St.
  (662) 473-9994

Fat Possum, the self-proclaimed bad boys of the blues business, have moved from their original digs at 603 S. 16th St., Oxford, to this suburban location. Owners Bruce Watson and Matthew Johnson try to maintain their company's image by being hostile to the public and the press. But they have been known to be nice to visitors who show up at the door, sometimes even selling them merchandise. (A better place to shop for Fat Possum merchandise is at **Off Square Books**, 1110 Van Buren, Oxford.)

Founded in the 1990s, Fat Possum found its niche in selling Mississippi blues to suburban white youths nationally. To accomplish that, it often plays up its artists' jail records, gun enthusiasm and non-conformity and tries to cast blues as a variety of punk music. Sometimes it even pairs bluesmen with punkers, as on *A Ass Pocket of Whiskey*, on which R. L. Burnside plays with the Jon Spencer Blues Explosion. But despite such commercialism, and its branching out into other genres, Fat Possum has released a lot of fine blues albums. Among those are the works of Burnside, Junior Kimbrough, Cedell Davis, Paul "Wine" Jones, and T-Model Ford, the award-winning comeback CD by Solomon Burke, and reissues of earlier artists such as Fred McDowell and Robert Pete Williams.

The Water Valley Casey Jones Railroad Museum
South Main St.
(662) 473-2849

To get there: From the intersection of highways 6 and 7 in Oxford, take Highway 7 south. Continue on it for 17.2 miles, making sure to stay on 7 when the road forks. When you see the sign for Water Valley, follow it and drive 1.7 miles from the highway to Main Street. Turn right (south) onto Main Street and go 0.8 mile to the museum, a gray building with a red caboose behind it.

Open from 2 to 4 P.M. Thursdays through Saturdays (admission is free; donations are accepted), the museum is in the original Water Valley Depot, which was Casey Jones's base of operations from 1888 to April 30, 1900, when he died in a crash near Vaughan, Mississippi. There were hundreds of train crashes, many of them fatal, in 1900. But one of them is still famous today, with dozens of songs and two museums dedicated to it (the other is in Jackson, Tennessee).

The wreck that killed Casey Jones was not especially newsworthy or deadly (only one person, Jones, was killed). We remember it today only because Wallace "Wash" Saunders, a black engine wiper, wrote "The Ballad of Casey Jones" for his dead friend, a thirty-six-year-old white engineer. A traveling engineer heard Saunders sing the song and gave it to his brother, a vaudeville entertainer. Copyrighted by Frank and Bert Leighton, the song became a hit (on sheet music, in those days before recording) immediately. Legend has it that Saunders sold it for a pint of gin—but he may not have received even that.

The wreck has been commemorated musically in many more songs, of all genres, in the years since. (One non-blues version and a movie place the wreck in California, for some reason.) In 1928, bluesman Furry Lewis made it a poignant two-part epic, "Kassie Jones," recasting the accident as a family tragedy:

> *This morning I heard someone was dying, Mrs. Kassie's children on the doorstep crying:*
> *"Mama, Mama, I can't keep from crying. Papa got killed on the Southern line.*
> *On the Southern line. Papa got killed on the Southern line."*

Mississippi John Hurt also interpreted the accident in song. Titled "Talking Casey," Hurt atypically uses a slide on the number, using it to mimic the sounds of the train, the sheep that get on the track, and Jones cursing at them.

This small, well-tended museum has plenty of photos and artifacts relating to railroad history, and a whistle that might have belonged to Jones. It also recently acquired the train's bell and many other artifacts from the Casey Jones Museum in Vaughan, which has closed. The curators, J. K. Gurner and his son Jack, know a lot about the Jones incident and are happy to talk about it with visitors.

Abbeville

- **Shaw's Disco 9000**
  Highway 310
  (662) 551-1758

  To get there: From the intersection of highways 7 and 310, turn west on 310 and go about 50 yards, to the second turn-off on the right.

This jook sometimes features live blues or R&B on Fridays and Sundays, continuing the tradition of the burned-down, beloved Junior Kimbrough's in nearby Chulahoma.

Holly Springs

For a town of only seven thousand, Holly Springs is an interesting place. The Kimbrough and Burnside families, purveyors of the distinctive Hill Country blues, all live in the area. The world's best-known jook joint, Junior Kimbrough's, was near here (until it burned down). The town also has a weird record store and a bizarre Elvis museum. It also boasts two radio stations that sometimes play blues: WKRA, 92.7 FM, "Key 93," a commercial station that slips blues into its regular programming and has a blues show on Saturday mornings, and Rust College's noncommercial WURC, 88.1 FM.

The **Kudzu Festival,** held in November on the Holly Springs town square, includes authentic hill-country blues acts and a barbecue competition. **Kenny Brown's Hill Country Picnic,** organized by R. L. Burnside's longtime guitarist Brown, a local resident, happens in nearby Potts Camp on Fourth of July weekend.

- **Aikei Pro's Records Shop**
  125 N. Center St.
  (no phone)

Aikei Pro's is just a block and a half off the town square, yet it is invisible and unknown even to many downtown Holly Springs merchants. So don't bother asking anyone how to get there. Just walk or drive north from the Holly Springs town square, on Center Street. Keep going until you see the store on the right. It has a big

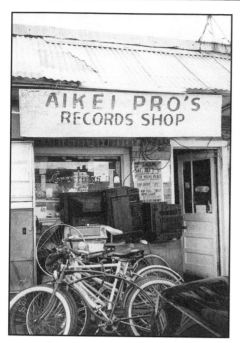

You can buy almost anything at Aikei Pro's Records Shop, Holly Springs

wooden sign and a tin roof, and people are hanging out in front. There is also a row of old bicycles for sale.

The owner, Aikei Pro (born David Caldwell, he renamed himself a Japanicized "Walker Bros.," he explains, as if that clears things up), might be hanging out in front of the store. Or he might be inside. If you arrive during regular business hours and find the doors locked, knock loudly. Or ask one of the people out front to help you find or rouse Aikei Pro.

When you enter, you'll think you're in a storage room or a workshop; disassembled car radios and stereo components lie in stacks all over the floor. But no, this awesomely cluttered space is the main room of a unique retail establishment. Records are everywhere—in piles, on racks, in piles on racks, under radios, behind radios. There are well-worn used records, old records still in their wrappers, empty record sleeves, sleeves with two or three records inside, 45s, cassettes, eight-tracks. There even are a few CDs, although Aikei Pro explains that he hasn't yet bought into the CD craze. "CDs can get old and scratched, and then you can't play them anymore," he explains. "A record, no matter how old it is, you can clean it up and it plays good as new."

Aikei Pro was a good friend of the late Junior Kimbrough, who often would hang out at the record store. Aikei Pro also is a serious fan of the music of Kimbrough and other North Mississippi blues artists. He collects books and articles about the area's blues tradition, and somehow finds them in the store, immediately, when he wants to show them to someone. Like most record store owners, Aikei Pro will talk about music for hours.

And talking with him is easier than shopping in his store. To really look through the records, you have to climb over or around the heaps of radios, move piles of records to get to other piles, carefully pick through precarious stacks. It is rather like archaeological digging, and the payoffs can be equally exciting. There are blues and gospel records, including ones by local performers. But you also might find Chet Atkins, El Chicano, or the Fat Boys amidst Leadbelly, Eddie Shaw, or Ray Charles. Of course, the records are not in alphabetical order. They are just piled all over the place. Prices are not marked.

Besides records, you also might find the pair of cowboy boots or roller skates you've been seeking, a peacock clock, a set of guitar strings, or an old issue of *Living Blues*. Don't forget to check out the bicycles outside. And if your car radio needs repair or replacement, this is the place.

• Graceland Too
200 E. Gholson Ave. at Randolph St.

Located in a residential area near the town square, this museum is in an old two-story white wooden house with a white cinder-block fence and stone lions in front. "Yes We're Open," the sign says. And it's true. They are open twenty-four hours a day, seven days a week (keep knocking if you get no answer, or come back in ten minutes and try again).

Owner Paul McLeod, with his slicked-back hair, sideburns, and paunch, doesn't really look like Elvis, but he somehow reminds you of him. His son, Elvis Aron Presley McLeod, comes even closer. These two men devote themselves to Elvis full time. Besides giving tours, they scan newspapers and monitor TV broadcasts just in case there is any reference to Elvis. If there is, they file it.

The house is full of records, books, clothing, photos, and artifacts with *some* connection, often tangential, to Elvis. The amazing part is not the collection but the level of human obsession. You may come to laugh but leave with a tear in your eye, touched by Paul McLeod's tremendous passion for his subject. Admission, which includes a tour, comes with a money-back guarantee. On your third visit, McLeod takes your picture in an Elvis-type jacket. The photo goes on the wall, and you become a lifetime member with free admission privileges.

Jessica McMorris (left), a great-niece of Mississippi John Hurt, and fellow student Dominique Howard working at Rust College radio station WURC, Holly Springs

- **Rust College**
  150 Rust Ave.
  (662) 252-8000

Established in 1866, this is the state's oldest historically black college and one of the five oldest in the nation. The Rust College Quartet made some fine religious "race" recordings in the 1920s, and the college still has a top-notch student gospel choir. The Northeast Mississippi Blues and Gospel Music Folk Festival, organized by Sylvester Oliver, an ethnomusicologist and Rust professor, was a favorite festival of many blues cognoscenti in the 1980s through the mid-1990s (unfortunately, it has not been held lately, but there is some talk of resuming it). The school's radio station, WURC, 88.1 FM (662-252-5881), includes gospel, jazz, and occasionally blues in its programming.

- **Chewalla Rib Shack (the original Junior Kimbrough's jook joint)**
  East of Holly Springs

  To get there: From the Holly Springs town square, drive east on Van Dorn. At the next traffic light, turn left onto Randolph. Proceed north to the first blinking traffic light, and turn right onto Salem Road, which is Highway 4. Continue on that out of town. After 1.3 miles the road splits. Bear to the right, following the sign for Chewalla Lake. You will be on Higdon Road. About 3 miles from the split, on the right, you will come to 2644 Higdon

Road, a big, modern log house. Chewalla Rib Shack is the small, red-stained, very old log cabin just past it. There is no sign.

Chewalla Rib Shack is the original Junior Kimbrough's jook joint. Don't go there hungry—the kitchen has been closed for years, along with the rest of the building. Its value is historic. For a few years in the early nineties, this one-room shack was the home of the blues.

The Chewalla Rib Shack's history began much earlier, how-ever—in about the 1820s, when someone picked up an ax and hewed rough logs from cypress, then fitted them together, Lincoln Logs-style, to build a six-room house near Byhalia.

About 160 years later, Sammy Greer, a counselor and football coach at Holly Springs High School, was on a fishing trip when he came across the remains of that house in the woods. With the prop-erty owner's permission, Greer began dismantling the house and hauling it off to his place near Holly Springs. "Every time I knocked off a log, a snake was sitting there," he says. "I killed thirty-six snakes while I was taking it apart. They ran me off one day."

But he persevered and salvaged enough of the logs to recon-struct a smaller version of the house. The corners of the logs still fit together snugly. Greer lived in the log cabin for a few years in the 1980s before turning it into a grocery store. Then he met bluesman Junior Kimbrough, who had been hosting all-day-and-all-night drinking-and-dancing sessions Sundays at his own home. Kimbrough wanted to move the sessions somewhere. Greer wanted to cook and sell barbecue. The two men teamed up to cre-ate the Chewalla Rib Shack, Kimbrough's first actual jook joint. The place opened in June 1990. But first, Kimbrough advised Greer on interior design. "I had it decorated with antiques, real nice," Greer says. "Junior, he said to clear it. 'That ain't gonna work with the type of people we're going to be getting in here.'"

The place was successful immediately. "They'd be jam-packed like sardines in a can," Greer says. People would arrive early in the day, driving in from miles away, and drink and socialize on the grounds until the musicians arrived. Since the shack was so small, many people would remain outside all evening, digging on the mu-sic. Those who had too much to drink were welcome to lie down and sleep it off on the grounds, or in one of the two tiny "cathouses" in the back and to the left. Kimbrough himself lived for a while in the cathouse on the right. "The law was not going to bother you. I was the police here," Greer explains. "We never had any problems. We'd go all night, selling beer and food and bootleg whiskey."

In the 1991 documentary *Deep Blues*, Jessie Mae Hemphill performs two solo numbers at Chewalla Rib Shack. Junior Kimbrough, who hadn't yet made an album, also plays there in the film. "If you want to hear him, you have to go jookin'," Robert Palmer, the narrator, advises.

After a few years, Greer became tired of the jook joint business. Kimbrough moved his jook to a bigger building which has since burned down.

The Chewalla Rib Shack remains standing, as it probably would even if a tornado hit. A tragedy befell the antique cypress structure a few years ago, however. Greer had been renting it out, and one day he came home to a smiling tenant and a red-stained shack. "He said, 'Look—I stained the logs for you. Doesn't it look nice?'" Greer recalls. "I fell down on my knees and said, 'Oh, my God! You ruined my shack!' I ran him out the same day." Greer has since spent hundreds of dollars and hours bleaching and sandblasting, but a red stain remains on Marshall County's original house of blues.

The house is on private property and is guarded by a dog, so look at it from the street, unless you have permission to get closer. There are tentative plans to reopen it as a take-out restaurant.

Chulahoma

• Junior Kimbrough's Jook Joint

To get there: From the intersection of highways 78 and 7 on the south edge of Holly Springs, drive south on 7, 1½ miles, to Highway 4, then west on 4 for 10 miles. Junior's was just past Muse Road, on the north side of the road.

Until a fire destroyed it on April 6, 2000, Junior's was perhaps the wildest blues spot in the world. A 130-year-old building, it had served as a horse stable, a general store, a cocktail lounge, and perhaps as a church at various times before David "Junior" Kimbrough took it over and turned it into a jook joint in the early 1990s (he relocated here from the Chewalla Rib Shack east of Holly Springs).

Every Sunday night during those years, people danced to Kimbrough's "cotton patch blues"—a hypnotic, groove-based style.

"My songs, they have just the one chord, there's none of that fancy stuff you hear now, with lots of chords in one song," Kimbrough once told an interviewer. "If I find another chord I leave it for another song."

After Kimbrough died on January 17, 1998, at age sixty-seven, his music and his jook joint lived on. Two of his sons—drummer/jook joint manager Kinney and singer-guitarist David (who recorded a 1994 album, *I Got the Dog in Me*, as David Malone)—kept it going strong, with help from relatives, neighbors, and visitors. Among those neighbors was R. L. Burnside, who often played here.

An arson-caused fire destroyed the building, which was uninsured, along with the musical instruments, sound system, and many priceless mementos, including the late Johnny Hughes's paintings on the wood rafters. The fire also closed the business. Despite worldwide sympathy, offers to help and support for the music, plans to rebuild or replace the jook joint never were carried out.

Hudsonville

- ## Junior Kimbrough's Grave

    To get there: From Holly Springs, drive 10 miles north on Highway 7. One mile past Bolden's Grocery, turn left on Clear Creek Road. Go 1 mile, then left on Kimbrough Church Road for 1/3 mile. You will see a small graveyard on the left. Pull in on the dirt road and park. Walk straight in, away from Kimbrough Church Road and about 20 yards to the left.

Junior Kimbrough, the patriarch of Holly Springs blues, is buried in a small country cemetery, with his brother Felix and Felix's wife, Irene, lying next to him. The front of Kimbrough's headstone reads:

MEET ME IN THE CITY
In Memory of legendary
Bluesman
David "Junior" Kimbrough
July 28, 1930
Jan. 17, 1998

The back reads:

"Junior Kimbrough is
The beginning and
end of all music."

Street sign near Junior Kimbrough's grave, Hudsonville

"Meet Me in the City" is one of Kimbrough's songs. The quotation on the back is by Charlie Feathers, a white rockabilly artist who grew up in this area and admitted being greatly influenced by Kimbrough. The headstone was erected in February 1999, about a year after Kimbrough's death, with funds raised from his fans in Oxford. Visitors often leave bottles of beer in tribute.

Como

- **Fred McDowell's Grave**

  To get there: From Interstate 55 take exit 257, the Como exit, and proceed west on Highway 310, through Como, for 4.5 miles, to Hammond Hill Road. Go north three miles to the intersection of Hammond Hill and Tate-Panola Road. Hammond Hill M. B. Church is on the northeast corner; the church cemetery is on the northwest corner. Park in the church parking lot and walk across the street to the cemetery. Walk over the knoll and into the small, crowded cemetery, which is surrounded by fields. McDowell's grave is in the middle of a row toward the back.

About three feet tall, the stone has a photo of the blues singer and the inscription:

"MISSISSIPPI FRED"
McDowell
Jan. 12, 1904–July 3, 1972

Below the date is the Masonic symbol, reflecting McDowell's proud status as a high-level member of that organization. Under that is another inscription:

Ester Mae McDowell
1906–1980

Despite their identical middle names, Ester Mae is not the same person as Annie Mae McDowell, the wife who accompanied McDowell on his gospel recordings. Toward the end of his life, McDowell left Annie Mae for Ester Mae. He had no children with either wife, but Annie Mae's children are the heirs to whatever royalties his recordings and songs continue to generate.

McDowell adapted the old spiritual "You Got to

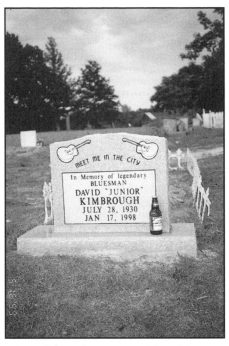

Junior Kimbrough's grave, with beer left in tribute, Hudsonville

Move" to his style. His version was, in turn, covered by the Rolling Stones, making it by far the best-known song in McDowell's repertoire. His estate collected royalties on the Stones' cover, which appeared on their hit album *Sticky Fingers* in 1972, the year of McDowell's death. The back of his gravestone bears a verse from the song:

You may be high,
You may be low,
You may be rich, child
You may be poor
But when the Lord
Gets ready
You got to move

Fred McDowell was born in 1906 in Rossville, Tennessee. He took up guitar at about age twenty and moved to Memphis in the late 1920s, but somehow was not among the many bluesmen recorded in that era. He moved to Hudsonville, Mississippi, in

Back side of Mississippi Fred McDowell's grave, Como

about 1940 and to Como in the 1950s. He played strictly locally until 1959, when Alan Lomax stopped by and recorded him. A few years later, Chris Strachwitz of Arhoolie Records also recorded McDowell, and his career took off.

In the 1960s, McDowell performed at colleges and festivals throughout the United States and Europe. But he continued to live in a trailer in Como, where fans and aspiring musicians—including Bonnie Raitt, who based her slide style on his—would stop by to visit and listen to him play. And, despite his international success, McDowell continued to work at the Stuckey's store and gas station that stood on the southeast corner of Highway 310 and Interstate 55. His agent, Dick Waterman, once asked him why he kept the job.

"All my friends are here, so you know I'm going to be here," Mc-Dowell told him. "There's nothing for me to do at that trailer all day. And if a car comes in and needs gas, I might as well go fill it up. I'm going to be here anyway. They give me thirty-two dollars a week, and I'm just *stealing* that money, Dick." Stuckey's also served as an office for McDowell, who did not have a telephone at home. The other employees got used to receiving calls from people with strange accents: "We got Paris, France, on the phone, Fred."

Senatobia

- ## Jessie Mae Hemphill's Grave

  To get there: On Highway 51 just south of Senatobia, on the east side of the road, look for the entrance to Senatobia Memorial Cemetery. Park as soon as you enter. Look for her large stone to the left of the entrance, close to the street.

Decorated with an electric guitar, music notes, and an inset picture, the grave marker reads:

JESSIE MAE HEMPHILL

Oct 18 1923

July 22 2006

"When we all rise together and face the rising sun,
Lord, help the poor and needy in this land."

Song written and composed by Jessie

Jessie Mae Hemphill, "the She-Wolf," was the granddaughter of Sid Hemphill, a fife-and-drum musician recorded by Alan Lomax. And she was the niece of Rosa Lee Hill, a singer-guitarist also recorded by Lomax. Jessie Mae Hemphill learned music from, and worked with, both of these musical relatives. She sat in occasionally with other artists and at fife-and-drum picnics, and played at family gatherings. But it was not until around 1980, when she was in her late fifties, that she began recording and performing professionally.

Singing and playing guitar and foot-controlled tambourine, Hemphill made hypnotic music, firmly within the Hill Country style but with the fife-and-drum rhythmic influence and a woman's perspective. She made several acclaimed albums, toured North America and Europe several times and appeared on *Mister Rogers' Neighborhood* and in the movie *Deep Blues*. In 1993 Hemphill suffered a stroke that prevented her from playing guitar. She also renounced blues in favor of church music for a while. But, urged on by artists who admired her, she began to sing the blues again, and to play the tambourine.

Harmontown

- ## R. L. Burnside's Grave

  To get there: From Highway 55 in Como, drive about 20 miles east on Highway 310. Or from Highway 7 between Holly Springs and Abbeville, drive

Melvin Burnside, bounty hunter and jook joint manager, at the grave of his father, bluesman R. L. Burnside, Harmontown

about 10 miles west on Highway 310. Turn south at a sign for Free Springs United Methodist Church. That church is half a mile south of the highway, but go past that church and its cemetery and continue straight down the middle road another half a mile to Free Springs CME Church. Park and walk straight back from the church, to the graves on the right.

Taught by Fred Mc-Dowell and inspired by John Lee Hooker and Muddy Waters, R. L. Burnside began playing in his youth but didn't become well known until he was well into his sixties. With his friend and neighbor Junior Kimbrough, Burnside became one of the icons of North Mississippi Hill Country Blues, which took over the blues world in the 1990s.

A visit to Burnside's bucolic grave in a remote village shows just how far he came. The internationally popular blues artist asked to be buried here, flanked by the unmarked graves of his mother Josie Gardiner and daughter Sandra K. Burnside.

His heart-shaped stone, decorated with two guitars, reads:

THE LEGEND
R. L. (Rural)
Burnside
Nov. 23, 1926
Sept 1, 2005
In Loving Memory

For most of his life, Burnside made his living as a sharecropper and fisherman, playing music on the side. He made some solo acoustic recordings (which many fans consider his best) in the 1960s and some with an electric family band in the 1980s. But he broke through with his appearance in the 1990 documentary *Deep Blues* and his subsequent tours and albums. Beyond establishing himself as a major blues artist, Burnside re-established Mississippi as the home of the blues and the jook joint as the heart of it. Every Burnside performance included long jokes and traditional toasts, along with some of the most vital blues since the early days of Hooker and Waters.

Gravel Springs

- **Othar Turner's Picnics**
  (662) 562-7606

  To get there: Take Interstate 55 to the Como exit (number 257) and proceed east, away from the town of Como, on Highway 310. After 2½ miles, turn north onto Hunter Chapel Road. The road's name changes to Gravel Springs Road when you cross the county line. Keep going, 4 miles total, over a narrow wood bridge and past Hunter Chapel on your right, until you get to the first stop sign, O. B. McClinton Road. Turn right and drive about half a mile, until you see a lot of parked cars and hear music. Park on the road and walk onto the farm, on the south side of the road. (This is a private residence. Please don't drop in anytime except on the picnic weekend.)

Of the many astounding discoveries of Alan Lomax's long and illustrious career—including making the first recordings of Muddy Waters and Fred McDowell—Lomax considers the discovery of the African American fife-and-drum tradition his major accomplishment.

The origins of this music remain obscure. It sounds nothing like the martial fife-and-drum sound associated with colonial New England. And the fife used by black southerners is not carved from wood, but cut from natural cane. The cane is hollowed out, and the finger holes are burned in, with a hot poker. The player blows the fife flute-style, creating a soaring sound that can be heard over the drums for miles around. Two snare drummers and a bass drummer keep the swinging beat.

The music is associated with summer picnics held on farms in the North Mississippi hills. Animals are butchered and barbecued; beer and moonshine are served; the fife and drums play; and the people dance, drawn to the festivities by the sound of the music. "And I didn't want to miss nothing," recalled John Bowden, who was born in the area in 1903 and played fife until the 1970s. "I hear a drum hit, and, man, I just, *whew*, I'd have a fit."

Lomax discovered fife-and-drum music at one of these picnics, hosted by Sid Hemphill in 1942 (Hemphill's granddaughter, Jessie Mae Hemphill, played drum in her grandfather's groups before becoming a popular blues singer-guitarist). The picnics were common in those days. Now the tradition remains in the hands of one remarkable family.

The head of that family was Othar Turner, who died February 26, 2003, at the age of ninety-four. He made and played a mean fife (or "fice," as he pronounced it), sang the blues and spirituals, and led the world's premier fife-and-drum ensemble, the Rising Star Fife and Drum Band. Turner was also, in the 1980s, perhaps the unlikeliest-ever guest on the television program *Mister Rogers' Neighborhood*. Drummers Abe Young and Jessie Mae Hemphill accompanied him on the show.

The group usually included at least one of Turner's children and one of his grandchildren. Throughout his later years, Turner showed no sign of imminent retirement, but there was another talented fife player waiting in the wings—his granddaughter Sharda Thomas, born in 1990, who has mastered the physically demanding instrument and also has the poise, confidence, and charisma to lead the band and charm the listeners.

Besides doing farm work and playing music, Turner also threw great picnics at his farm. Despite Turner's death, the family still holds the annual picnics on the last weekend of August. They feature live music from the family band, which alternates sets with electric blues jams by local musicians or perhaps a disc jockey. Home-raised goat and pig barbecue is served, along with coleslaw and cold beer or soft drinks to wash it down.

The picnics last all weekend, starting on Friday night, picking up again Saturday afternoon and going way into the night, and then again on Sunday. Admission is free, and food and drink are sold at very reasonable prices.

People stand around and talk with friends, drink, eat, dance, and laugh. As the night goes on, the dancing becomes wilder. The fife-and-drum musicians move slowly around the lot as they play, and the dancers follow them, gyrating in response and spurring on the musicians to keep the beat going. These are community

events, held so that the neighbors can have fun. Visitors from outside are welcome. But don't expect things to happen when you
want them to. This is a picnic, not a concert. And you are a guest,
not a customer. Relax, be friendly, have fun, and ask permission
before sticking a camera in someone's face.

Sardis

• Sardis Courthouse
215 Pocahontas St. (Pocahontas is parallel to and just across the railroad
tracks from Main St.)

Sardis no longer has a county jail. Prisoners are taken to the jail
at the other county seat, Batesville. But before this building was
built in 1972, the site had an old courthouse dating from the early
1900s, with a jail behind it.

That jail is where Robert Lockwood, Jr., and Sonny Boy
Williamson II were sentenced to twenty-one days for vagrancy in
about 1935. As Lockwood later told writer Robert Palmer, they
were locked up on a Friday:

> On Saturday, we went up on the second floor and raised the
> jailhouse windows and started playing. In a matter of minutes, the jail-
> house was surrounded with people. There was a little fence down there,
> about as big as the one on the side of my yard, and the people started
> throwing nickels and dimes and quarters over that fence. The trusty
> went out there and picked the money up, and we knew he didn't bring it
> all to us. We knew *he* got fat, but when he turned it in to us, we had
> made four hundred dollars. That day. The next night, the high sheriff
> and the deputy sheriff came and asked us did we want to go out and
> make some money. Sid and Ed was their names. And for the next
> twenty-one days, they took us out to serenade for the whites, every night
> but Sunday. They'd take up the money for us, pass the hat, make the
> people not put nothin' less than a dollar in it. And then they'd take us
> back and put us in jail. Now, mind you, they was bustin' places for corn
> whiskey right and left, and they gave us a whole gallon of that. We had
> girls comin' to the jailhouse and spendin' the night. We was eatin' from a
> hotel down the street. So it really wasn't like bein' in no jailhouse. But it
> was terrible 'cause it was against our will.

The town still has a historic downtown, reminiscent of what it
must have looked like when Lockwood and Sonny Boy were there
playing the jailhouse blues.

Hernando-Nesbit

- ## Gus Cannon's Grave

  To get there: From Interstate 55, take exit 284, Nesbit Road–N. Hernando. Go west onto Pleasant Hill Road. Drive 0.2 mile to Highway 51 and turn right. One mile up the road, on the left, there is a large cemetery between two churches, across from the Place Pub. The first church is Oak Grove M. B., 2541 N. Highway 51. Cannon is buried about halfway back from the road and a quarter of the way in from the right.

He has two stones—one upright and one flat. The upright one has an engraved drawing of a jug over a banjo and says:

> Gus Cannon 1874–1979
> Baby Let Your Mind Roll On
> Composer—songwriter—jug band pioneer
> Pride of Memphis—Beale Street Balladeer

The small flat stone, right in front of the large upright one, reads:

> Gus Cannon
> September, 1875
> Oct. 15, 1979
> May he rest in peace.

Note that the two stones disagree on the year of Cannon's birth—and both might be way off. Most sources list September 12, 1885, as the date of his birth. Whichever date is correct, Gus Cannon was one of the oldest blues singers to record. His main instrument, the banjo, predates the guitar in African American musical tradition. Cannon also played the jug, on a rack around his neck. With the incredible harpist Noah Lewis and guitarist Ashley Thompson, Cannon formed Cannon's Jug Stompers. They were a premier jug band of the 1920s, with such hits as "Walk Right In" and "Viola Lee Blues."

- ## Joe Callicott's Grave

  To get there: Callicott's grave is near Interstate 55's exit 284, the same exit as Gus Cannon's grave, but they are on opposite sides of the interstate. To get to Callicott's, head east on Pleasant Hill Road for 3.2 miles, to Getwell Road, and turn left. Go 0.4 mile to Mount Olive C. M. E. Church, on the left. Park at the church and go up the sidewalk that leads into the small cemetery north of it. Walk straight in from where the sidewalk ends. Callicott's grave is almost at the far side.

The stone reads:

JESUS ON MY BOND
Mississippi
Joe
Callicott
1899–1969
An original medicine show 'songster' who played through the vast Delta from 1918 until his death Recorded for Arhoolie Records

This cemetery has quite a few hand-carved or hand-painted stones that you might find interesting. Callicott's headstone, however, like those of many

Handmade grave marker in cemetery where bluesman Joe Callicott is buried, Mount Olive C. M. E. Church, Pleasant Hill

blues singers, was professionally inscribed, and is bigger and more modern than most of those around it. This is not because blues artists' families have the means for such extravagance, but because the stones are usually erected by fans or record companies, often long after the musician's death.

"Mississippi" Joe Callicott was born in Nesbit, lived there most of his life, and is buried there. Callicott was friends with Frank Stokes and Garfield Akers, fellow North Mississippi bluesmen. He recorded "Traveling Mama Blues" and "Fare Thee Well Blues" in 1930—his only recording session until 1967, a few years before his death, when folklorist George Mitchell tracked him down in Nesbit and recorded him. One of Callicott's songs from the later session, which he called "Love My Baby Blues," has been covered by Ry Cooder as "France Chance." Callicott's complete recorded works are available on *Mississippi Delta Blues, Vol. 2, "Blow My Blues Away."*

RECOMMENDED READING

Albertson, Chris. *Bessie*. New York: Stein and Day, 1972.

Booth, Stanley. *Rythm Oil: A Journey through the Music of the American South*. New York: Pantheon Books, 1991.

Bowman, Rob. Booklet in *Malaco Records: The Last Soul Company* (CD box set). Jackson, Miss.: Malaco Records, 1999.

———. *Soulsville, U.S.A.: The Story of Stax Records*. New York: Schirmer Books, 1997.

Broonzy, William. *Big Bill Blues: William Broonzy's Story as Told to Yannick Bruynoghe*. New York: Da Capo Press, 1992.

Calt, Stephen. *I'd Rather Be the Devil: Skip James and the Blues*. New York: Da Capo Press, 1994.

Calt, Stephen, and Gayle Dean Wardlow. *King of the Delta Blues: The Life and Music of Charlie Patton*. Newton, N.J.: Rock Chapel Press, 1988.

Charters, Samuel. *The Blues Makers*. New York: Da Capo Press, 1991.

Danchin, Sebastian. *'Blues Boy': The Life and Music of B. B. King*. Jackson: University Press of Mississippi, 1998.

Davis, Francis. *The History of the Blues: The Roots, the Music, the People from Charley Patton to Robert Cray*. New York: Hyperion, 1995.

Doughty, Junior. "Junior's Juke Joint." Web site. www.deltablues.net

Edwards, Honeyboy (as told to Janis Martinson and Michael Robert Frank). *The World Don't Owe Me Nothing: The Life and Times of Delta Bluesman Honeyboy Edwards*. Chicago: Chicago Review Press, 1997.

Erlewine, Michael, Vladimir Bogdanov, Chris Woodstra, and Cub Koda, eds. *AMG All Music Guide to the Blues: The Experts' Guide to the Best Blues Recordings.* San Francisco: Miller Freeman Books, 1996.

Evans, David. *Big Road Blues: Tradition and Creativity in the Folk Blues.* Berkeley: University of California Press, 1982.

Ferris, William. *Blues from the Delta.* New York: Da Capo Press, 1984.

Garon, Paul, and Beth Garon. *Woman with Guitar: Memphis Minnie's Blues.* New York: Da Capo Press, 1992.

Guralnick, Peter. *Last Train to Memphis: The Rise of Elvis Presley.* Boston: Little, Brown and Co., 1994.

———. *Searching for Robert Johnson.* New York: E. P. Dutton, 1989.

Handy, W. C. *Father of the Blues: An Autobiography.* New York: Da Capo Press, 1941.

King, B. B., with David Ritz. *Blues All Around Me: The Autobiography of B. B. King.* New York: Avon Books, 1996.

LaVere, Stephen C. Liner notes to *Robert Johnson: The Complete Recordings.* New York: Columbia Records, 1990.

Levine, Lawrence W. *Black Culture and Black Consciousness: Afro-American Folk Thought from Slavery to Freedom.* New York: Oxford University Press, 1977.

Lomax, Alan. *The Land Where the Blues Began.* New York: Pantheon Books, 1993.

McKee, Margaret, and Fred Chisenhall. *Beale Black & Blue.* Baton Rouge: Louisiana State University Press, 1981.

Mitchell, George. *Blow My Blues Away.* Baton Rouge: Louisiana State University Press, 1971.

Oliver, Paul. *Blues Fell This Morning: Meaning in the Blues.* New York: Cambridge University Press, 1960.

———. *Conversation with the Blues.* New York: Cambridge University Press, 1965.

———. *The Story of the Blues.* Boston: Northeastern University Press, 1969.

Oshinsky, David M. *"Worse than Slavery": Parchman Farm and the Ordeal of Jim Crow Justice.* New York: Free Press, 1996.

Palmer, Robert. *Deep Blues.* New York: Penguin, 1981.

Peabody, Charles. "Notes on Negro Music." *Journal of American Folk-Lore* 16 (1903): 148–52.

Raichelson, Richard M. *Beale Street Talks: A Walking Tour Down the Home of the Blues.* Memphis: Arcadia Records, 1994.

Ryan, Marc. *Trumpet Records: An Illustrated History with Discography.* Milford, N. H.: Big Nickel Productions, 1992.

Thompson, Robert Farris. *Flash of the Spirit: African and Afro-American Art and Philosophy.* New York: Vintage Books, 1984.

Tooze, Sandra B. *Muddy Waters: The Mojo Man.* Toronto: ECW Press, 1997.

Trynka, Paul. *Portrait of the Blues.* New York: Da Capo Press, 1996.

Wardlow, Gayle Dean. *Chasin' That Devil Music: Searching for the Blues.* San Francisco: Miller Freeman, 1998.

Wilson, Charles Reagan, and William Ferris. *Encyclopedia of Southern Culture.* Chapel Hill: University of North Carolina Press, 1989.

RECOMMENDED LISTENING

To get in the mood for your trip, to listen to as you drive down Highway 61, and to bring back memories when you get home, here are some recordings to get you started in the Mississippi blues. The albums on this list include great music by most of the artists discussed in this book. All are available on CD and highly recommended by the author.

Cannon's Jug Stompers, *Cannon's Jug Stompers (1927–1930)*. Herwin 208. One of the rare banjo players in the blues (sometimes he even used a slide on it), Gus Cannon worked with the extraordinary harpist Noah Lewis and other musicians to create these charming, often beautiful songs that they stomped out on the streets of Memphis.

Bo Carter, *Greatest Hits, 1930–1940*. Yazoo 1014. The prolific but now-underappreciated Carter was one of the dominant bluesmen of the 1930s, combining dazzling and unusual guitar work with erotically teasing lyrics. This collection includes a few tunes by the Mississippi Sheiks, a string band that Carter belonged to part time.

John Lee Hooker, *The Legendary Modern Recordings 1948–1954*. Virgin 39658. Hooker, a Clarksdale native, probably made more recordings and more money than any other bluesman. This is the one to get for a full dose of that heavy, foot-stomping, solo electric-guitar boogie. It's a sound imitated by many, but no one else does it like this.

Mississippi John Hurt, *Avalon Blues: The Complete 1928 Okeh Recordings.* Sony 64986. "Well sir, I just make it sound like I think it should," is how Hurt once explained his prodigious, unique talents to an interviewer. Although he remained a fine performer right up to his death in 1966, these recordings (cleaned up sonically) are the ones that established his warm, folksy style and deceptively intricate guitar playing.

Robert Johnson, *King of the Delta Blues Singers.* Columbia/ Legacy CK 65746. Sixteen tracks by the late-1930s artist whose life, myth, and music epitomize the blues for many people. This clean-sounding collection leaves out the back-to-back alternate tracks that make some other Johnson sets laborious to listen to.

Frank Frost, *Jelly Roll Blues.* Paula 20. In the mid-1960s, when everyone thought the blues' heart had moved to Chicago, out came this laid-back but thoroughly modern set from Helena, Arkansas bluesman Frost—with the great, rarely recorded Arthur Williams on harp.

Skip James, *Complete Early Recordings.* Yazoo 2009. The eerie, otherworldly sounds of this enigmatic Bentonia singer-guitarist-pianist are something everyone needs to hear. James recorded again in the 1960s, but these 1931 recordings are his most brilliant. Some of the tracks are quite scratchy, but the music is masterful.

Paul "Wine" Jones, *Mule.* Epitaph 80305. This album of powerful, 1990s electric jook-joint blues has a raw, unfinished quality that only adds to its appeal. As they used to suggest on 1960s rock albums—play this record at maximum volume!

Junior Kimbrough, *All Night Long.* Fat Possum 1002. With his son Kinney on drums and neighbor Garry Burnside (son of bluesman R. L.) on bass, Junior Kimbrough's first album, which he didn't make until he was in his 60s, captures the feel of this North Mississippi bluesman's hypnotic, deceptively simple sound.

Albert King, *King of the Blues Guitar.* Atlantic 8213-2. This one has King backed by Booker T and the MGs and the Memphis Horns—the Stax sound at its bluesiest. The CD includes all of King's classic LP *Born Under a Bad Sign,* plus all of his Stax singles.

B. B. King, *Great Moments with B. B. King.* MCA MCAD–4124. There is a baffling array of B. B. King CDs available, but this compilation of his 1960s work is a good one to start with. It includes a live version of his "Gambler's Blues," which kicks off with a long, burning guitar solo that might be his best ever.

Fred and Annie Mae McDowell, *My Home Is in the Delta.* Testament 2208 Fred McDowell's rock-solid North Mississippi sound continues to resonate through his influence on R. L. Burnside, Junior Kimbrough, Bonnie Raitt, and others, as well as through his own large catalog of powerful recordings. This haunting collection, with his wife helping on vocals, offers blues and spirituals.

Memphis Jug Band, *Memphis Jug Band.* Yazoo 1067. On the verge of chaos but somehow always right, this great jug band featured funny lyrics, snappy vocal interplay, harp and kazoo solos soaring over the guitars, and, anchoring it all, that booming jug bass line.

Memphis Minnie, *Bumble Bee.* Indigo 2005. A good sampling by this prolific, influential but often underrated guitar virtuoso and hip blueswoman who was one of the dominant blues artists of the 1930s. "When the Levee Breaks," "Black Rat Swing," and the dazzling instrumental "Let's Go to Town" are among the many classic tracks here.

Little Milton, *Greatest Hits.* Malaco 7477. Milton Campbell had made some wild music for Sun in the 1950s, but the 1960s' Chess tracks on this album capture the period when he had found his own voice and was turning out exquisite work such as "Annie Mae's Café," "The Blues Is Alright" and "Walking the Backstreets and Crying." One of the blues' finest electric guitarists and singers, Milton for some reason has yet to "cross over" to white American and foreign audiences the way his old buddy B. B. King has.

Little Brother Montgomery, *Complete Recorded Works (1930–1936).* Document 5109. This Louisiana singer-pianist became a Chicago blues fixture from the 1940s on. Before that, he spent a lot of time in Mississippi—especially Jackson and Vicksburg, the riverside town that inspired him to write the lovely "Vicksburg Blues." Montgomery was a virtuoso who has influenced every other blues pianist since.

Charley Patton, *Founder of the Delta Blues.* Yazoo 1020. To ears accustomed to modern recordings, it will take awhile to get past the surface scratches (yes, even on a CD—these were mastered from worn 78s, since no masters survived) and muddy recording values. But take the time and let your ears adjust and hear the music. Patton was the Delta blues' first star, and still one of the most impassioned artists ever to enter a studio. His songs are varied, intricate, entertaining, and inimitable.

Lonnie Pitchford, *All Around Man.* Rooster Blues 2629. This dazzling 1994 album presents the awesomely talented young bluesman on Robert Johnson–style acoustic numbers, full-band electric blues, one-string romps, introspective piano, and even fake harmonica. Unfortunately Pitchford died (in 1998 at age 43) before he could make a second album—but he sure packs a ton of music into this one.

Jimmie Rodgers, *The Essential Jimmie Rodgers.* RCA 67500. White blues did not begin with Stevie Ray Vaughan or even with Elvis Presley, as this collection proves. This white Mississippian became a huge pop star in the late 1920s and is still credited as the Father of *Country* Music. Yet he was actually singing his own style of the blues, with yodels added.

Bobby Rush, *Best of Bobby Rush.* La Jam 6. There isn't yet a good representation culled from Rush's hundreds of recordings, many of which are no longer in print. This one includes a few of the chittlin' circuit king's suggestive hits—"Sue" and "What's Good for the Goose . . . "—but misses many others. Pick it up to hold you over until you get to see his live show. Featuring booty-shaking dancers, frequent costume changes, hilarious stories and interplay with the audience, a Rush show is something that can never really be captured on a recording, anyway.

Bessie Smith, *Essential Bessie Smith.* Columbia/Legacy 64922. Although she was born in Chattanooga, Tennessee, the Empress of the Blues died in Mississippi and often performed here. This two-CD set is a good introduction to this powerful, sophisticated-yet-downhome singer of sassy, witty songs, who fit into both the blues and jazz worlds.

James "Son" Thomas, *Beefsteak Blues.* Evidence 26095. This high-voiced downhome bluesman was beloved throughout Mississippi and, in the final decade before his 1993 death, to festival-goers throughout the world. Yet there is not much of his work available on commercial recordings. This collection gives a good sample of his electric and acoustic playing, and a glimpse of his eccentric personality.

Mose Vinson, *Piano Man*. Center for Southern Folklore. Born in 1917, this piano man played at countless jooks and parties, sat in on many of the classic Sun recordings of the 1940s and 1950s (he worked at the studio as a janitor but his musical ability was noticed), and in his final years was the house act at Memphis's Center for Southern Folklore. He waited until 1997 to release his first solo album. It is worth the wait.

Muddy Waters, *The Complete Plantation Recordings*. MCA 9344. This fascinating recording captures Waters in 1941–42, before he left Stovall's plantation (outside Clarksdale) to move to Chicago and plug in his guitar. There are solo and group acoustic pieces, and interviews with Waters by Alan Lomax and John Work (Waters, thinking the Library of Congress folklorists were revenuers out to bust him for moonshining, gives brief answers).

Muddy Waters, *His Best: 1947–1955*. Chess/MCA 9370. This one gives you the magnificent music Waters made after his move to Chicago. All of the classics such as "Rollin' and Tumblin'," "I Can't Be Satisfied," "I Just Want to Make Love to You," and "Rollin' Stone" are here. Fellow Mississippians Willie Dixon, Jimmy Rogers, and Otis Spann are part of Waters's Chicago band, along with the exquisite Louisiana-born harpist Little Walter. If you own only one blues album, this should be the one.

Bukka White, *The Complete Bukka White*. Columbia CK–52782. Solo or accompanied by Washboard Sam, White sang his heart out and pounded away at his metal guitar on this collection of personal songs he recorded just after his release from Parchman prison in 1940.

Big Joe Williams, *Shake Your Boogie*. Arhoolie CD–315. Ancient-sounding yet always fresh, Big Joe was a true original who added three extra strings to his guitar and then played it percussively. He also had a wry humor, a knack for writing topical songs, and even a flair for religious material. These recordings from the 1960s capture his essence.

Sonny Boy Williamson II, *King Biscuit Time*. Arhoolie CD–310. This one includes Sonny Boy's early 1950s classics such as "Nine Below Zero," "Eyesight to the Blind," and "Mighty Long Time" (with the amazing Cliff Bivens *singing* the bass part); a piece of a live King Biscuit Time radio broadcast; "Sonny Boy's Christmas Blues"; and a great cover photo.

Howlin' Wolf, *Howlin' Wolf/Moanin' in the Moonlight*. MCA/Chess 5908. Wolf's growling vocals, moans, harp, and killer band-leading make him, along with Muddy Waters, one of the architects of Chicago blues. Most of the songs here have been covered by dozens of blues and rock acts, but there's really no duplicating Wolf's magic. Wolf's lead guitarist, Hubert Sumlin, was Eric Clapton's idol—and this collection shows why.

Various artists, *Blues Masters, Volume 12: Memphis Blues*. Rhino 71129. A terrific intro to Memphis blues and jug-band music from the 1920s through the 1950s. Includes the Beale Street Sheiks' "Mr. Crump Don't Like It," B. B. King's very early "When Your Baby Packs Up and Goes" (before he became a lead-guitar soloist), and great tracks by Furry Lewis, Rufus Thomas, Howlin' Wolf and others.

Various artists, *Masters of the Delta Blues: The Friends of Charlie Patton*. Yazoo 2002. A wonderful collection of the giants of the early Delta blues— Son House, Tommy Johnson, Louise Johnson, Bukka White, Willie Brown, and the mysterious Kid Bailey. With this and a Charley Patton CD, you'll have a good picture of Mississippi blues in the 1920s and early 1930s.

Various artists, *Mississippi Delta Blues "Blow My Blues Away,"* *Vol. 2.* Arhoolie CD 402. This album presents the amazing first recordings of R. L. Burnside, on acoustic guitar at his home in 1967. Joe Callicott, a North Mississippi artist who recorded in 1930 and then again in the sixties, also is included here. And as a bonus, there are a few electric covers of Tommy Johnson songs by the Houston Stackhouse/Robert Nighthawk/Peck Curtis trio.

Various artists, *Sun Records Collection*. Rhino 71780. This three-CD set gives you Elvis Presley's early, bluesy tracks and puts them in context with all the great blues, rockabilly, and country-Western that came out of Sam Phillips's studio. B. B. King, Jerry Lee Lewis, Charlie Rich, Howlin' Wolf, Rufus Thomas, "Doctor" Isaiah Ross, Carl Perkins, Rosco Gordon, Roy Orbison, Little Milton, Carl Mann, Sleepy John Estes, and Johnny Cash are all here.

INDEX

References to illustrations appear in *italics*.

259